AF477705

KEROUAC BEAT PAINTING

KEROUAC
BEAT
PAINTING

Edited by
Sandrina Bandera
Alessandro Castiglioni
Emma Zanella

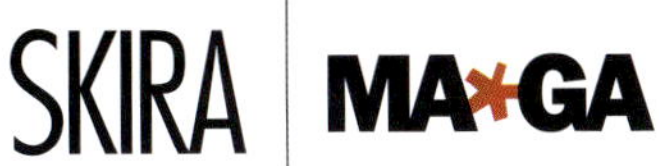

Cover
Untitled, n.d.
oil on paper, 24 x 32 cm
(detail fig. 25)

Design
Marcello Francone

Editorial Coordination
Vincenza Russo

Editing
Piera Tenconi and Niahm Blande

Layout
Evelina Laviano

Translations
Lauren Sunstein and
Darcy Lynn Di Mona
for *Scriptum*, Rome

First published in Italy in 2018 by
Skira editore S.p.A.
Palazzo Casati Stampa
via Torino 61
20123 Milano
Italy
www.skira.net

Printed and bound in Italy.
First edition

ISBN: 978-88-572-3779-4

Distributed in USA, Canada,
Central & South America by
ARTBOOK | D.A.P. 75 Broad Street
Suite 630, New York, NY 10004, USA.
Distributed elsewhere in the world
by Thames and Hudson Ltd.,
181A High Holborn, London
WC1V 7QX, United Kingdom.

KEROUAC BEAT PAINTING

Gallarate, Museo MA*GA
3 December 2017 – 22 April 2018

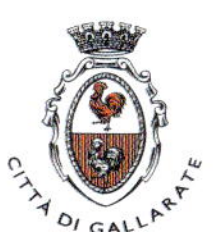

Mayor
Andrea Cassani

Councillor for Culture
Isabella Peroni

Culture Section Chief
Manuela Solinas

Fondazione Galleria d'Arte
Moderna e Contemporanea
"Silvio Zanella"

Founding Members
Città di Gallarate
MiBACT

Co-founding Members
Lombardy Region
Province of Varese

President
Sandrina Bandera

Director
Emma Zanella

Management Board
Sandrina Bandera, President
Cristina Boracchi
Mauro Croci
Francesca Raimondi
Francesco Tedeschi

Auditor
Guido Senaldi

*Scientific Technical
Committee*
Andrea Cassani, President
Giovanni Orsini
Emma Zanella
Luciano Caramel
Paolo Lamberti
Luca Molinari

*Collection Curation
and Management*
Giulia Formenti,
Senior Conservator
Laura Carrù, Registrar

*Exhibitions, Events
and Communication*
Vittoria Broggini,
Curator Conservator

*Marketing and Private
Events*
Daniela Costantini

Education Department
Lorena Giuranna, Chief
Children and Families
Marika Brocca
Elena Scandroglio
Adult Training
Francesca Chiara

Research and Web Projects
Alessandro Castiglioni

*Secretariat and
Administration*
Monica Colombo

Library
Daniela Anselmi

Security and Reception
Gilles Ielo
Alberto Vernale
Sofia Mele
Monica Ghiraldini
Michela Morelli

Installation
Giacomo Zaniboni

Graphic Design Studio
MMG Design, Gallarate

Press Office
CLP, Relazioni Pubbliche,
Milan

Web Site
LabUCdesign

Financial Consultant
Studio Trotti, Busto Arsizio

Employment Consultant
Studio Colombo, Gallarate

Surveillance
IVNG, Gallarate

Housekeeping
Olexandra Zaliska

President
Luca Missoni

Board of Directors
Lino Bozzola
Brunella Cardani
Enrico Consolandi
Mario Lainati
Luca Missoni
Emma Zanella,
ex-officio member
Sandrina Bandera,
ex-officio member

Founding Members
Francesco Aspesi
Franca Bellorini
Lino Bozzola
Cecilia Cagnoni Luoni
Brunella Cardani
Enrico Consolandi
Carla Micaela Donaio
Paolo Gasparoli
Piero Giardini
Nicola Giuliano
Mario Lainati
Paolo Alberto Lamberti
Giuseppe Merlini
Luca Missoni
Rosita Missoni
Marcello Morandini
Giovanni Orsini
Maurizio Pastorelli
Cinzia Puricelli
Alfredo Sardella
Massimiliano Serati
Angelo Zanella

*Organization and Treasury
Secretariat*
Daniela Costantini

Exhibition curated by
Sandrina Bandera
Alessandro Castiglioni
Emma Zanella

Honorary Committee
Roberto Maroni, *President
of the Lombardy Region*
Carla Di Francesco,
Secretary General, MiBACT
Andrea Cassani, *Mayor
of Gallarate*
Raffaele Cattaneo, *Council
President of the Lombardy
Region*
Gunnar Vincenzi, *President
of the Province of Varese*
Isabella Peroni, *Gallarate
Councillor for Culture*
Antonio Lampis, *Museum
Director General, MiBACT*
Fabio De Chirico, *Director
General of Contemporary
Art and Architecture and
Urban Outskirts, MiBACT*
Marco Edoardo Minoja,
*Director Secretary General
of Lombardy, MiBACT*
Stefano L'Occaso, *Director
of Museum Hub Lombardy*
Antonella Ranaldi,
*Superintendent of
Archeology, Fine Arts,
and Landscape, Milan*
Luca Rinaldi, *Superintendent
of Archeology, Fine Arts,
and Landscape CO, LC, MB,
PV, SO, VA*
Maurizio Savoja,
*Superintendent Director
of Archives and Libraries
of Lombardy*

Scientific Committee
Enrico Camporesi
Stefania Benini
Franco Buffoni
Francesco Tedeschi

Catalog Texts
Sandrina Bandera
Stefania Benini
Franco Buffoni
Enrico Camporesi
Dario Franceschini
Virginia Hill
Ada Masoero
John Shen-Sampas
Arminio Sciolli
Francesco Tedeschi

Sections and Work Entries
Alessandro Castiglioni

Organization
Monica Faccini
Paola Pastorelli Auser
for MA*GA

*Conservation of Works
on Display*
Laura Carrù
Giulia Formenti

Communication and Events
Vittoria Broggini

Educational Activities
Marika Brocca
Alessandro Castiglioni
Francesca Chiara
Lorena Giuranna
Elena Scandroglio

Installation
Claudio Mascero
Giacomo Zaniboni

Graphic Design Studio
MMG Design, Gallarate

Press Office
CLP, Relazioni Pubbliche,
Milan

Social Media
Erika La Rosa

Graphic Design Installation
Art Massa Studio, Gallarate

Insurance
BIG Broker Insurance Group
– CiaccioArte

Shipping
Liguigli Fine Art, Lodi

Photography
Michele Lamassa

*Auser for MA*GA*
Paola Pastorelli
Sandra Amoedo
Angela Bellora
Carolina Bianchi
Franca Ermelinda Caso
Valentino Cerasani
Mirko Ceriotti
Elena Galazzi
Daniela Magni
Giuseppe Paccione
Maria Teresa Saielli
Luisa Simoventi
Lorena Soffritti
Genny Randisi
Antonella Sanzone
Elena Semenova

Social Team
Erika La Rosa
Marta Bergamin
Sara Biancardi
Christian Bianci
Marco Caccianiga
Edoardo Carabelli
Myriam De Salvo
Martina Filaferro
Luca Gadda
Gaia Gandolfi
Nicol Girardi
Lorenzo Imperiale
Simona Livrieri
Sarah Lombardo
Pietro Maurino
Ester Miri
Emmanuele Occhipinti
Lorenzo Padovan
Matteo Papatola
Riccardo Planca
Silvia Porro
Alessandro Saltafossi

The organizers and curators
would like to thank the
lenders of the works who
made this exhibition
possible, in particular
Arminio e Paolo Sciolli
(Il Rivellino), EFG Art
Collection Svizzera,
The Museum of Fine Arts
Huston, RAI Teche,
Archivio Corriere della Sera
Fernanda Pivano

Thanks to
Marika Armini
Raffaella Bentivoglio Ravasio
Cristina Boracchi
Santa Brumermane
Ilaria Bruno
Walter Camarda
Daniela Cecchini
Massimo e Gabriele Ciaccio
Luca Ciardiello
Giuseppe Curonici
Luciano Fontana
Martin Kunz
Enrico Maria Mancuso
Donatella Manzan
Francesca Martinoli
Andrea Mascetti
Luca Morari
Sergio Pagani
Simonetta Romagnolo
Maurizio Savoja
Davide Simone
Paola Strada
Francesca Tramma

Special thanks to
John Shen-Sampas

In our collective imagination, Jack Kerouac is the icon of a restless and rebellious generation, the symbol of the Beat movement. *On the Road*, which legends hold was written in just three weeks on a roll of telex paper, is a long seller that still casts its spell on young people today, thanks to the yearning for freedom, the value of friendship, the Wanderlust and search for authenticity that it represents.

Yet Kerouac is an extraordinarily complex figure, an intellectual who resists all attempts at being pigeonholed or forced to conform, with an eclectic talent that found expression in an array of different mediums. The novelty of this exhibition is its success in putting all this versatility on display. To start with, it gives visitors the chance to admire Kerouac's drawings and paintings with the benefit of input from many different sources: art historians, poets, philologists and translators, artists, filmmakers and visual arts experts. It's a priceless opportunity to relive the cultural climate of those times and the dreams and contradictions of the "beat-up and beatific," as well as discover a lesser-known but equally fascinating side of Kerouac and his personal and artistic journey.

This exhibition is further proof, if any is needed, of MA*GA's commitment to contemporary art, as it turns the spotlight on an artist whose career left an indelible impression on our own more recent past, and whose works dialogue with those of the museum's superb permanent collection. MA*GA is an exhibition space that is open to culture and cultural exchanges. It is a major player on its own city's scene with an international calling as well; I won't hesitate to call it one of Italy's most important institutions devoted to contemporary art.

Dario Franceschini
Minister of Cultural Heritage and Activities and Tourism

I was enormously curious to explore Jack Kerouac's career as a painter, and
I was duly astonished to learn that this was hardly a minor interest of his, but on
a par with and parallel to the preeminent literary career we all know so well.
Say "Kerouac", and you summon up that longing for freedom, that life on the
road that characterizes the Beat Generation, the cultural movement that kept its
hold on an entire generation of artists from the 1950s to the 1970s. The exhibition
at MA*GA is the perfect opportunity to acquaint oneself with the author of
On the Road far from his beloved road, inside a museum that is the first in Italy
to offer a solo exhibition so rich in artworks and significance. For our museum, the
importance of the show is twofold: Kerouac's mystique is a surefire draw to attract
new visitors to the venue, and it also signals the new direction undertaken by
MA*GA president Sandrina Bandera, who was handed a mandate to cast her net
wide, combining an international dimension with an awareness of the museum's
local roots.
Those who visit the exhibition *Kerouac. Beat Painting* will be invited to undertake
a journey quite different from those described in his own novels: a voyage and
a kaleidoscope of emotions I recommend for one and all.
To paraphrase Kerouac himself: *Right or wrong, this is the exhibition.*

Andrea Cassani
Mayor of Gallarate (province of Varese)

The exhibition at MA*GA goes well beyond the analysis and display of Jack Kerouac's paintings and drawings. It is an expedition into the territory of the Beat Generation, starting with the American writer's (little-known) output as a painter and moving on to embrace Kerouac's personal items; film and music; and his relationship with European culture and in particular that of Italy.
It is therefore an honor for our museum of contemporary art to host these artworks by Kerouac, set off by a stunning arrangement by the great British filmmaker Peter Greenaway, photographs by Ettore Sottsass and a video of the interview that the Italian critic and translator Fernanda Pivano conducted with Kerouac himself for RAI Television, a firsthand account of the Italian journey undertaken by the author of *On the Road* and his friend and fellow Beat Allen Ginsberg. And apropos of the influence of Italy on Kerouac, among the portraits of celebrities such as Joan Crawford and Truman Capote on show from December 2017 to April 2018, there is also one of Cardinal Montini.
This original and comprehensive exhibition of works, never displayed in Italy before, is something entirely new that once again sees MA*GA the protagonist of a major cultural event.
I wish to thank MA*GA president Sandrina Bandera, director Emma Zanella and Alessandro Castiglioni, curators of the exhibition, for their zeal and utter commitment to this latest project. Thanks as well to all those who helped make this exhibition a reality, in particular the museum's patrons and the newly founded Friends of the MA*GA Museum Association; they believed in the museum and its cultural mission.

Isabella Peroni
Gallarate Councillor for Culture

A passion for art and culture and the desire to support them, in recognition of their enormous social and educational value, fueled the decision to create the Friends of the MA*GA Museum Association, of which I am president, on June 6, 2017. We want people to know about MA*GA. We intend to see it prosper and support it in all its vibrancy and potential. At this museum, which I have been familiar with as a visitor for some time now, I'm proud to say that the socio-cultural milieu is quite sophisticated, and education is key to the museum's agenda.
It's wonderful to see young people and students in the rooms of the museum and at its café, and lingering outside as well (which you find in English-speaking countries); in fact the outdoor areas do even more to promote socialization. And it's quite stimulating to observe this dialogue between an institution with a history rooted in its surrounding area and its present-day efforts to seek out more and more fresh contacts that will allow it to sink its roots even further in the living fabric of this city. Indeed, MA*GA is expanding its own borders well beyond the city that actually hosts it. On this occasion it acquaints us with the United States in the 1950s, the decade that spawned the Beat Generation and the age that saw individuals in growing numbers refuse to follow society's rules, making a clean break with the past.
My own parents, Ottavio and Rosita Missoni, were also caught up in this spirit of revolution and introduced a radical break with the traditions of the fashion world starting in the mid-1950s and up to the early 1970s, making many innovations in the culture of clothing. As exponents of the avant-garde of Italian fashion, they contributed first-hand to the major shift in the industry that gave rise to prêt-à-porter and the triumph of Milan as Italy's fashion capital, replacing Florence.
It is all proof that concurrently with the Beats in the U.S., in Italy the artistic and cultural avant-garde was instilling a new vitality in the society of the day, offering people the chance to become familiar with new ideas, satisfy their curiosity and feel free to experiment.
This is precisely the spirit that inspires MA*GA and is sure to take us far beyond our present horizons.

Luca Missoni
President of the Friends of the MA*GA Museum Association

Contents

Why This Exhibition?

Foreword

Sandrina Bandera
Emma Zanella

In a first for Italy, the exhibition *Kerouac. Beat Painting* and the catalog accompanying it present a series of never-before-seen artworks, images and studies representing the visual art of Jack Kerouac, one of the twentieth-century's greatest writers and one of the founders of the Beat Generation, the literary and artistic movement that scandalized the Puritan mentality of the United States, and shocked Europe as well, starting in the late 1940s.

This exhibition is part of the museum's broader agenda concerning its exhibitions and the research behind them: on the one hand, it aims to foster the exploration of unfamiliar aspects of contemporary visual culture; on the other hand, it seeks to describe the evocative interactions between different fields of artistic expression, specifically the crossover between painting and literature. Thus understood, *Kerouac. Beat Painting* picks up where *Ritmo sopra a tutto* left off. The 2016 exhibition curated by Franco Buffoni, in fact, examined the relationship between art and poetry in Italian culture in the second half of the twentieth century.

The nearly one hundred works by Kerouac on display, dating to the late 1950s and early 1960s, include pieces of paper of different sizes containing both drawings and paintings; the film *Pull My Daisy* (Robert Frank and Alfred Leslie, 1959), written by and starring Kerouac; and the well-known TV interview conducted by critic and translator Fernanda Pivano, as well as excerpts from Kerouac's writings and some of his personal effects, all rounded out by a thorough critical apparatus.[1]

We make no pretense of faithfully reconstructing Kerouac's complex career as an artist, since our chief concern is to provide an original interpretation of this major writer/artist, one that shows Kerouac in a new light, with his writings, paintings, drawings, scripts and his own voice all placed in a single, impetuous creative flow that admits no barriers, obstacles or classifications. The works on display, therefore, should not be approached using an art critic's traditional methods, but seen with one's eye and one's mind, the two tools capable of perceiving the powerful world of Kerouac's art. After all, Kerouac felt the need to convey his ideas and feelings through an array of tools and visions, seeing artistic expression in its totality.

His drawings and paintings complement and round out his writings, showing the latter from a whole new angle that is stimulating and vital.

As further proof of the potency of Kerouac's art, the exhibition opens with a tribute by another great artist, Peter Greenaway, the director and screenwriter, and a highly skilled draughtsman himself. His own drawings are mainly visions and interpretations that project Kerouac into the future, in an energetic burst of fantasy that could well lead to new artworks, new directions and possibly even new films by this auteur filmmaker.

Considering the complexity of this corpus of artworks, the curators decided to display and consequently publish the artworks by arranging the sections of the exhibition thematically, allowing for a wide-ranging analysis of the connections between Kerouac's literary works, artistic output and his own life story. These sections are interspersed with essays written for the occasion by experts from different areas, devoted to Kerouac's own works and, more broadly speaking, to the larger question of the relationship between American and European art in the immediate post-WWII period. The first section, "A Personal Album," brings together a series of portraits Kerouac made of friends and celebrities as well, some of whom he had met and others he had come across in the magazines of his day, particularly *Life*. Parallel to this section, the opening essay in the catalog by curator Sandrina Bandera, "Jack Kerouac: Surprising Cultural Interactions," looks at the sources of his art and the importance of the history of European art to his own background as an artist. The exhibition next turns to the film *Pull My Daisy* by Robert Frank and Alfred Leslie (1959), a freewheeling improvisation of a scene from a play script by Jack Kerouac that was never performed. Kerouac himself dubs all the characters and comments on their actions as he goes. The film is elucidated by the essay "*Is the Word Holy? On Kerouac's voice in Pull My Daisy*" by Enrico Camporesi, who has fresh ideas about Kerouac's use of voice and improvisation. Another essay in the catalog by critic Francesco Tedeschi is also concerned with improvisation; it leads off the fourth section of the exhibition, "Abstract Expressionism," featuring works which clearly show the gradual transition from figurative art, albeit freer, yet still recognizable, to the use of improvised and decidedly abstract lines and shapes.

The focal point of the exhibition actually consists of two quite different yet complementary sections, "Visions of Jack" and "Beat Painting," which explore the dimension of sacredness and other aspects of Beat culture.

In "Visions of Jack," the artworks, accompanied by an introduction by Stefania Benini, reflect the main religious themes, both Catholic and Buddhist, with which Kerouac's writings and artworks are permeated. These themes become the hallmarks of his graphic art and paintings and include the angel, the Holy Ghost, the cross, Buddha, the dying Christ, Mary Magdalene and so forth, all proof of the complex cultural universe in which the writer was immersed, and his own desire to give shape to a transcendent reality.

The totalizing perception of reality, in which personal plans, interests and models for life overlap to the point of canceling each other out, can be seen most clearly in the section "Beat Painting," explored in depth in the essays by Franco Buffoni, who looks at the history of Kerouac's involvement with Italian culture and the culture of his day, and by Virginia Hill, who explains the ties between the Beat Generation – and Kerouac, above all – and fashion and style in general.

The exhibition concludes with a famous interview with Kerouac by Fernanda Pivano in 1966, for RAI Television, reproduced courtesy of the RAI Teche Archives, along with a series of photographs by Ettore Sottsass, taken in the same year, when Kerouac came to Italy.

Kerouac's legacy is alive and well today in our mind's eye, and not just from a literary point of view, but in the perception of the world and the coming of age of an entire generation inspired and energized, then and now, by Kerouac and the Beat movement.

Three personal accounts published in the catalog bear out the lasting impact of that legacy. The first is a touching interview with sculptor Arnaldo Pomodoro, conducted by Ada Masoero. The artist reminisces about Kerouac and what he meant to the American youth culture during the student protest movement, when a young Pomodoro was teaching at Stanford University in California as an artist-in-residence.

The second is an account by a major collector of Kerouac's artworks, Arminio Sciolli, enamored of the writer and what he represented long before he became his most ardent supporter and collector, along with his brother Paolo.

Lastly, John Shen-Sampas reminds us that these artworks were a gift from Kerouac to his brother-in-law John Sampas.

By the same token, Kerouac's enduring relevance and his warm following that includes a host of artists, intellectuals, writers and musicians have prompted us to devote an event running parallel to the exhibition, called *My Kerouac*, reserved for what Kerouac represents today, to both young people and the generation of his own day. This will be an unstructured, freely conceived space for further reflection, where ideas and associations will be conveyed by graphic art, photographs and other visual art, along with performances and writings by anyone interested in adding to the vibrancy of our exhibition: a fluid space that corresponds to the writer's own creative flow.

We would like to thank everyone who collaborated on this project for the hard work, professionalism and dedication they put into the selection of artworks and other exhibits for the show, particularly those who loaned their own artworks, Arminio and Paolo Sciolli as well as the EFG Art Collection – Switzerland, The Museum of Fine Arts – Houston; and the archives of the *Corriere della Sera* and the RAI Teche. We are also grateful to the experts who brought their own enthusiasm to the project, writing essays that we believe are crucial to the understanding of Kerouac's literary and artistic output. Besides, we thank the museum's supporters, Ricola, BIG srl, The Friends of the MA*GA Museum, the Fondazione Cariplo, the Heritage Art Foundation, and Castaldi Lighting, all of whom helped make this exhibition possible, as well as the many educational initiatives connected with it.

Lastly, we'd like to thank the Municipality of Gallarate, MiBACT, the Lombardy Region, the Province of Varese, and the founding members of the museum, whose participation is vital to the museum's success. Special thanks go to Andrea Cassani and Isabella Peroni, respectively Mayor and Gallarate Councillor for Culture, as well as Andrea Mascetti, who represents the Fondazione Cariplo, which first put us in touch with the collectors of Kerouac's artworks. We wish to thank Minister of Culture Dario Franceschini wholeheartedly for choosing to write an essay that was not just "institutional" but "from the writer Franceschini to the writer Kerouac."

[1] Artworks on display in the exhibition but not published in the catalog: Robert Frank, *New Mexico 45 Route 285*, 1955–56 (printed in the 1970s), silver gelatin on paper, 36.5 x 25 cm, EFG Art Collection, Switzerland; Robert Frank and Alfred Leslie, *Pull My Daisy*, 1959, film, 28", The Museum of Fine Arts, Houston; and the interview with Jack Kerouac by Fernanda Pivano in "Segnalibro 1966-1967", October 17, 1966, courtesy of RAI Teche Archives.

John Shen-Sampas
Supporting and Preserving the Mementos of Kerouac

Jack Kerouac, the legendary writer of *On The Road* and other books that inspired a generation of American youths to pursue liberty and dreams, is little known for his artistic endeavors in paintings and drawings. However, when he passed away in 1969, he left a trove of portraitures, drawings and sketches behind. For the first time, those treasures are gathered and displayed in a methodical way so that his genius, not only in writing but also in visual arts, is shown.

Crowned as the father of the "Beat Generation," Kerouac, till this day, remains one of the most read American authors, for his prosaic passages, radical ideology and inspirational adventures. However, understanding of Kerouac and his influence will not be complete without examining his burning desire to be a painter. As a 9-year old, Jack drew a self-portrait. Later, he voiced that he'd rather be a painter than a writer. When *On The Road* was finished, he had already drawn a cover for the book. Throughout his journals and notebooks, illustrative sketches abound. His angelic portrait of Stella Kerouac seemingly supine while propping her head reminds viewers of the Canova sculpture of Pauline Bonaparte. The blue departing angel and the rays of black darkness surrounding it reveal his true self as an introvert.

He drew his techniques from old masters and his contemporaries such as Stanley Twardowicz and Willem De Kooning, while maintaining originality and mastery in his works.

"Stream of Consciousness," reinvented by Kerouac, is evident in his drawings and sketches. The focus on what consciousness directs you towards rather than that you as a being control your consciousness gave his works a sense of liberation. Details are not as important as concept. His sketches betray Jack's deep connection with the eastern culture, which in many ways, emphasize concept and ideas while downplaying realism and details. His sketches flow and resonate with meanings oftentimes implied by a string of lines and a collection of curves. His paintings rivet viewers with a masterful play of colors and light. Deep down, Jack was a true believer of divinity, which in no way contradicts his desire to be free. Religious themes crop up in many of his works and many a time he conspicuously titled his works after the themes. Catholicism and Buddhism are mixed. Western and Eastern influences compete in his works. To him, spirituality and humanity have no temporal or physical boundary. It is the whole that interests him.

The collection of works shown in this exhibit was given to John Sampas, Kerouac's brother-in-law, as gifts by Kerouac himself. As the executor for the Jack Kerouac estate, Mr. Sampas, over the past two decades, heralded Kerouac's works and helped to maintain Kerouac's relevance and significance in American Culture. He passed away earlier this year at the age of 84. This introduction is dedicated to him for his excellent work as a champion and chaperone of Kerouac.

Greenwich, Connecticut, September 30, 2017

Arminio Sciolli
A Rebel's Dream: Collecting the Paintings of Jack Kerouac

I remember the Beatles. They're my first childhood memories, in Paris, maybe in 1962. Sheila would sing *Hello Petite Fille*, the uncensored version, at home, by the badly-dressed long-hairs who sang in English, while my father and the strict French schoolteachers required us to practically shave our heads. I would watch the Beatles and listen to their songs on the sly, and the same held for Bergman films on television, which I watched perfectly camouflaged under the couch, or *Doctor Zhivago*, which I got to see with my mother because she couldn't find a babysitter. I would dream of Julie Christie and other Nordic Valkyries who would spring me from school – me: the budding "yéyé" singer.

I think that about wraps it up, since everything that follows is just how I executed my plan to rebel against short hair, anorexic girls, and the whole system.

At the Lycée Chateaubriand in Rome, when we first read *On the Road* in English class in 1973, I learned that the Beatles were originally going to call themselves the Beetles, but that after reading Kerouac they decided to fall in with the Beatniks. Meanwhile, my posters of the *White Album*, by Avedon, were ripped off the walls of my bedroom, and my sneakers were relegated to serving for sports activities only. The photograph signed by the Fab Four was buried in the netherworld of my first record library.

And I still listen to the Beatles, just like I still have a weakness for blondes. So it's clear that when I went to the splendid Book Fair organized by Marcello Dell'Utri at the Permanente in Milan in 2007, to give a hand to Andrea Del Lago with some of my Beat books, I fell helplessly in love with the painting *The Slouch Hat* by Kerouac, on display at the Lame Duck Books stand and already put on hold by Johnny Depp...

But then the subprime mortgage crisis of 2007 came along, Lehman Brothers went bust, taking America's leading financial institutions down with it, and my brother Paolo and I were there to pick up the pieces. We bought five floors of a gallery belonging to AIG, in temporary receivership under the TARP program, in Locarno, and then we contacted John Sampas, the last of the Kerouac clan in Lowell, to see if he had a memento or two that we could display. By now the recession had put a stop to acquisitions by film stars or public libraries, and the Kerouac collection of paintings was intact. Surrounded by the skepticism of the "experts," Paolo and I ignored all their advice and threw ourselves into the acquisition of the collection, tightening our belts for years to come, paying in installments (struggling to, anyway) for the entire deal consisting of 100 drawings, paintings and personal items, including the tennis shoes worn by Kerouac, the writer who would write in English, although his mother tongue was French.

Sadly, John Sampas died a few months ago, but I feel moved to thank him anyway, by way of his son John Shen-Sampas, for his father's patience and trust in us. I am also very grateful to all those who believed in the bona fide artistic talent of Jean-Louis Lebris de Kérouac: Consuelo Císcar at the IVAM in Valencia, above all; Jean-Jacques Lebel, who imported the Beats into Europe, Peter Weibel at the ZKM in Karlsruhe; Jean-Olivier Despres, director of the Gagosian Gallery in Paris; Jim Canary, the keeper of the "scroll" of *On the Road*, and, on the Italian front, Sandrina Bandera and Emma Zanella, president and director of MA*GA, respectively, for also believing in the dream of one rebellious child. Last but not least, I'd like to thank my parents for listening to me for once, possibly through the intercession of Pope Paul VI, a portrait of whom, painted by Kerouac when he was still a cardinal, is on display in the exhibition.

To conclude, we hope to take the installation *On the Road* to the 2020 Dubai EXPO: it's a vision of Peter Greenaway's, on a journey of which we fondly hope the present exhibition will be just the first leg.

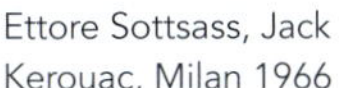

Ettore Sottsass, Jack
Kerouac, Milan 1966

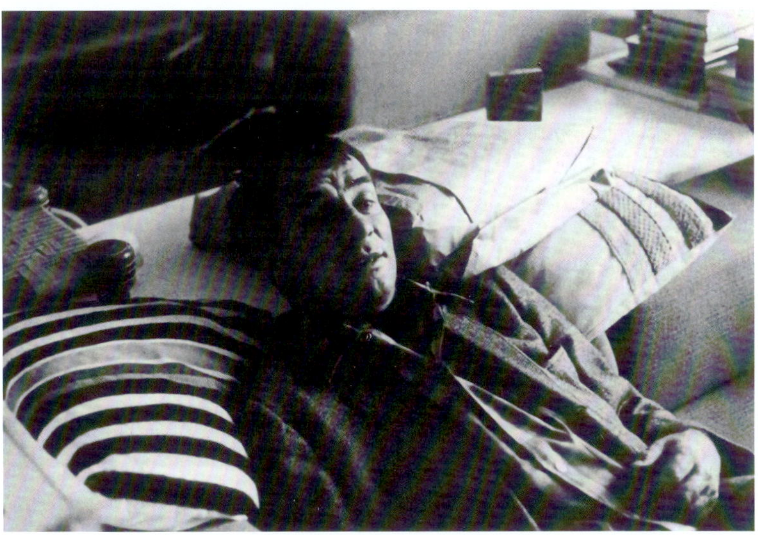

Between Past, Present and Future: a Voyage

Peter Greenaway
On the Road

The catalog opens with a remarkable tribute to Jack Kerouac: an unpublished drawing by Peter Greenaway dedicated to *On the Road*. The British artist and filmmaker has produced a series of sketches, storyboards and writings for his new project: the creation of a video screening on the move, which concentrates on the car featured in *On the Road*. The iconic vehicle thus becomes a film set and a screening venue for a video that reinterprets Kerouac's journey while it is in motion, on a sort of imaginary circuit through the locations in the novel itself.

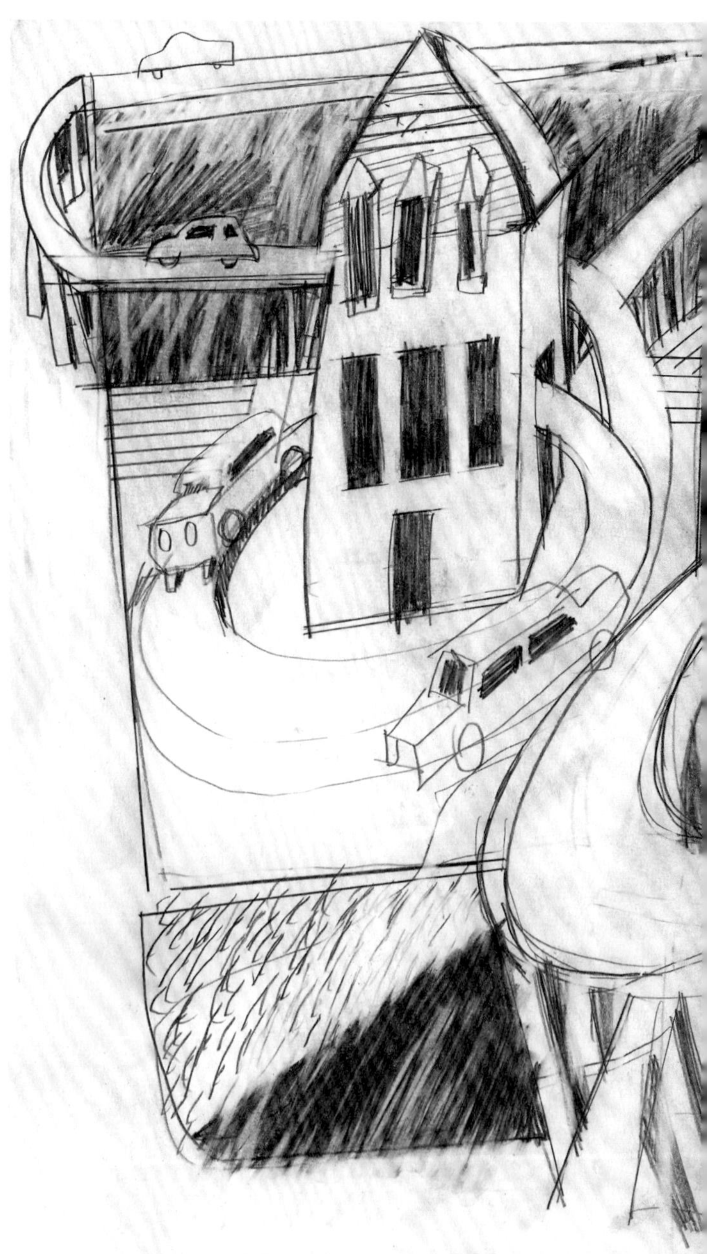

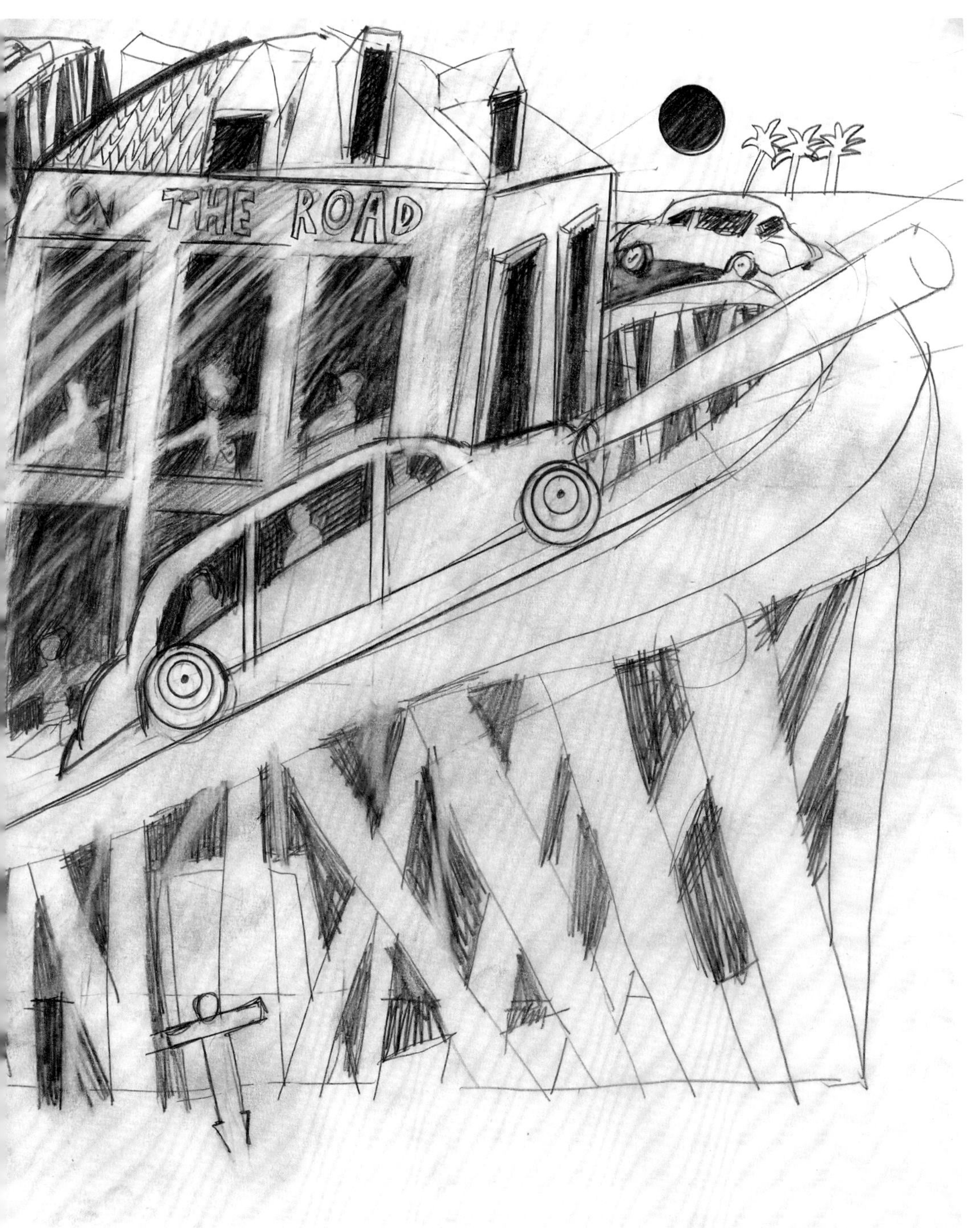
ON THE ROAD

Jack Kerouac: Surprising Cultural Interactions

Sandrina Bandera

All that old road from the past unreeling dizzily, as if the cup of life had been overturned and everything gone mad.[1]

How can we revisit the evolution of Kerouac's painting? An overly detailed exhibition, arranged thematically, would only reinforce the illusion of an inexorable logic that negates all prospects of creativity, ignoring the fact that Kerouac's hallmark was just this invention of his own determinism and his defiance of the laws of evolution. Vice versa, a chronological treatment reflecting the vitality of the writer's individual creative endeavors would turn into a mere sequence of works and, realistically speaking, a fragmentary one, if we bear in mind the limited scope of this exhibition, confined to just under one hundred of Kerouac's myriad drawings and paintings, and making no pretense, therefore, as sizable as it is, of reconstructing his multifarious artistic activity in its entirely. A clear outline of Kerouac's artworks would simply get bogged down in the tangle of the inventions and contrasts inherent to Kerouac's written works, which the author himself considered to ideally belong to a single autobiographical narrative bearing the title *The Duluoz Legend*,[2] composed to reflect his own life experience and that of his group of friends who were the founders of the Beat Generation. In the end we opted for a thematic exhibition with a chronological treatment of the works in the various sections of the exhibition themselves, the idea being to reconstruct a narrative in which the written works and the forays into figurative art would perfectly coincide: different aspects of the same poetic journey.

Decidedly autobiographical, therefore, and part of a creative whole that admitted no boundaries between life and art, these artworks of Kerouac's need to be interpreted in this light, and in light of the other essays in the catalog as well, bearing in mind, moreover, that Kerouac, the founder of Beat culture, was ultimately undone by a troubled existence in which his own drinking and drug use didn't do him any favors and unleashed his inner demons. Nor should we forget that he was closely associated with a group of people involved in a number of homicides in a few short years, which implicated him as well, as shall be seen later in this essay. Besides, Kerouac had other problems with the law when he refused to acknowledge the child born to him and his wife Joan Haverty (whom he married and promptly left in 1950), despite his paternity being confirmed by court-ordered tests.[3] His flouting of conventions, matched by those of his milieu, was extremely disruptive to his life and his career as an artist, pervaded by an inexorable sensation of sadness. A passage from *On the Road* aptly conveys this underlying emotion: "I realized that these were all the snapshots which our children would look at one day [...] never dreaming the raggedy madness and riot of our actual lives, our actual night, the hell of it, the senseless nightmare road. All of it inside endless and beginningless emptiness [...] 'Good-bye, Good-bye'. Dean walked off in the long red dusk [...] I gaped into the bleakness of my own days. I had an awful long way to go too."[4]

It was Fernanda Pivano in her introduction to the first Italian translation in 1959 who first observed that the author of this instant bestseller had immediately become a symbol "of an aesthetic revival, a way of life, the mores of these rebels without a cause."[5] Pivano had also seen through the critics' usual association between the Beat Generation and the Dadaist/Expressionist ideas of which Henry Miller was commonly held to be the leading exponent (or so she considered him). Miller was in fact the founder of an intellectual/anarchist community in Big Sur, California, that inspired Kerouac to isolate himself for a time and write a novel. In reality, the young artists whom Pivano met and whose works she translated fought a tireless battle against the prevailing conformism and bourgeois values of their day and struggled to impose their own esthetic credo even before their morality.[6]

It would be wrongheaded, therefore, to read these artworks using an art critic's traditional method, when they are actually an essential part of that potent entity known as Jack Kerouac. These works are like the limbs of a single body spinning on its own axis, so dynamic that it needs an abundance of different tools to express itself.

Kerouac's drawings, taken separately, could be said to belong – on the philosophical level as well – to that alternative twentieth-century movement that looks to graffiti and children's drawings. Indeed, in light of this wide-ranging retrospective, perhaps the time has come for us to realize that if we want finally to start to take stock of the Kerouac revolution, we can no longer refrain from analyzing his creativity as a whole. His drawings and paintings round out his career as a writer; they make up what Gérard Genette[7] calls the "paratext", that apparatus of elements necessary to the written text itself: the illustrations, footnotes, forewords, introductions and post-scripts. Hence these illustrations corroborate, explain and enliven the texts by their author. Taking certain European artists such as Klee or Picabia as their model (to mention two cultural extremes), many American artists, particularly between 1945 and 1975, viewed the written word as a vital and highly stimulating feature of a work of art,[8] not just a necessary mediation but *one* with the artwork itself.[9]

This was certainly the case of several writers in Kerouac's milieu, and was typical of the rebels who gave rise to Beat culture, such as Gregory Corso, Peter Orlovsky, William S. Burroughs, Allen Ginsberg, Lawrence Ferlinghetti, and obviously Kerouac himself.[10] They all accompanied their own writings with drawings, paintings, photographs, music, sounds, rhythm, recordings and films. The same text typed on a typewriter needed to be interpreted in terms of its graphic guise even before considering its content, along with the sound and rhythm of the typing itself (the bebop clickety click of the keys and the bell sounding at the end of a line), and the aesthetic form the writing took (akin to a stage performance executed while holding one's breath, in a virtually ecstatic state)[11] all this in edition to being the draft of a text. The most representative example was surely the *Scroll*, the first draft of *On the Road*, which Kerouac finished on April 26, 1951, after a three-week tour-de-force consisting of typing non-stop and not sleeping at all, under the effect of Benzedrine. The punctuation-free text was typed on a continuous scroll of tracing paper.[12]

Again, it would be a serious mistake to consider these illustrations and sketches as divorced from the artist's writings, judging them, that is, merely from a stylistic point of view or from that of the subjects they portray. The artworks are an integral part of the writings and should be interpreted in the same way as Kerouac's own writing style, for which he coined the term "spontaneous prose": the composition of sentences by association, in a stream of words free from syntactic constraints and with all the immediacy of a rushing river.

Just like his literary works, the artworks by the founder of the Beat Generation reflect his desire to distance himself from America's rigid social structure in his own day and try to fill the void left by the death of his brother Gerard when he was a child – he still could not get past his grief – as well as seek out those highs offered variously by drugs (Benzedrine and marijuana), religious syncretism (Catholicism and Buddhism) and a desire to travel that verged on the obsessive.

Indeed, Kerouac's entire output, be it written, drawn, painted or even set to music, is – as startling as this first of a number of surprising incongruencies may seem – a sort of Proustian search for times past: an immersion in his own personal world made up of experiences and memories that could be traced back to his hometown and his college years, peopled by Hemingway, Dickens, Joyce, Tolstoy, Dostoevsky and Thomas Wolfe.[13] There was an air of modernity to those college years and a desire to flout conventions, the most obvious hallmarks of his boisterous set.

His hometown, Lowell, Massachusetts, clearly emerges in his artworks and can be found in the domestic setting of many of his descriptions, along with the strong sense of the family's importance that is a constant in his novels, where Mémère is a fixture, the symbol of stability hovering in the background, no matter how scandalous the action becomes. Kerouac's past also shines through in his many figurative references to the greatest landscape painter in nineteenth-century America, James McNeill Whistler, born in Lowell, just like Kerouac, in 1834. Another echo of the past is his recollection of his father and his printing business, where Jack acquired a liking for the whir of the printing presses at an early age. And if he liked to call himself a "jazz poet," thanks to his love of jazz, Duke Ellington, Louis Armstrong, Charlie Parker, and Lester Young[14] – or even the bebop style of his prose, which took shape on the typed scroll that contained the first draft of *On the Road* – it all just might come down, in part, to that rhythmic clicking of his father's printing presses, which had been branded onto his imagination as a child.

This precedent of the printing press went hand in hand with Kerouac's ability to pick up on all the most modern and revolutionary aspects of the culture of his day, a knack he shared with his group of friends that formed the original nucleus of the Beat Generation, William S. Burroughs and Allen Ginsberg. He'd met them in 1944, along with Lucien Carr, a character who would cause enormous trouble when he initiated Kerouac into his alternative lifestyle. It's a matter of record that in the same year Kerouac was charged with covering up a crime and arrested for hiding the weapon Carr had used to kill his insistent lover; and that when Kerouac's father refused to bail him out of prison, the family of a wealthy heiress he married and just as quickly divorced two months later picked up the bill.[15] Kerouac's friendship with Burroughs got him into more trouble in 1949, when the former didn't think twice about fleeing to Mexico, where Burroughs, a married man yet homosexual, had gone to avoid a drug charge, just after killing his wife in a game of William Tell (only to do very little jail time). With all the drugs Kerouac brought into the house, Burroughs was forced to pull up stakes once more to avoid going back to prison.[16]

Nevertheless, it was thanks to these early fellow travelers that Kerouac discovered a love for literature and the avant-garde, as well as a commitment to an alternative view of culture. Through them, and his gang at Columbia University, he became acquainted with Breton, Proust, Blake, and Apollinaire, and grasped the symbolic value of the life of Van Gogh as well as the modernity of Cézanne's paintings. The critics call this kind of group a "rootstock," a sort of constellation with no particular hierarchy, around which the new Beat Generation sprang up.

The surrealism that can be detected in the public performance of October 7, 1955, which officially set the Beat Revolution in motion, must have been picked up by the group courtesy of André Breton's *Manifesto*, which Breton publicized during his stay in New York. In this text, almost prophetic in its use of automatic writing practiced by the Beat writers, Breton provocatively described the liberating power of the act of writing itself: "Have writing materials brought to you. Put yourself in as passive, or receptive, a state of mind as you can... Write quickly, without any preconceived subject, fast enough that you will not remember what you're writing and be tempted to reread what you have written. The first sentence will come spontaneously..." The argument that Breton and Picabia possibly influenced the Beat movement is one of the strong points of the exhibition *Beat Generation: New York, San Francisco, Paris* which was recently held at the Pompidou.[17] It suggests that the founder of Surrealism's concept of an automatic, uninterrupted flow of words, with no punctuation whatsoever, was the precursor of Kerouac's spontaneous prose – an argument that has prompted second thoughts about the tradition that sees the Beat Generation as an isolated phenomenon, and a solely American one, as Ginsberg's spontaneous poetry theory suggested. The Beat culture's automatic writing and continuous flow of words, in fact, have the same destructive effect as Surrealism itself, the same violence of uncontrolled psychic energies.[18] As proof of how familiar Kerouac was with the founder of Surrealism, a look at his autobiographical novel *Satori in Paris* (1966) may suffice. Here Kerouac describes what amounted to a picaresque, even hallucinatory journey he made to France in 1965, to discover his family roots. The story hinges on the meeting between the protagonist and an art dealer who is not identified, but is said to be an acquaintance of André Breton's.[19]

The Beat writers became acquainted with the counter-culture thanks in part to the English translation of Antonin Artaud's 1947 biography of Van Gogh[20] in 1949. This work must have created a scandal in America at that time and exerted a crucial influence on Kerouac himself. In this new critical appraisal of Van Gogh, in fact, Artaud attempted to overturn the prevailing theory, dear to the society of his day, that Van Gogh had gone mad, and it seems that Kerouac thought very highly of the Dutch painter himself, if we can believe the frequent notes and dedications for some of his sketches (not on display here, regrettably, but known from photographs) that praised Van Gogh. Even more importantly, certain rare yet unforgettable descriptions of landscapes in Kerouac's writings also reveal the painter's influence.

Much like an arrow shot into the air, Kerouac's life describes a sort of trajectory that manages to combine tradition and a journey into one's memories with the glorification of an alternative lifestyle, at a time in history – the two decades from the early 1950s to the late 1960s – that appears remote today, yet oddly similar, rightfully belonging to the history of culture, hence to the past, while extremely contemporary as well.

It's not surprising, therefore, that Kerouac's novels challenged the certainties of post-war society and launched a number of trends: the hippies' lifestyle and the youth culture of the 1960s, the protests in 1968 and the pacifist movements, and in general the radical rethinking of society that we still consider the momentous beginning of the enormous social changes to affect the modern world.

The past in Kerouac's works is always present, represented by his education in Catholic schools, his attachment to his mother tongue, French (in which he wrote the earliest version of *On the Road*), his knowledge of European culture and his interest in nineteenth-century painting – all elements that frequently surface in passages throughout his writings.

Certain unforgettable passages from *On the Road*, for example, have an unexpected lyricism, considering the harsh context of Kerouac's novels, resulting in landscapes that appear to have been filtered through the magical sensibility of James Whistler: "We were in the mountains: there was a heaven of sunrise, cool purple airs, red mountainsides, emerald pastures in valleys, dew, and transmuting clouds of gold";[21] or "and [we] returned to the tremendous darkness, and the stars overhead were pure and bright because of the increasingly thin air as we mounted the high hill of the western plateau [...] and no trees obstructing any low-leveled stars anywhere. And once I saw a moody white-faced cow in the sage by the road as we flitted by."[22] It is Van Gogh's palette that shines through in other memorable descriptions by the founder of the Beat Generation: "Soon it got dusk, a grapy dusk, a purple dusk over tangerine groves and long melon fields; the sun the color of pressed grapes, slashed with burgundy red [...] I stuck my head out the window and took deep breaths of the fragrant air. It was the most beautiful of all moments."[23]

Kerouac's whole personality was imbued with the noble tradition of European culture, which he had made his own, and didn't hide it. He portrayed that tradition as if it were a painting, fragmented glimpses of which he alternated with the clanking of modern machinery, the screeching of engines and the smell of gasoline: "The opera was *Fidelio*. 'What gloom!' cried the baritone [whose name was D'Annunzio],[24] rising out of the dungeon under a groaning stone. I cried for it. That's how I see life too. I was so interested in the opera that for a while I forgot the circumstances of my crazy life and got lost in the great mournful sounds of Beethoven and the rich Rembrandt tones of his story."[25] Even Dostoevsky, symbol of ethics and morality in contemporary thought, has a place in Kerouac's imagination and finds his way into the latter's references to his novels as a sort of a fairy-tale figure, a virtual *topos*, turned into a caricature that was palatable to America in that age, and to the Beat Generation: "He asked me, 'What's the name of that Russian author you're always talking about – the one who put the newspapers in his shoe and walked around in a stovepipe hat he found in a garbage pail?' This was an exaggeration of what I'd told Remi of Dostoevski."[26] This European culture was so entrenched in Jack's generation that it even fascinated the character who was easily the craziest in his novels, Dean Moriarty in *On the Road*,[27] in reality a stand-in for Neal Cassady, Kerouac's long-time friend whom he had met in 1946 when the latter was a twenty-year-old parking attendant in New York, living in a furnished room with his sixteen-year-old wife. Cassady, who had done time in a reform school for stealing cars, had a literary bent – a true outsider who provided the literary inspiration for *On the Road*, the entire plot hinging on his character: "...suddenly I noticed the hush in the room and looked around and saw a battered book on the radio. I knew it was Dean's high-eternity-in-the-afternoon Proust. As in a dream I saw him tiptoe in from the dark hall in his stocking feet...'Ah,' he said....'[I] have many things to say to you in fact with my own little bangtail mind I've been reading this gone Proust all the way across the country and digging a great number of things...'"[28] It was a culture filtered through a close acquaintance with art, museums and galleries, as was only fitting for a thirty-year-old American well-versed in the culture of the Old World: "Marylou was... waiting like a longbodied emaciated Modigliani surrealist woman in a serious room."[29] The comparison of the female character to a Modigliani figure is even more sophisticated and surprising in light of the fact that Marylou was actually a flashy blonde bombshell along the lines of Marilyn Monroe!

The education of this group of young men so thirsty for knowledge at Columbia University must have owed a considerable amount to the teaching of Meyer Schapiro, who taught art history there from the 1930s up to 1973. Schapiro was a remarkable figure with a boundless intellectual curiosity that made him possibly the leading academic on the American university scene in those post-war years. An enthusiastic champion of the relationship between society, with its different values and ways of viewing the world, and art, to which he applied his remarkable philological perspective, drawing on a range of humanistic disciplines (ethnology, psychoanalysis, semiotics), Schapiro largely confined his studies to medieval art and contemporary art. It was he who aroused the Beats' interest particularly in Van Gogh and Cézanne, whose works Schapiro considered to be the foundations of modern art (as his two monographs in 1950 and 1952 attest). Schapiro's philological interpretation of Cézanne's paintings made a deep impression on Ginsberg, who was enthralled by the French artist's technique and his alternation/juxtaposition of dashes of color and neutral spaces, which could be seen to epitomize a modern anti-academic method and a syncopated musical rhythm that could be extended to prosody as well.[30] Kerouac himself was fascinated by Cézanne and Van Gogh when he traveled to Provence and Paris and later sent an emotional postcard to Ginsberg and Burroughs from New York in May 1957, in which he described Arles, where Cézanne had lived, as being "exactly like his paintings," and "Van Gogh's house" with the "endless row of cypress trees and yellow tulips in the window," and lastly Montmartre, where, grasping the value of founding a counter-culture community, he wrote "they were all together: Van Gogh, Cézanne, Rousseau, Lautrec, Seurat, Gauguin."[31]

Moreover, Kerouac's graphic art was surely stimulated by the esteemed professor's method and broadness of outlook when he taught medieval European art, freely interpreting history in a way that is still vital and fascinating today. Schapiro's research into historical periods so removed from each other, as were the Middle Ages and his own day, may seem surprising, but was actually quite typical of his generation, a habit of mind shared by other high-profile academics, such as, to confine ourselves to Italy, Vittorio Viale and Franco Russoli. Indeed, in his studies of both past and present, what came to the fore was Schapiro's perception of the ways history and society prevailed over the development of art forms. Schapiro had a notorious falling out with Alfred Barr,[32] the long-time director of MoMA, after the latter's 1936 exhibition *The Nature of Abstract Art*, an occasion for the American public to see abstract European painting, from Picasso's Cubism to Kandinsky, for the first time. These artworks were presented as the inevitable result of the evolution of art from figurative to abstract, their historical framework and provenance having no bearing whatsoever on their appraisal. Schapiro came out with a seminal study, *The Nature of Abstract Art*, in which he refuted Barr's conclusions, claiming that the evolution of society and temporal dynamics were closely entwined with works of art themselves. For example, in Schapiro's view Impressionism reflected the social changes in France in the 1880s, with society no longer revolving around the family and the church but open spaces, factories, markets, and the middle classes instead.

Another fundamental influence on the Beat Generation's anti-academic leanings was Schapiro's other main interest in pre-classical art, such as primitive art, and Byzantine and medieval art (with their simpler design and lack of spatial perspective), in all of which he saw the symbol of the search to express one's inner life, and proposed these art forms as figurative models for the artists of his own day. The Beat culture shared Schapiro's enthusiasm, as can be clearly seen in Kerouac's graphic works and paintings on display here, and Pivano described Kerouac's "writing with a fresh intensity, applied to primordial words [...], a return, in common with all the arts, to original, pure forms [...] and an elimination of the superfluous in the language."[33] By looking at Schapiro's ideas, and his continual perception of the spontaneous flow of social context in works of art (as in Courbet's *naïveté*),[34] it may be easier to understand the Beat philosophy and the Beats' rebellious impulse, which, despite the fact that its members were enamored of culture, took the form of hitchhiking, wearing torn, filthy jeans, street talk, the continuous flow of spontaneous prose based on free association, and endowed with a musical rhythm, plus a Christian-Buddhist syncretism, drugs, and the underground (to borrow the title of a piece written by Kerouac in 1953). These were all tools of open rebellion, tools in the possession of the have-nots and the misfits and everyone on the fringes of a normal, bourgeois existence, as Camporesi observed,[35] using the list as a formula to define the existential attitude and the intimate convictions of the Beat generation. That generation challenged the "pre-established order" of social conventions, to borrow a term of Barry Miles's,[36] and Western civilization is seen in its decline, just as it was described in a famous bestseller widely read in French intellectual circles (and French was Kerouac's native tongue) after being translated from the original German in 1948. Oswald Spengler's *The Decline of the West* (originally published in 1922) was a book Kerouac read in his college years thanks to a loan from Burroughs, earmarked for his education.[37] And considering the essential unity of all his artistic endeavors, what Kerouac wrote about his own writing techniques must hold true for these drawings and paintings on display as well. He touched on the subject in what may be considered his manifesto, "Essential and Spontaneous Prose," published in the

Evergreen Review in 1958,[38] following the publication of *The Subterraneans*. This novel came complete with an introduction by Henry Miller, who praised Kerouac's ability to "rape" the immaculate American prose of the day, and do so inexorably and definitively. This semi-autobiographical novel revolved around a doomed love story featuring an African-American woman from the streets, who cheated on Kerouac with Gregory Corso (Yuri Glicorich in the novel), Corso being another Beat writer with a past, including reform school and jail time, along with a love for Shelley. Writing, declared Kerouac on the subject of his own methods, has to draw on initial memories – his friends called him the "Great Rememberer" due to his ability to *recall even the slightest of details thanks to sketches in his notebooks* --- and then proceed through various ascending levels with the constant underlying aim of being wholly captured by whatever one perceives and sees (the "picture"), in a merging of sensations, images and feelings, using "the language of the river current of sounds, words, darkness, leading to the future," modeled after "Jazz and bop, in the sense that a tenor sax breathes in and then blows a phrase into his saxophone until his breath runs out, which is the point when his musical phrase is complete." By the way, it is of some interest to recall that this masterpiece by Kerouac, written with Dostoevsky's *Notes from the Underground* in mind and inspired by Zen Buddhism as well, was censured for "obscenity" when it was published in Italy by Feltrinelli's Comete imprint, only to be absolved thanks to the "lyrical beauty of some of its images."

These introductory remarks make it easier to understand Kerouac's drawings and paintings, which should be considered as the starting point – in a poetical sense, not chronological – of each of his creations, be it a text, a piece of music, or a chorus.

First of all, there are his religious subjects, never cited by critics since they consider them extraneous to the poetics of the author of *On the Road*: these Christian images (Kerouac is known to have been a Catholic, Figs. 12–17) and Buddhist images (Figs. 18, 20, 21), featuring angels in flight, apparitions, crosses and saints, and decidedly inspired (the Buddhist subjects as well) by the iconography of the gold jewelry, reliquaries and medieval Christian manuscripts discussed in Meyer Schapiro's classes and articles.[39] Above all, thanks to photographs of these items and other black and white images documenting them, they would be perceived by Kerouac, and become part of his visual repertoire, through their iconography and two-dimensionality, not because of their chromatic values. This keen interest in these art objects is borne out by the fact that the founders of the Beat movement were habitual museum-goers who took notes on what they saw in their writings, in letters they sent each other and on photographs. We know, for example, that the group went to see the Maya codices and the *Pietà* by Carlo Crivelli at the Metropolitan Museum of New York in 1953, from a handwritten reference in the lower border of gelatin by Ginsberg.[40] The presence of apparitions by angels or Satanic snakes, or even an interest in the Buddha himself, all emerging so clearly from his sketches, were also underscored in nearly all Kerouac's writings, such as, to name just a few, *Book of Dreams* in 1960, *Visions of Cody* in 1951–52 (published in 1960) or *Wake Up: A Life of the Buddha* in 1955 (published after his death), and were a constant in the work of Kerouac and his milieu. A clearly-stated assertion by Pivano comes in handy to explain this phenomenon. "Their Buddhist contemplation and the search for truth is just a way to escape from their surroundings, in an extreme attempt to fulfill themselves and assert their own personalities, threatened by [...] collectivism and the relentless march of science towards forms that give less and less importance to [...] the individual."[41] Kerouac lyrically expressed this yearning in his writings, and, as the exhibition reveals, also in his drawings and paintings: "We were on the roof of America and all we could do was yell, I guess – across the night, eastward over the Plains, where somewhere an old man with white hair was probably walking toward us with the Word, and would arrive any minute and make us silent."[42]

Next in importance in Kerouac's figurative art are the numerous portraits and other depictions of his Beat friends (Figs. 1–11), as if to underscore that other hallmark of the Beat Generation, after their rebelliousness and attraction to the dregs of society: the sense of belonging to a tight-knit group. Although beyond the scope of the present study, which looks at the crossover between art forms, this sense of belonging played a remarkable role, as did the group itself, which shared the spirit of rebellion and the same ambitions involving literature, music, poetry, film, street culture, spontaneity, and the cult of travel as a metaphor for universal drives.[43] A departure for Kerouac is his 1959 portrait of Truman Capote (Fig. 5), outside of his group. In this case, the resemblance is distorted due to the use of a spiral motif with a strongly negative connotation, as if to express Kerouac's anger at Capote's criticism of his work. The model for this spiral form for the portrait is most likely to be found in the work of one of the artists the Beat Generation most admired, William Blake – perhaps for the *noir* quality of his art. In particular, Blake's illustration for Dante's *Inferno* in the frontispiece for Canto XIX was a significant source of visual inspiration for Kerouac and his fellow Beat Ginsberg.[44]

In a number of his works Kerouac exhibits an overwhelming fascination with Picasso,[45] perhaps because the latter was able to express primordial forms and concepts powerfully and with a master's touch. Kerouac had probably become acquainted with Picasso's *Guernica*, that archetype of rebellion, when it was displayed at the MoMA during the Second World War. Indeed, he would prove to be an acute observer of Picasso's work; stylistically speaking, some of his drawings seem to be derived from the clean lines against a white background found in the graphic art created by Picasso for the prints accompanying an edition of *Don Quixote* in 1955, on the occasion of the 350th anniversary of Cervantes' birth (Figs. 38, 42).

Another fundamental milestone in Kerouac's career as an artist is his discovery of Abstract Art, as can be seen in a group of artworks that are quite similar in terms of their bright, dense colors, elongated brushstrokes that don't always cover the canvas, and a generous use of a creamy white paint that was almost three-dimensional. Although his sketches must have been an integral part of his own drafts of his novels from the start, Kerouac's introduction to painting dated to 1958–60, the result of his infatuation with Dody Muller, newly widowed in 1958; she and her husband Jean Muller had both been fairly well-known painters in Abstract Art circles, and they acquainted Kerouac with the likes of Willem de Kooning, Franz Kline, Robert Motherwell, Stanley (whom Kerouac called Stash) Twardowicz, and others. It was in this environment that Kerouac must have learned the fundamentals of painting, and there exist firsthand accounts of his methodical approach, dividing the task into different phases: prep, sketch, and application of the layers of paint. As Twardowicz recalled in a note: "He would draw the image first, then paint it. [...] He felt better with the security of a drawing to work from. [...] He didn't like abstraction. I think he tried to understand it, but he had no interest in painting that way [...] and he really liked the painters, Franz Kline was his favorite, they were good friends. He did a woodcut at Franz's studio once. I remember him cutting himself carving the wood, his hand slipped..."[46]

For this reason, Kerouac's art has much in common with that of Willem de Kooning. The former's *Untitled* (Figs. 51–63) works are truly quite similar to de Kooning's *Women*, as far as their lines and sense of drama are concerned. In another example, there is clearly a close connection between the explosive, universal images of Adolph Gottlieb – "simple impressions of complex thought" – and Kerouac's painting *Untitled,* with its blue hand and blue circle against a dark background, with splashes of red (Fig. 25).

An inseparable part of Kerouac's creativity, painting was constantly on his mind, from as early as 1952, when he wrote a letter about his approach to depicting reality to John Clellon Holmes, the reporter who wrote an article for *The New York Times* the same year, "This is the Beat Generation," considered the group's manifesto. His method, wrote Kerouac to Clellon Holmes, was exactly the same as a painter's. "I am Rubens and this is my Netherlands. I've been drawing pictures of the scene." In another note he wrote to Allen Ginsberg the same year, he noted, "Your abstraction is more superior. Save the pastels..."[47] In the same way, when Kerouac was learning painting technique from Dody Muller many years later, and jotted down in a notebook (on January 27, 1959) the various steps in creating a painting, he was really mapping out an approach that metaphorically applies to writing as well: "1) ONLY USE BRUSH, no knife to mash and spead and obliterate brush stokees, nofingers to press in lines that aren't real; 2) USE BRUSH SPONTANEOUSLY: i.e. without drawing, without long pause or delay, without erasing... pile it on; 3) FIGURE MEETS BACKGROUND OR VISA VERSA (sic) BY THE BRUSH; 4) PAINT WHAT YOU SEE IN FRONT OF YOU. NO FICTION; 5) STOP WHEN YOU WANT TO 'IMPROVE' – IT'S DONE."[48]

There is something about these artworks that alludes to the unfinished, in fact, as if they really *were* trial runs, while in reality they already belong to Kerouac's poetic universe: that world in which all is fleeting and must be caught, instantly, before one moves on to future experiences. It's an image inspired by a passage from *On the Road*, the end of the fifth chapter in Part Three: "Our battered suitcases were piled on the sidewalk again; we had longer ways to go. But no matter, the road is life."[49]

I'd like to conclude by evoking two paintings that would seem to be exceptions, given the obvious Renoir-like impressionistic touches and the *fauvist* notes right out of Matisse (Figs. 26 and 28); in any case, they both share a *joie de vivre* which stands out from the rest of Kerouac's work. Yet even these two paintings of young women *en plein-air*, especially the one with the green dress (Fig. 28), with none of the German Expressionist feel of the other, can be compared to writings that are just as lyrical and poetic, such as a famous passage from *On the Road* (Part One, chapter ten) that is far removed from the transgressive morality we might expect from Kerouac and the Beat Generation: "My moments in Denver were coming to an end...I stretched out on the grass of an old church with a bunch of hobos...I wanted to go and get Rita again and tell her a lot more things...Not courting talk – real straight talk about souls, for life is holy and every moment is precious." Yet this poetic, romantic abandon will be revealed to be the briefest of flashes, just as the two paintings mentioned above stand out as exceptions to the rest of his work. Indeed, in this very same passage, just a few lines down, Kerouac seems to revert to his cult-like devotion to the idea of the journey as life itself, the only hope he has of breaking with his past and freeing himself from all the rhetoric revolving around conventions: "I heard the Denver and Rio Grande locomotive howling off to the mountains. I wanted to pursue my star further."[50]

1 J. Kerouac, *On the Road* (London: Penguin Essentials, 2011), p. 213 (Part III, chapter 9). [Translator's Note: The author consulted the Italian translation of *On the Road*, *Sulla strada*, translated by M. Caramella and published in 1959 by Mondadori with an introduction by Fernanda Pivano. The quotations from *On the Road* in English in this essay are taken from J. Kerouac, *On the Road* (London: Penguin Essentials, 2011).]

2 J. Kerouac, *Big Sur* (San Francisco: Farrar, Straus and Cudahy, 1962), p. 1. "My work comprises one vast book like Proust's except that my rememberances are written on the run instead of afterwards in a sickbed. Because of the objections of my early publishers I was not allowed to use the same personae names in each work [...] [they] are just chapters in the whole work which I call The Duluoz Legend [...] seen through the eyes of poor Ti Jean (me), otherwise known as Jack Duluoz [...]."

3 B. Miles, " Les écrivains de la Beat Generation dans les années 1950-1960. Une introduction ", *Beat Generation. New York, San Francisco, Paris*, exhibition catalog (Paris: Centre Pompidou; Karlsruhe: ZHM, 2016–17), Paris, 2016, pp. 14–27, p. 21.

4 Kerouac, *On the Road*, pp. 231–32 (Part IV, chapter 1, conclusion).

5 F. Pivano, in *Postfazione* (corresponding to her 1958 *Prefazione*, updated in consequent editions) to J. Kerouac, *Sulla strada* (Milan: Mondadori, 1959), p. 366.

6 From F. Pivano in J. Kerouac, *Sulla strada*, pp. 369–70 (paraphrase).

7 G. Genette, *L'oeuvre de l'art, 2: La relation esthétique* (Paris 1997), edition consulted published in Bologna 1998, p. 8.

8 H. Rosenberg, "Art and Words," *The De-Definition of Art* (Chicago: The University of Chicago Press, 1972).

9 D. Riout, *L'arte del ventesimo secolo. Protagonisti, temi, correnti*, first edition in French, Paris: Gallimard, 2000, edition consulted Turin: Einaudi, 2002, p. 283.

10 The first exhibition of artworks by the Beat poets was held in 1994 at the 80 East Washington Square East Gallery at New York University (E. Adler, *Departed Angels. Jack Kerouac, The Lost Paintings* (New York: Thunder's Mouth Press, 2004), p. 158).

11 Ph.-A. Michaud, "Odds and Ends," *Beat Generation*, pp. 36–49, pp. 37–38.

12 Sold in 2001, after being held by the New York Public Library, it is now privately owned and is frequently displayed as a star exhibit in American libraries.

13 See Kerouac's own description in a 1951 letter to Cassady cited in H. Cunnel, "Stavolta veloce: Jack Kerouac e la composizione di 'Sulla strada,'" in J. Kerouac, *On the Road. Il "rotolo" del 1951*, Ed. H. Cunnel, afterword by F. Pivano, first English edition 2007, Italian edition consulted Milan: Mondadori, 2010, pp. V-CVI, pp. XXV-XXVI.

14 See J. Kerouac, *On the Road*, p. 218 (Part III, chapter 10).

15 B. Miles, "Les écrivains de la Beat Generation dans les années 1950-1960. Une introduction," *Beat Generation*, pp. 14–27, pp. 18–19.

16 B. Miles, "Les écrivains de la Beat Generation," pp. 22–23.

17 J.J. Lebel, " Dadaïstes, surréalistes, clochards célestes et compagnie ", *Beat Generation*, pp. 86–95.

18 Lebel, *Beat Generation*, p. 88.

19 Adler, *Departed Angels*, p. 231.

20 On the role Artaud played in the U.S. in the 1950s, see C. Tomkins, *Robert Rauschenberg. Un ritratto* (Milan: Johan & Levi, 2005), p. 135.

21 Kerouac, *On the Road*, p. 149 (Part II, chapter 8).

22 Kerouac, *On the Road*, p. 28 (Part I, chapter 4).

23 Kerouac, *On the Road*, p. 72 (Part I, chapter 12).

24 Kerouac, *On the Road*, p. 49 (Part I, chapter 9).

25 Kerouac, *On the Road*, pp. 46–47 (Part I, chapter 9).

26 Kerouac, *On the Road*, p. 62 (Part I, chapter 11).

27 Neal Cassady can also be found in other

novels by Kerouac: *Visions of Cody, The Dharma Buns, Big Sur* and *Desolation Angels*.

[28] Kerouac, *On the Road*, p. 278 (Part V).

[29] Kerouac, *On the Road*, p. 4 (Part I, chapter 1).

[30] Lebel, *Beat Generation*, p. 91.

[31] Adler, *Departed Angels*, p. 234: "Be sure to dig the Cezanne country which looks (anyway in Spring) exactly like paintings, and Arles too, [van Gogh home] the restless afternoon cypress, yellow tulips in window boxes, amazing… Montmarte will call me back… and that was where van Gogh, Cezanne, Rousseau, Lautrec, Seurat and Gauguin were, all together, wheeling their paintings upstreet in the wheelbarrows…"

[32] This subject has been extensively addressed in F. Tedeschi, *La scuola di New York. Origini, vicende, protagonisti* (Milan: Vita e Pensiero, 2003), pp. 41–42.

[33] F. Pivano, "La 'beat generation,'" afterword to Kerouac, *Sulla strada*, pp. 365–89, p. 389.

[34] M. Schapiro, " *Courbet* et l'imagerie populaire. Etude sur le réalisme e la naïveté " (1940) republished in *Style, artiste e societé*, Paris, 1982, pp. 273 ff.

[35] In particular, E. Camporesi, "Man, I'm beat," *Beat Generation*, p. 98.

[36] Miles, "Les écrivains de la Beat Generation," p. 27.

[37] Miles, "Les écrivains de la Beat Generation," p. 19.

[38] An example of escalation in Kerouac's writing technique:

BELIEF & TECHNIQUE FOR MODERN PROSE
Jack Kerouac

1. Scribbled secret notebooks, and wild typewritten pages, for yr own joy; 2. Submissive to everything, open, listening; 3. Try never get drunk outside yr own house; 4. Be in love with yr life; 5. Something that you feel will find its own form; 6. Be crazy dumbsaint of the mind; 7. Blow as deep as you want to blow; 8. Write what you want bottomless from bottom of the mind; 9. The unspeakable visions of the individual; 10. No time for poetry but exactly what is; 11. Visionary tics shivering in the chest; 12. In tranced fixation dreaming upon object before you; 13. Remove literary, grammatical and syntactical inhibition; 14. Like Proust be an old teahead of time; 15. Telling the true story of the world in interior monolog; 16. The jewel center of interest is the eye within the eye; 17. Write in recollection and amazement for yourself; 18. Work from pithy middle eye out, swimming in language sea; 19. Accept loss forever; 20. Believe in the holy contour of life; 21. Struggle to sketch the flow that already exists intact in mind; 22. Dont think of words when you stop but to see picture better; 23. Keep track of every day the date emblazoned in yr morning; 24. No fear or shame in the dignity of yr experience, language & knowledge; 25. Write for the world to read and see yr exact pictures of it; 26. Bookmovie is the movie in words, the visu of American form; 27. In praise of Character in the Bleak inhuman Loneliness; 28. Composing wild, undisciplined, pure, coming in from under, crazier the better; 29. You're a Genius all the time; 30. Writer-Director of Earthly movies Sponsored & Angeled in Heaven.

[39] There are numerous examples of Schapiro's interest in the Middle Ages. Among others, "The Romanesque Sculpture of Moissac," in *The Art Bulletin*, vol. XIII, 1931, pp. 248–351; "From Mozarabic to Romanesque in Silos," in *The Art Bulletin*, vol. XXI, 1939, pp. 312–74; "The Sculptures of Souillac," in *Medieval Studies in Memory of A. Kingsley Porter*, ed. W.R.W. Koelher (Cambridge (Mass.): Harvard University Press, 1939), vol. II, pp. 359–87; "New documents on St. Gilles," in *The Art Bulletin*, vol. XIX, 1937, pp. 414–31.

[40] See the gelatin silver print (Archives of the National Gallery of Art in Washington, inv. Davies 2008.103.6), made by Allen Ginsberg in 1953, published in *Beat Generation*, bottom p. 117.

[41] Pivano, "La 'beat generation,'" p. 387.

[42] Kerouac, *On the Road*, p. 49 (Part I, chapter 9).

[43] G. Tibergihier, "Dinamo Beat," *Beat generation*, pp. 28–35, pp. 33–35.

[44] As is well known, Kerouac and Ginsberg called these "visions of Blake" and "divine spirits," attained while on drugs, "new visions."

[45] Adler, *Departed Angels*, p. 241.

[46] Texts found in Adler, *Departed Angels*, pp. 145–46.

[47] Citations from Adler, *Departed Angels*, p. 142.

[48] Adler, *Departed Angels*, p. 142.

[49] Kerouac, *On the Road*, p. 192 (Part III, chapter 5).

[50] Kerouac, *On the Road*, p. 51 (Part I, chapter 10).

Kerouac. Beat Painting

Franco Buffoni

Jacques Querouaques, Picaresque Anarchist

"Do you like Jackson Pollock?", a young Beatnik asked Kerouac the last time he was in Milan, in 1966, during a book presentation at the Libreria Cavour. "Of course I do! He draws much better than I do. And once we even got drunk together." His translator Luciano Bianciardi was with him at the time.

"I'll make the aorist tenses blare like the brass, and play the imperfect tenses like bagpipes," Bianciardi had written in one of the most ironic, rhythmical passages in *Vita agra* [It's a Hard Life] (1962), after evoking – Frenchifying his name as Jacques Querouaques – the American poet whose *Swinging* from *On the Road* he had just translated for the publishing house Guanda. "[I'll make] the present tenses swerve from the moan of the flute to the trill of the violin to the thick pasty sound of the cello, and make the future tenses, full of hope, thunder like the drums and the kettledrums." (It should be remembered that when he was in Italy, Kerouac would sporadically break into the old French spoken by his Breton grandfather who had emigrated to Canada.)

Despite being a novel, one that can be read even as a screenplay – and a film of the same name was made by Carlo Lizzani in 1964, starring Ugo Tognazzi – *It's a Hard Life* – the title referring to the harsh, miserable existence of a translator – makes a number of shrewd observations on stylistics and translation studies. Such as the following: "Translating is what it is usually called today. But in the fourteenth century the word was putting a text into the vernacular, because the word 'translate' sounded too Latin, and Latinisms were to be avoided – only to be in demand again in the fifteenth century, and there are those who still seek them out today. True, because those clever translators did things for a good reason, and in carrying ideas from an unknown language over to a known language, they thought they would be making them intelligible to most people." The famous first line from Chapter 8 of *It's a Hard Life* comes to this tongue-in-cheek conclusion: "But today most translations couldn't be called vulgarizations except in jest, given that they start with a forest language, which is crystal clear and of the people, and turn it into a half-dead language, which isn't any people's at all; it's their translation that could use a new vulgarization."

Needless to say, the "forest language" that is "crystal clear and of the people" which is being translated is the English of Jack Kerouac, Henry Miller and Saul Bellow, while the half-dead language into which the English is being translated is Italian, which belongs to no people – not, at least, as it has come down to us, literarily speaking.

The fact is that Bianciardi always talks and writes for a reason. When he Frenchifies Kerouac's surname, it's because the latter's grandfather was French-Canadian; his real name was Jean-Louis Lebris de Kérouac and he had married an American Indian woman.

Let's look for a moment at this half-dead language that belongs to no people at all: it's the Italian of Pietro Bembo and the Accademia della Crusca; it is a child of Petrarchism; it is incapable of breeding with that other quite vibrant and popular tradition that considered Italian dialects the expression of the true soul of the Italians (albeit so very different from one another). Bembo the poet on one side, Ruzante the playwright on the other.

Bianciardi would have us think about this very point: how well-nigh impossible it is to render the immediacy of a "genuine" language like Kerouac's in an Italian that is necessarily polysyllabic and literary. Bianciardi himself admitted that at first he had simply tried to render Kerouac's jazz rhythms in an acrobatic Italian. Only later, when he couldn't get that music out of his head, did he realize that Kerouac was a master, and it was due to that bodily trace of Kerouac still to be found in the American language.

Just think: today English-language poets like Simon Armitage – keeping up a tradition that goes back to Tony Harrison and Auden before him – still poetize their comments on the news of the day in the pages of the *Guardian*.

The point is, there's a big difference between Italian, with its enormous literary tradition, and a language like English which – welding one concrete noun to another – cheekily calls the famous marine mammal a "sperm-whale."

"I had to learn, as Balzac did, that one must write volumes before signing one's own name." Henry Miller made that remark, but Bianciardi showed he agreed by translating several books, including *The Portable Jack Kerouac* and Miller's own *Tropic of Capricorn*, before writing one of his own.

"A dog was barking in the distance, and you could hear the muffled rasping of the crickets," is a line we come across opening Bianciardi's novel *Il lavoro culturale* (1957). The author was so sensitive to metrics in his formative years that he managed to create a solid style for himself as a writer, inside of which – in perfect synchrony – the unconscious-conscious-preconscious dynamic measured out the metrics of a line, right up to the hendecasyllabic explosion of the Italian: "Come un sordo limio il canto dei grilli."

Did this also occur when Bianciardi translated Kerouac? Was Bianciardi the kind of translator who adapts his own style to that of the author he is translating, or tends to impose his own style instead? We can fairly safely say that neither is the case. Bianciardi instinctively established a dialectical relationship between his style and the style of the writer he was translating, without imposing anything, yet without being imposed upon either.

In Bianciardi's translation of Maugham's *The Gentleman in the Parlour* we find: "Lungi da me l'idea di dar consigli al lettore, ma dirò di passata che nel romanzo picaresco i personaggi son tratti dalla feccia della società, e i protagonisti campano di espedienti. Di solito sono scritti in prima persona" [Far be it from me to offer the reader advice, but I will say in passing that the characters in picaresque novels are treated like the dregs of society, and the main characters get by on their own wits. The novels are usually written in the first person.] Bianciardi is wholly involved: anarchist that he is, he feels like a *picaro* [rogue] himself. The poietic encounter (the encounter between poetics) with Kerouac – Kerouac, the picaresque anarchist of *On the Road* who lives by his wits – is thus a meeting of minds:

"Dobbiamo andare e non fermarci finché non siamo arrivati."
"Dove andiamo?"
"Non lo so, ma dobbiamo andare."

["We have to go away and not stop till we get there."
"Where are we going?"
"I don't know, but we have to go."]

This Kerouac, by the way, is always on the brink of transcending his anarchy and picaresqueness to become, as in the above passage, a creation of Beckett's. After all, there was the startling, epic coincidence of the two writer's books coming out almost at the same time, *On the Road* in 1951 and *Waiting for Godot* in 1952.

Years ago, when Dario Fo received the Nobel Prize, people wondered about the source of his language as a playwright. And once that source was narrowed down to a specific time and place (Milan's Brera neighborhood in the 1950s), it was suggested that Bianciardi, above all others, was the crafter of that language, followed by other names including Arbasino, Simonetta, Tadini, Del Buono, Scerbanenco, and even Vittorio Sereni and Sandro Sinigaglia. Indeed, one of the most ardent weavers of the bohemian language known as the "Brera *scapigliatura*" was Grosseto-born Bianciardi. Precisely because he was not from Milan, Bianciardi chemically reacted with the milieu to produce some superb language and style: "Scatenare contro i torracchioni del centro, contro i padroni mori e timbergecchi [...] e fare piazza pulita d'ogni ingiustizia, d'ogni sporcizia, d'ogni nequizia." [Lash out against the tower-dwellers of downtown and the Moorish, timber-heavy landlords [...] and root out all injustice, filth and evil." That language and style would spill over into his translations, of Kerouac's novels above all.

Elsewhere I have explained why I feel that the tools of linguistic theory are inadequate when applied to literary translation. They can be up to the task in the case of a translation from one esperanto to another, or one source language to another target language, by means of a process of decodification, hence re-codification. However, translating from the language that was once Chaucer's and Shakespeare's to the language once Tasso's and Petrarch's calls for far more sophisticated, empirical tools: that poietic encounter seen above, and the concept of the movement of language over time; above all, the notion of the stratification of language must be foremost in the translator's thoughts. In Bianciardi's novel *It's a Hard Life*, that notion is epitomized by the architectural stratification he summons up when he recalls that the building housing Grosseto's library was formerly a training college for Jesuits, and before that the provostry for the Humiliati, and at the outset a meadow known as the Braida del Guercio. The ability to transfer this description to language is surely Luciano Bianciardi's most masterful intuition as a narrator. And his ability to wed his own cultured, humanistic anarchy to its desperate yankee variant, that of Jacques Querouaques, in its totality, stands as Bianciardi's keenest intuition concerning translation studies.

Thank you, Nanda

"We won!" Nanda Pivano cried, although she hardly had the breath in her body, on that day in 2008, when she learned that Barack Obama had been elected president of the United States of America.

Yes, we won, Nanda. And it's a good thing you died with your dream come true instead of sticking around for the calamity of January 2017, when a new president took office. You were born in 1917, and it wouldn't have been a proper celebration of your one-hundredth birthday.

So stay by our side with your twentieth century that started with *Spoon River* and militant anti-fascism, and proceeded through Kerouac and Gregory Corso, Henry Miller and Erica Jong, Bob Dylan and Lou Reed, Picasso and Ettore Sottsass, only to wind up with Brett Easton Ellis and Jay McInerney and your personal album and autobiography *The Beat Goes On*, which you would have liked to call *Why I Didn't Go to Bed...with Hemingway*.

"By now America had unfurled before me and it seemed impossible that the fraud of dictatorship could ever kill so many of our individual talents. Roosevelt's American dream had taken over our souls and our illusions. Maybe we'd gotten it all wrong; maybe there was nothing to get right; maybe Alberto Mondadori, our magnificent and ill-fated publisher, had tried to help us dream our dreams. I did translations for him with one idea in my mind: seeing the books go to print. And with one desire: sharing my dreams with young people who were immune to the trials and tribulations I had had to endure myself." So wrote Fernanda Pivano in her *The Beat Goes On*, published in 2004 and edited by Guido Harari.

One such trial for Nanda Pivano was her arrest for translating Hemingway's *A Farewell to Arms*, which was judged too pacifist and denigratory of the honor of the Italian army. And of course prison, during which she discovered a trick of Cesare Pavese's for getting around Fascist censorship: a simple yet effective initial "s," which, in the eyes of the "clerical Fascists" of the era, turned an *Antologia di Spoon River* into a more palatable *Antologia di S. River*.

All irony aside, an arrest is an arrest, and jail is jail, has been and will always be. Just imagine the experience in those darkest of times. Even more obscene, that arrest and prison time, for an upstanding young woman with a degree in English literature (with a thesis on Melville's *Moby Dick*) as well as a philosophy degree (and a thesis on existentialism, with Nicola Abbagnano as her supervisor). "*The Spoon River Anthology* was blacklisted in Italy too," Pivano recalled years later. "Its theme was peace, it was against war, against capitalism, against everything conformism entailed in general. It was everything the government didn't allow us to think about, so they threw me into prison. And I'm very glad they did."

The funny thing is that it all started as a joke, or a challenge, when a young Nanda asked her mentor, Cesare Pavese, to explain the difference between English and American literature. By way of an answer, Pavese handed her that slim volume by Edgar Lee Masters. Which Nanda opened at random, half-way through, electrified by the verses: "Kissing her with my soul upon my lips / It suddenly took flight." "Who knows why those lines awed me?" the translator mused many years on. "It's so hard to explain teenagers' reactions."

In fact, talking to teenagers and talking about them (only to learn at a later date, perhaps, that that so very surprising passage from *Spoon River*, E. L. Masters had lifted it from the Palatine Anthology) was Fernanda Pivano's true calling, as early as the Fascist jails, on through her militant radicalism in the 1970s, and up to her enviable old age at the turn of the new millennium. And she always treated "her" poets the same way: like fragile if brilliant adolescents who had grown up in too much of a hurry, and it showed – after Hemingway scolded her at the Gritti Palace in Venice in 1947, with a "Daughter, you might have spared me this one!" when he learned she was a teetotaler.

And so Nanda became the "pal" of an odd assortment of alcoholics, drug addicts and sexually promiscuous individuals who nevertheless went by the names of Allen Ginsberg, Jack Kerouac, William Burroughs, Gregory Corso, Lawrence Ferlinghetti, and Charles Bukowski. She, of all people, faithful to the same man her entire life, the architect and designer Ettore Sottsass, whom she married in 1949, and with whom she produced a series of memorable photographs whenever her hard-living geniuses toured Italy.

It's not hard to imagine how Italian academia reacted to her translations and the company she kept. As her popularity grew (actually, the popularity of her translations) among younger readers, so grew the snobbery and a certain dismissive attitude towards her, until she was practically shut out from pursuing a standard academic career (not that she ever wanted one, however); the tough part was that she was also shut out of simple invitations to conferences and seminars. Above all, lest we forget, Pivano dealt with "translations." Here was a term that academia considered reductive, even disagreeable. It would not be until the early 1990s that translations would qualify as credentials; before then, they were worse than useless when applying for a teaching position, and if an applicant insisted, they actually became a boomerang.

How may we define and describe Fernanda Pivano's translation method? That method which enabled her to familiarize Italians with the four basic categories of dissent in America in the 1950s and 1960s and legitimate them in their eyes? There was **black dissent**, whose spokesperson, courtesy of Pivano, became Richard Wright; then there was **pacifist/non-violent dissent** (our own Ginsberg and Kerouac); then **gay dissent** and **feminist dissent**. Pivano, who translated and befriended the literary lights of the day, turned out translations that managed to convey and even legitimate the deeper spirit of such protests and their hidden motivations, laying the groundwork for that explosion that would rock Italian society, as well, in the late 1960s – and leave it unrecognizable.

It was a translation method that I like to call the poietic encounter: the meeting of two *poiein*, two poetic "plans of action" that suggest translation should be understood as a literary subproduct no longer, but an *Überleben* instead: an "afterlife" of the text itself. My belief being that translation is not so much a formal exercise as an existential experience, which allows it to overcome those traditional and sterile dichotomies that inevitably lead to a standoff. On the one hand, the idea that style and poetic "ineffability" get lost in translation; on the other, the belief that the only thing that can be conveyed is content. Pivano didn't ask the question: "How can I reproduce the style?" Because in her view, literary translation could not be conceptually reduced to being an operation that reproduces a text. She saw it as a process, one that shifted over time – flowering, then flowering a second time – with no distinction between "original" and "copy," but two texts, each with its own artistic dignity. As is clearly seen in that famous notebook with Pivano's earliest versions of *Spoon River* poems, which she hid in a desk at the publisher's, Einaudi in Turin, so Pavese wouldn't find it – or perhaps so he *would* find it.

Of the five basic notions underlying modern translation studies (intertextuality, poetics, the movement of language over time, rhythm and avant-texte), and at a time when these terms were not yet in use, Pivano instinctively resorted to the avant-texte, which involved firsthand experience and an ongoing collaboration with living authors, in a sort of applied socio-biographical method. This meant she could appropriate the process by which the text germinated and grew, in all its various stages, in a sort of sympathetic adherence not only to the text itself, as a finished work, but to its formativity. And she evidently got it right, both in theory and in practice, if she came up with lines like this:

> Immagina di essere alto un metro e cinquantotto
> e di avere iniziato a lavorare come garzone in una drogheria
> studiando legge a lume di candela,
> finché non sei diventato avvocato.

[Suppose you just stood 5 feet two
And had worked your way as a grocery clerk
Studying law by candlelight
Until you became an attorney at law?]

[*Spoon River Anthology*, 94. Judge Selah Lively]

Pivano was firmly convinced that, above and beyond the issue of meter, a text actually *breathed*, deeply and to a rhythm, which enabled it to organize thought – and even mold it. From this perspective, there was no real distinction between translating prose and translating poetry, since the true difference was between a text endowed with its own breath, and its own rhythm, and a text bereft of both. Therefore it was crucial for a translator to impose a creative rhythm on a text, and *for* that text.

At this point I feel I must address the controversial relationship between Fernanda Pivano and poetry, understood as a literary genre, and from both an Italian and an "American" perspective. After all, Pivano cut her teeth reading Edgar Lee Masters and Jack Kerouac, and her tastes would later broaden to include Bob Dylan, while in Italy she was initiated into Cesare Pavese and would end up a fan of singers Vasco Rossi and Jovanotti. Her idea of poetry hardly coincided with that of John Ashbery or Andrea Zanzotto.

And while we are on the subject, that famous saying of Ezra Pound's comes to mind: "Italian poetry is in need of a good sandpapering." By that he meant to decry its verbosity, overwrought lyricism and syrupy sentimentality. That said, while we can summon up a fresh admiration for Pivano's courage and tenacity – together with Ettore Sottsass she did co-found the psychedelically- inclined review *Pianeta fresco*, a platform for the best in Italian beat poetry in 1967–68 – on the other hand, we certainly can't buy into her unyielding belief that "the only true poets writing today are singer-songwriters." And this at a time when Italy was enjoying its postwar economic boom, a time when the logical conclusion of the existential philosophy underlying *On the Road* might have been a hike around Kathmandu, or Dino Risi's road comedy *Il sorpasso*, starring Vittorio Gassman and Jean-Louis Trintignant.

Make no mistake: I like Pivano's "singer-songwriter friends" (to para-phrase the title of a popular book of hers that Mondadori published in 2005, edited by Stefano Senardi and Sergio Sacchi), be they Piero Ciampi, De André or Jovanotti. I've listened to their music and even enjoyed it on occasion. But Nanda, in whatever heaven you are in, hear me out: if you take a moment and reread their lyrics, without calculating the music adorning them and sometimes disguising them, you will see that there's very little poetry to be found there: "Piero, shoot him / Shoot him now /And if he doesn't die / Shoot him again."

Poor poetry! Let's help it survive – the real thing, that is: the thing that few probably read at all; since let's not forget that it's only real poetry that truly "invents" and renews language. Otherwise we run the risk of winding up with Gian Pieretti, a mediocre singer-songwriter Kerouac engaged for a travel-ing show of alcohol-fueled performances in 1963. Something Giovanni Raboni wrote admirably pertains to what we are discussing here: "Poetry is neither a state of mind a priori, nor a privileged condition, and neither a separate reality nor a better one. It's a language: a different language from the one we use every day to communicate; a far richer, far more complete, far more human language, one that is at once carefully premeditated and profoundly involuntary, with the ability to connect things that can be seen, and connect them to the unseen; and to relate the things we know to those we don't."

What is much more convincing, in our eyes, is Pivano's courageous position on the civil rights movement in the United States and also in Italy. Here she is utterly consistent, with no lapses of any kind. She would never give up her pacifist ideals. Those ideals come vividly back to life in the marvelous documentary *A Farewell to Beat*, made in 2001, on a road trip across America to uncover the few survivors of that era, and revisit the evocative backdrops to their adventures. What was it that Kerouac said about the peace movement? "Tolstoy invented it, then Gandhi copied it."

When Italy was still all about statues of the Madonna that shed real tears and clenched-fist salutes, Nanda Pivano put up a wild card like Gregory Corso since she knew he was a genius, despite his excesses and scrapes with the law. Allen Ginsberg was with Nanda in Spoleto in 1967, when he tried to give a flower to a carabiniere, who hauled him off to prison for offending public decency (the offense being the verses he had recited in public and Pivano had translated simultaneously). And who happened to be the publisher of that review *Pianeta fresco* mentioned earlier? None other than Angelo Pezzana, one of the four or five Italians to openly declare their homosexuality pre-1968.

This is why I am firmly convinced that if we take a comparative view of those "courageous" individuals born in the decade starting in 1910, Fernanda Pivano deserves a place of honor alongside, for example, Charles Olson and Judd Marmor. Olson, the Rector of Black Mountain College from 1951 to 1956, pulled off a coup, hosting and hence conferring academic dignity on the top American artists of the avant-garde of the day, from Allen Ginsberg to John Cage: figures who inspired acts of total rebellion and gay liberation. Judd Marmor was the psychiatrist who succeeded in getting homosexuality removed from the *Diagnostic and Statistical Manual of Mental Disorders* in 1973, which would ultimately lead to its being removed from the World Health Organization's own list in 1990, on May 17, the date that the entire civilized world now celebrates as the International Day against Homophobia – an anniversary to which Nanda Pivano would give her own interpretation in the last generous years of her life. So just like Jay McInerney, who devoted a whole article to Pivano in *The New Yorker* a few years ago, with an Italian title, "Grazie, Nanda," I, too, take this occasion to thank Nanda.

Into the Wild as the extreme consequence of the philosophy underlying *On the Road* (and St. Francis)

To define the huge impact of the *sapiens-sapiens* on the Earth, the custom is to refer to the Anthropocene, a young era, geologically speaking, that covers the last ten thousand years. Another term, "domestication," is also used to describe that symbiosis between man, plants and wild animals that resulted in our transformation from hunters and gatherers to farmers who subsequently lived in villages. As domestication during the Anthropocene progressed, nature started to retreat; those *sapiens-sapiens* turned their backs on the wild. In the future, there will likely only be room for domesticated animals. A few species – mice and rats, perhaps, along with crows, pigeons and a sparrow or two – are expected to survive by preserving their own ecological niches. By now, foxes and badgers are becoming urbanized. Even polar bears face very slim chances of being able to linger on in the wild.

Jon Krakauer's 1996 work of non-fiction, *Into the Wild,* shows how the concept of wilderness had been transformed in the late-twentieth-century collective imagination, departing from the romantic view of nature in its wildest sense. But the book also reveals the transformation of the very concept of narrative, from the canonical novel to docu-fiction, conceived as a script for a film version of the "story" that would inevitably follow. And so it did, in this case, when the film of the same name came out in 2007, artfully directed by Sean Penn. In short, what emerges from the account by Krakauer and the film by Penn is a concept of the wild crafted by the human imagination, showing how the arc of the Anthropocene produced a perception of nature as an environment evoking ancestral fears, yet still exerting a powerful appeal on contemporary humanity that at times rewards them with heightened sensations of physical and psychological well-being.

Indeed, who could possibly deny that Christopher Johnson McCandless, once he had become Alexander Supertramp and had finally reached Alaska, felt an extraordinary sense of physical and psychological well-being in his first few weeks in the wild? And if we ask which philosophy was driving Christopher's retreat, we soon discover that, apart from the inspiration of Kerouac himself, the exponents of that philosophy were the same as those who had inspired Kerouac.

Following in the footsteps of Thoreau, Jack London and Kerouac, then, twenty-four-year-old Chris, as the original photo shows, seen at the end of the film and probably taken by Chris himself, is leaning against the by now legendary "Magic Bus" from the 1940s, courtesy of the Fairbanks Transportation system, with an intense expression of pure, sublime well-being on his face. It's a sensation that the fine Californian actor Emile Hirsch conveys to perfection in several scenes in the film, even though, more often than not, he appears to channeling post-Kerouac road movies like *Easy Rider* instead. And it's a sensation that Krakauer ably traces to its own real source, when he quotes some of Chris' real words in his book: "I read somewhere... how important it is in life not necessarily to be strong... but to feel strong."

Seen in this light, certain conversations Chris has on the road – with the hippie couple, the young singer-songwriter who falls for him, and the loner war veteran who would like to adopt him – assume the status of parables. Actually, however, it's Chris' plain talk with the thresher operator from South Dakota, Wayne Westerberg, that most clearly reveals the McCandless quest for physical and psychological well-being, which proves to be a wholesale rejection of the version offered up by the highly evolved Anthropocene.

> Chris: I'm going to Alaska.
> Wayne: Alaska, Alaska? Or city Alaska? Because they do have markets in Alaska. The city of Alaska. Not in Alaska. In the city of Alaska, they have markets.
> Chris: No, man. Alaska, Alaska. I'm gonna be all the way out there, all the way fucking out there. Just on my own. You know, no fucking watch, no map, no axe, no nothing. No nothing. Just be out there. Just be out there in it. You know, big mountains, rivers, sky, game. Just be out there in it, you know? In the wild.
> Wayne: In the wild.
> Chris: Just wild!
> Wayne: Yeah. What are you doing when we're there? Now you're in the wild, what are we doing?
> Chris: You're just living, man. You're just there, in that moment, in that special place and time. Maybe when I get back, I can write a book about my travels.
> Wayne: Yeah. Why not?

Chris: You know, about getting out of this sick society. Society!
Wayne: [*coughs*] Society! Society!
Chris: Society, man! You know, society! 'Cause, you know what I don't understand? I don't understand why people, why every fucking person is so bad to each other so fucking often. It doesn't make sense to me. Judgment. Control. All that, the whole spectrum. Well, it just...
Wayne: What "people" we talking about?
Chris: You know, parents, hypocrites, politicians, pricks.
Wayne: [taps Chris' head] This is a mistake. It's a mistake to get too deep into all that kind of stuff. Alex, you're a hell of a young guy, a hell of a young guy. But I promise you this. You're a young guy.

This dialogue lends itself to two significant deductions, one of a semantic nature and the other of a social nature. The former tells us that the word "life," as understood by the advanced Anthropocene, comes down to "markets" for Wayne and a nasty "game" for Chris, which takes us straight back to the philosophical connection to Kerouac, as well as Thoreau and Jack London. The second deduction strikes at the root of Chris' motivation for rebelling as he does. The society understood as *homo homini lupus* is the one that his father, an ambitious aerospace engineer, summed up in two words: judgment and control. These are the very words that Chris, with his brand-new degree in anthropology, promptly decides to drop from his vocabulary, like Kerouac before him. He does it by degrees, starting with a two-year wander not so very different, in the end, from a grand tour – heading west, on the road – that will take in Oregon, Nevada, Arizona and South Dakota. Then he abruptly ups the stakes, abandoning his old car, Kerouac-style, and donating the $24,000 that represents his college savings, then becoming unreachable in any way. Not only does he break off with his family, he also cuts off his beloved sister Carine, whom he had always confided in as a teenager, and who will be present at his cremation, flying back to Virginia with Chris' ashes in her backpack.

Ten days hitching rides on slow freight trains, or thumbing rides on the highways, and Chris makes it to the North, for the last four month of his true existence ("no game") amid wild animals on the tundra and frozen, then swollen, rivers. His close encounter with a bear, who rears up on his haunches before a naked Chris then meekly withdraws into the wilderness once more, suggests a bold analogy with another twenty-year-old who lived seven centuries earlier, whose own "wild" was represented by: a) the pounding of Marmore waterfalls north of Rome, and b) the surrounding woods home to wolves instead of bears. The youth's aversion to and subsequent rebellion against his father is essentially the same: Ser Bernardone and the engineer Walt McCandless, two sides of the same coin.

This supreme act of rebellion against his father – surpassing and transcending every "beat rebellion" and taking it to its logical extreme – assumes the form of an urgent need to strip down and flee, naked as the day he was born, and Chris, like St. Francis seven centuries earlier, carries out his radical plan in ways that are quite similar to our saint's, even when adjusted for two different eras. Chris' young singer-songwriter thus corresponds to Saint Clare. However, there is a major difference: Francis relied on a powerful ideology that sustained him and in some way defended him, while Chris had nothing apart from the books in his head. Chris is just "a hell of a young guy," but even a hermit needs base competencies. Just think of all the ideological "buffers" – from Buddhism to Christianity and all the way to a syncretism that could even be inspiring on a visual level, as the present exhibition shows so well – that Kerouac himself made good use of. As to those various religious beliefs, it should be pointed out that for Kerouac their value was mainly emotional, esthetic-symbolic, or at most philosophical, as well as folkloristic. Kerouac would never have been able to admit or even, perhaps, understand the political weight of these beliefs. We can well imagine the effect that the word "concordato" [Translator's note: a word that recalls the Lateran Treaty of 1929], for example, which is totally alien to American culture, including the establishment, would have had on the anarchical Kerouac, who once said, "I believe in angels walking the earth, I believe in God, when I feel good. When I feel bad I curse Him and all the saints. I am Catholic. I'm also part Indian: this is why I feel at home anywhere in America."

As a recent autobiography by Julia Kristeva, recently published in Italy by Donzelli, observes: "Semiologists have demonstrated that human beings cannot be defined exclusively on the basis of the place they occupy in the production line or the social relations that derive from such a position; men and women are mainly constituted of the productivity inherent to speaking beings, that is to say, language and the creations derived from it: literature, the arts, law, codes of communication, and all kinds of expressions that constitute a sense or a non-sense."

St. Francis invented Italian literature, enabling art to sublimate that initial impulse of hatred of one's father, and the society he represents, into love, rendering it eternal. Kerouac did *not* invent American literature – that had been done for him by Walt Whitman and Emily Dickinson – yet it's safe to say that, together with Ginsberg, he invented a new way to present American literature to the Cold War Era, by means of a "wild rebellion." By contrast, Chris left us just his notes in a college notebook: notes that grow increasingly dramatic and conclusive as he realizes that he has eaten the wrong kind of roots, despite possessing an edible plant guide that he regularly consulted. Those wild potato roots were the inedible kind, so poisonous that nothing but immediate medical care could have saved him. This being completely out of the question, Chris lay down on his filthy mattress in the bus and looked up at the patch of sky he could see through a window. Touching his fingertips together, seeing his cracked, split fingernails: his stigmata.

Finale, with a few thoughts spared for Keats and Rimbaud

"So dirty and unkempt to be unimaginable, practically barefoot, so worn were the shoes on his feet; his jacket all torn behind, a fur cap on his head, a plaid blanket wrapped around his shoulders and a knapsack on his back: I cannot say what he looked like." So Mrs. Dillon described the appearance of one of England's purest romantic poets, John Keats, on his return from a wildly improbable hike through the Scottish Highlands in 1818. At the time of his own plunge into the wild, complete with a memorable white night spent with his friend Brown in Kirkcudbright, Junkets (a nickname for Keats that Leigh Hunt had jokingly bequeathed him) was exactly the same age as Chris in his Magic Bus and Kerouac his first time on the road. And, if you will, the same age as St. Francis when he gave up his worldly goods.

From the Highlands, Keats made an adventurous crossing to the wild islands Iona and Staff. That taste of raging winds straight out of a Shakespearian tempest, in an utterly impervious natural setting, cliffs and tundra pelted by the waves, would prove fatal to the poet who wrote *Endymion*. Once the journey was at an end, raging fevers would turn into pneumonia, and tell-tale blood would do the rest. Having studied medicine, Keats knew the difference between venous blood and arterial blood. Absorbing the prognosis, he nevertheless let his painter friend Severn convince him to play his last card: a milder climate. He came to Rome where he died a few weeks later, at the age of twenty-five.

Nevertheless, in the summer of 1819, after a brief respite, Keats had succeeded in sublimating his sacrifice into art. His overwhelming desire to flee from the frustrations ensuing from the negative reviews of his *Endymion*, combined with his venture "into the wild" in 1818, resulted in the sublime poetic achievement of *Ode to a Nightingale*:

> The same that oft-times hath
> Charm'd magic casements, opening on the foam
> Of perilous seas, in faery lands forlorn.

While another desperate rebel such as Rimbaud would write, a few decades later, "I will go into nature like a woman," with the intent of being penetrated and even "impregnated" by nature ("Si j'ai du goût ce n'est guère / Que pour la terre et les pierres"), Keats succeeds in concentrating his need to strip down and immerse himself in nature by evoking Ruth, the Biblical figure who epitomizes the feeling of being "sick for home," in endless solitude. And in a stupendous burst of lyricism he tells us that that song of sorrow and rejection is the same that has so often "charmed" magic windows, thrown open over the foam of restless seas in remote, enchanted lands. The adjective "forlorn" on which the seventh stanza ends, referring to those lands, at the beginning of the eighth and last stanza of the ode, in a slight yet enervating semantic shift, is reiterated by Keats but now refers to himself:

> Forlorn! The very word is like a bell
> To toll me back from thee to my sole self!

It has come down to solitude, therefore, in wild rebellion. And it's just his terror of solitude that confuses a hungry Chris McCandless as he looks for edible plants, convinced, like St. Francis, that the nature deity protecting wild fowls and bears would nourish him as well.

In Keats' ode, the word "forlorn" is weighed and analyzed like an inedible, poisonous root. Its gloomy sound echoes like the sound in a shell held to one's ear among the rocks of that "fairyland." However, while the remote lands may have been enchanted, the term "forlorn," referred to human corporeity, still means "rejected, abandoned, miserable," which makes us realize that art alone has the power to lift us above human corporeity and become eternal. Like St. Francis, who transforms the waters of the Marmore Falls, where he fails to cleanse himself, and sublimates them into a prayer that will be a milestone in Italian literature. Like Chris, perhaps, who – thanks to two artists, Krakauer and Penn – still haunts us with his photo in his plaid shirt, and with his notebook. And the same is just Kerouac's own achievement, when he sublimated his post-war wild rebellion – the same that Salinger saw come to nothing on that fatal day in 1951, in a field of rye – into literature "on the road."

A Personal Album

This first section brings together a series of portraits of real people who touched the life of Jack Kerouac, some actually encountered, others simply imagined. Regardless, together they bring to light significant aspects of his life story and the people and places he frequented, as well as his dreams and obsessions. Rather than being an all-encompassing vision, this gallery of faces, like an album of photographs, offers new bases for reflection on the author's life and work. Some recognizable figures were participants in Kerouac's life, such as William Burroughs and Dody Muller, while others populated his obsessive, mystic and oneiric imagination, such as Cardinal Montini, Truman Capote and Joan Crawford. (A.C.)

Arnaldo Pomodoro and the Beat Generation.
An Eye-witness Statement

Ada Masoero

Arnaldo Pomodoro is an ideal eye-witness of the epoch celebrated in this exhibition. Now in Milan, Pomodoro taught as artist-in-residence at Stanford University in California, in the heart of what is today Silicon Valley, in 1966. The following year, he was at Berkeley, another California university, in the same role.

Pomodoro had been to the United States before, in 1959, on a scholarship from the Italian Ministry of Foreign Affairs, and he returned several times in the 1960s,[1] to both the East and the West Coast, forming friendships with the greatest American artists of the moment.[2] Those two periods gave him the opportunity to experience the cultural movement of the student revolts and the hippies "in real time" and right there where it was all happening, that historic turning point in twentieth-century history which was the year 1968.

As Arnaldo Pomodoro tells it:

My trips in the United States were fundamental to the evolution of my work, on the one hand, from the experience of a space completely different from ours, and on the other, from my relationship with the American artistic and cultural movements of those years. While I was teaching at Stanford and Berkeley, I spent a lot of time with the poets and writers of the Beat Generation. The movement – with its extraordinary power of ideas, total freedom of behavior, and innovative spark – influenced me profoundly in a number of ways. I should say, though, that I had already had contact with Beat writers in Milan (Allen Ginsberg, Gregory Corso, Jack Kerouac...) through Fernanda Pivano and Ettore Sottsass. After she had translated *Spoon River Anthology*, "la Nanda," as we called her, met them personally and became the narrator of that new literary current and the lifestyle that went along with it.

In just a few years, on many trips, with an inexhaustible enthusiasm, she had single-handedly created a bridge between the American and Italian cultures, transmitting the great lessons of that movement that transformed our conception and perception of the world. When Ginsberg, little-known in Italy at the time, came to Milan on his way back from India, Nanda, Ettore and I organized a meeting in his honor at my studio. All dressed in white like a guru, he sat on the ground reciting his wonderful poems, accompanying his voice with the gentle sound of little bells and drums, like a shaman chanting... I remember that Nanda managed to get him into the most prestigious homes of Milan, and he charmed everyone, including even the well-bred ladies of the upper-crust and the snobbiest intellectuals.

Pomodoro still has vivid memories of those times in California:[3]

It was a truly extraordinary experience. In the course of a few months, in the unusually mild winter of 1966–67, everything changed. Everything was ablaze with innovation. I frequented poets and writers of the Beat Generation (Allen Ginsberg, Gregory Corso, Lawrence Ferlinghetti...) and was familiar with the student movement. Everyone was so alive, full of imagination and incredible confidence. Young people had the awareness and pride of being the anticipators of events and issues of opposition to industry, technology, wealth, conformity... I was enchanted by their naturalness, their improvised ways of dressing, their bare feet, their opposition to old-style professors – in brief, by the way they lived their lives so freely. Everything was meaningful, even the smallest thing or act: the mattress on the floor, houses without furniture, communes or nearly, their outfits with tennis shoes, Levi's, ponchos and Indian shirts, their concentration when they spoke, their sensitivity to nature... In San Francisco, I spent a lot of time with Lawrence Ferlinghetti at his City Lights Bookstore, the gathering place of the protagonists of the Beat Generation.

There is no need to insist how important Jack Kerouac's books were for the development of that culture and lifestyle. No one else succeeded so well in anticipating and interpreting the anxieties and utopias of the 1960s, for entire generations. His masterpiece, *On the Road*, and also *The Subterraneans*, were not only pivotal books in the history of twentieth-century literature and culture, introducing new narrative forms with immediate, spontaneous language and an explosive be-bop rhythm, but they also became a sort of manifesto of an entire literary, social, musical and cultural movement. Discovering Kerouac's drawings now, which I hadn't known before, has been a surprise but surely one that confirms the brilliance of this experimenter and builder of languages, operating outside of all pre-established models and limits.

Statements made by Arnaldo Pomodoro directly to Ada Masoero.

[1] In 1962, the Los Angeles gallery owner Felix Landau presented Arnaldo Pomodoro's first solo exhibition in the United States, which was followed by many others.
[2] His American friends and acquaintances beginning in the early 1960s included Mark Rothko, with whom he spent time in New York when both were working with the Marlborough Gallery, Barnett Newman, Franz Kline, Philip Guston, Jasper Johns, Robert Rauschenberg, Andy Warhol, Louise Nevelson, and Mark Di Suvero.
[3] The sculpture *Il Grande Ascolto*, 1967–68, was inspired by the gigantic radio telescope at the University of Berkeley in California, which fascinated Pomodoro.

1 *The Slouch Hat*, 1960 c.,
oil and charcoal on paper, 43 x 35.2 cm

The Slouch Hat introduces a sense of the everyday
in Kerouac's crowded life in New York between
the end of the 1950s and the beginning of the
1960s. The characters are sketched roughly, but
a synthetic gestural painting that closely recalls
that of Larry Rivers is added in places to the rapid
charcoal drawing. The scene shows a quintessential
Beat subject, evoking many photographs taken
in the famed Cedar Tavern in the Village in New
York, a meeting place for poets like Allen Ginsburg
and Bob Dylan as well as artists like de Kooning,
Twardowicz and Rivers. The reference to a "slouch"
hat also appears in one of Kerouac's poems from
1959, *I had a slouch hat too one time*, which he
read on the LP *Poetry for the Beat Generation*,
accompanied by the legendary Steve Allen
on the piano.

2 *Pfui*, n.d.,
pencil on paper,
9.2 x 8.4 cm

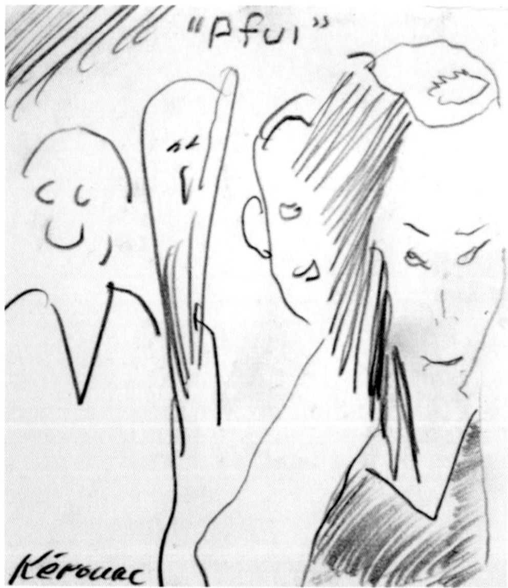

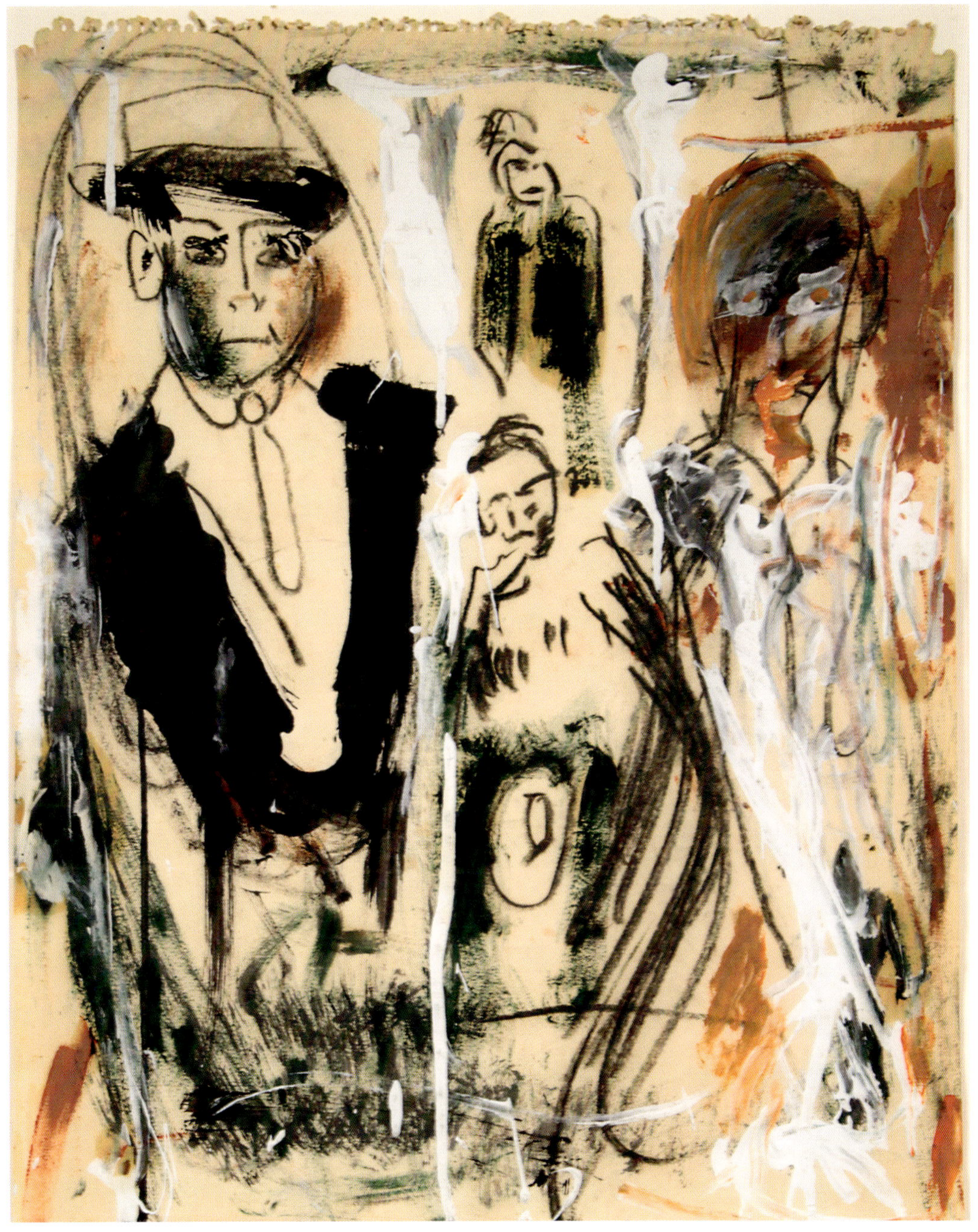

The portrait of Cardinal Montini, painted in 1959, was based on a photograph appearing in *Life* on 20 October 1958, when the magazine published a special report on the consistory that elected Giuseppe Roncalli as pope. What is striking about the portrait, painted in New York in Dody Muller's studio, is Kerouac's interest in this man who would play a central role in the history of Catholicism, who in fact, a few years later, in 1963, became Pope Paul VI. A letter sent by Kerouac to Allen Ginsberg on October 4, 1962 indicates the importance this painting had for Kerouac. In this expressionist portrait, Jack tried to merge the solemnity of the subject, not unlike the sacred nature of medieval painting, with the emotional and expressive power of the contemporary American painting that Kerouac was becoming familiar with through his friendship with Muller.

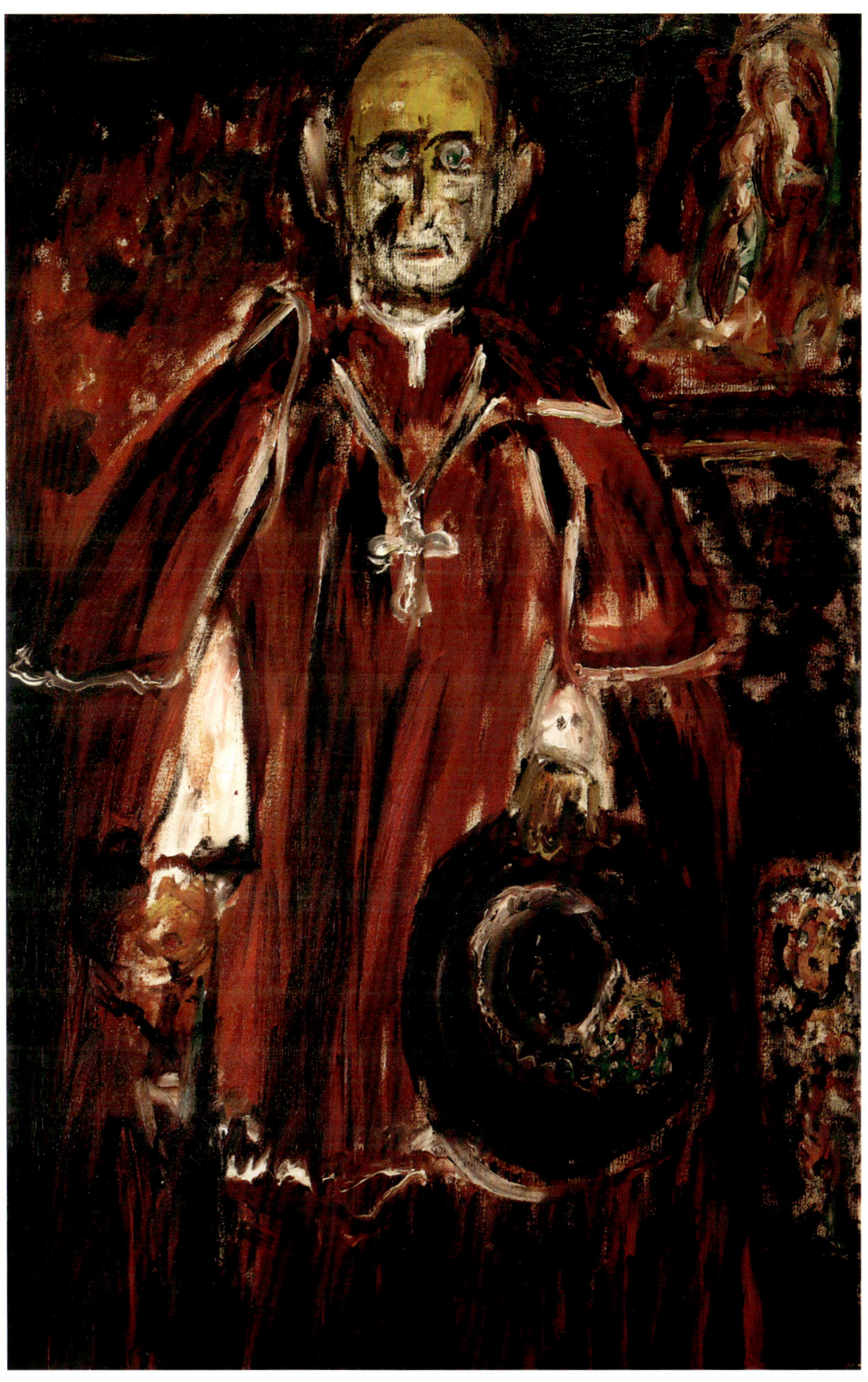

4 *Woman* (Joan Rawshanks) *in Blue
with Black Hat*, n.d.,
oil on canvas, 40.6 x 30.5 cm

62

Visions of Cody features a section dedicated
to Joan Rawshanks, which was republished in the
Transatlantic Review in the spring of 1962. While
strolling through San Francisco with Neal and
Carolyn Cassady in 1952, Kerouac happened upon
the set of the film *Sudden Fear*, where he met Joan
Crawford. In a play on words, Neal transformed the
name "Crawford" into "Rawshanks," the elusive,
cigarette-smoking character in Kerouac's story and
in this painting. *Femme fatale* of Hollywood cinema
between the world wars, Crawford also appears in
The Origins of the Beat Generation (in *The Beat
Book: Writings from the Beat Generation*, Anne
Waldman, ed. Shambhala, 2007) as the recurring
image of "a woman with a cigarette at sticky lips."

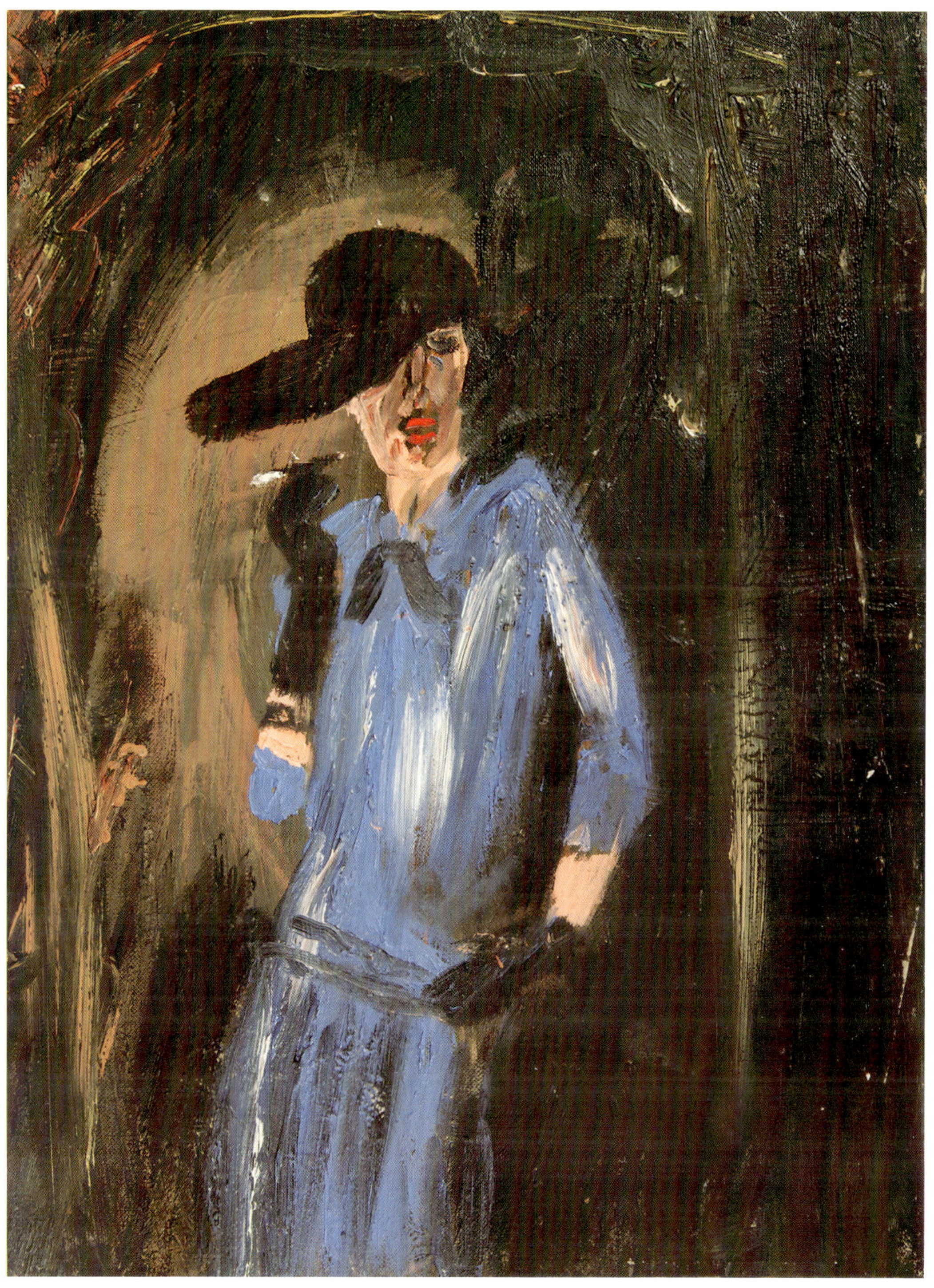

64

The portrait of Truman Capote has a dynamic,
almost violent quality, a gestural mass of lines
whose centripetal movement recalls the circularity
of Roger Higgins' famous photograph of Capote.
The painting was probably a response to the
many criticisms Capote directed at the authors of
the Beat Generation. He was particularly vitriolic
against Kerouac between 1958–59, immediately
after the release of *On the Road*, whose success
overshadowed Capote's *Breakfast at Tiffany's*.
In an interview with David Susskind on the
WNTA-TV program *Open End*, Capote famously
branded the writing of the Beat authors as
mere "type-writing."

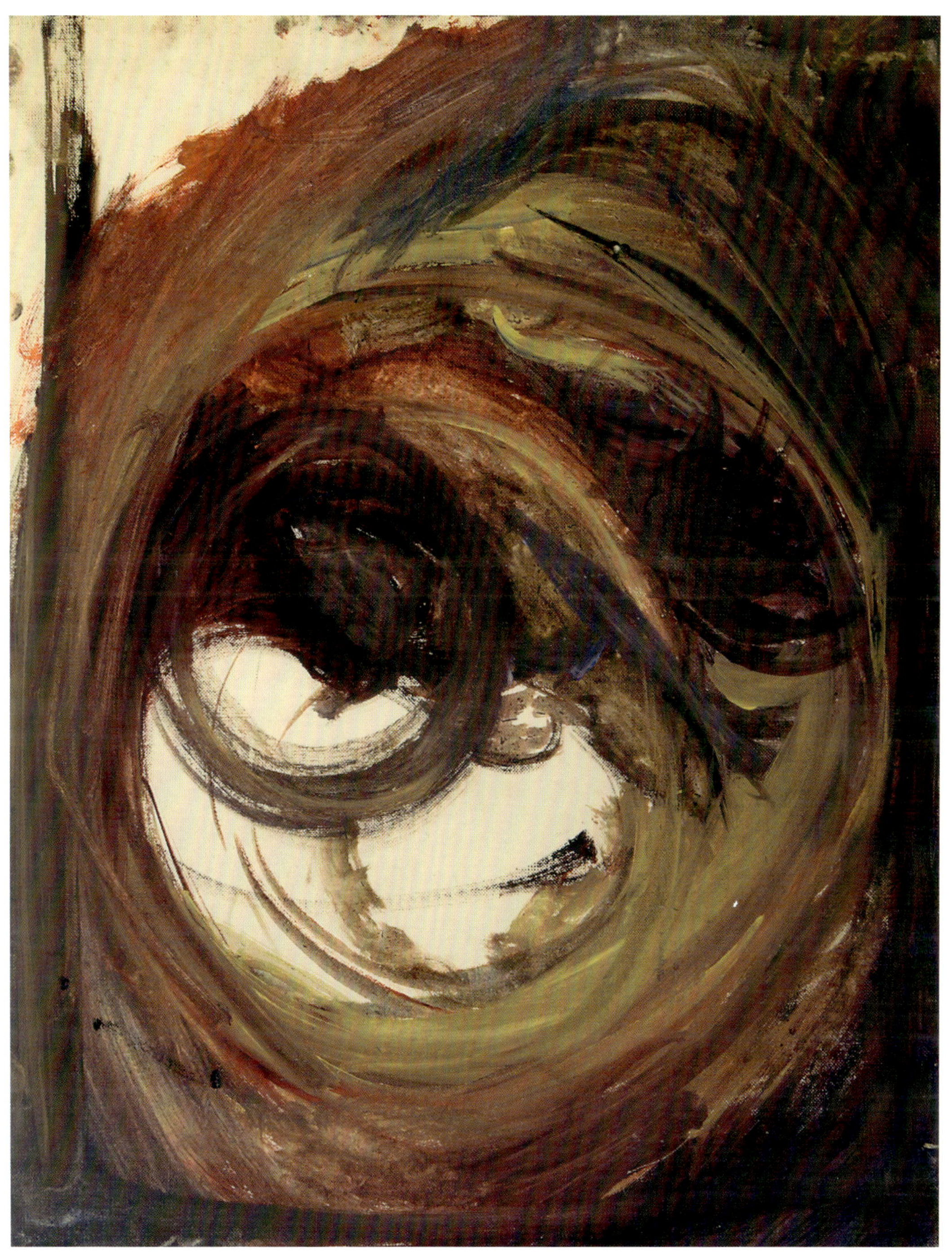

The Silly Eye is an enigmatic painting. A character
seen in full profile looks out vacantly, his wide-
open eye outlined in a brash yellow. Careful
comparison with other portraits by Kerouac (Fig. 7)
indicates that the subject in this painting is William
Burroughs. In a diary entry dated October 20,
1959, Jack specified that the term "silly" refers to
the empty eye with its dilated pupil, accentuated
by the use of yellow, which alludes to a distinct
alteration in the character's psychophysical state.

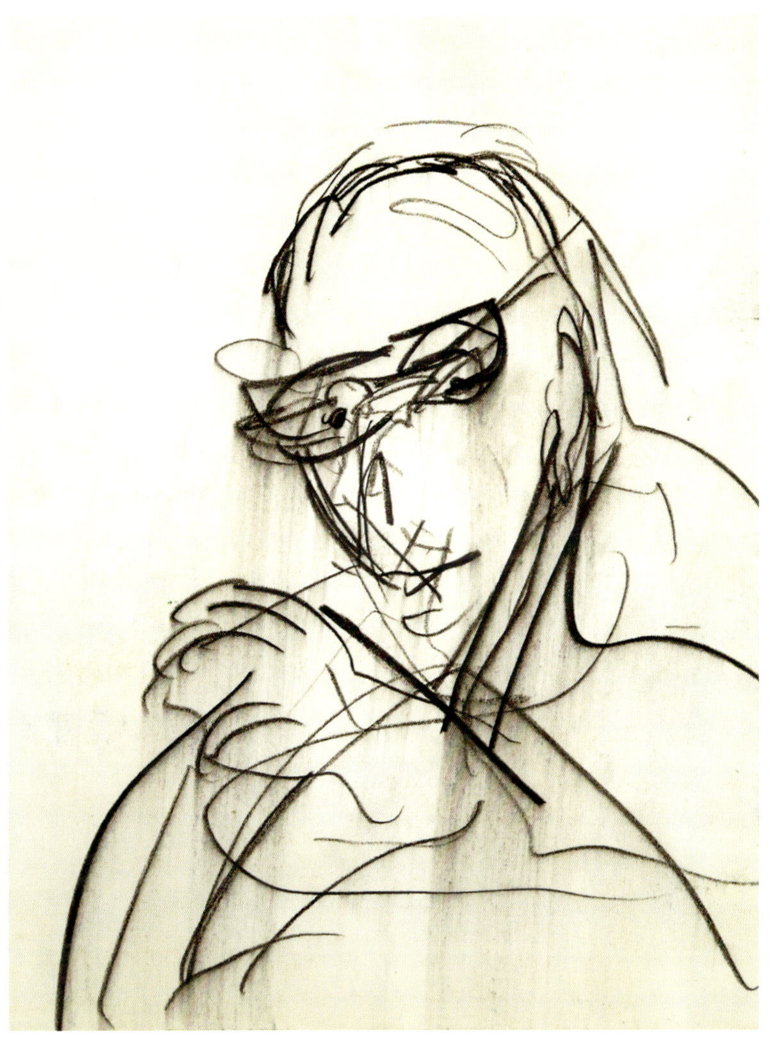

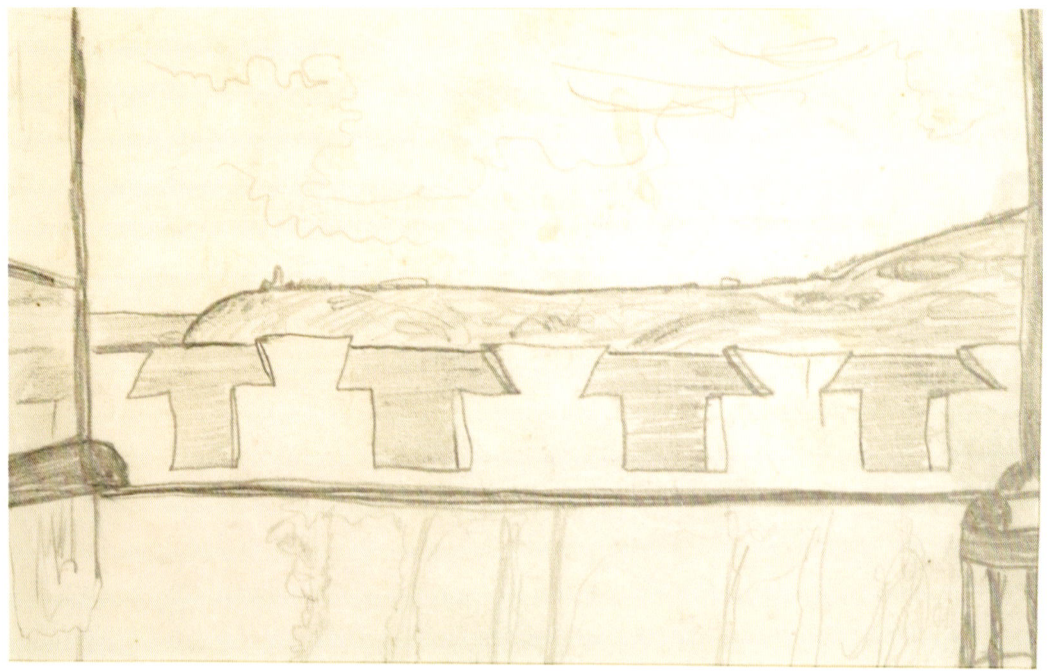

After the second portrait of Burroughs (Fig. 7)
comes this small drawing of a Mediterranean
landscape. Specifically, it is a view of Tangiers,
probably seen from Hotel El Muniria, where
Kerouac went in 1957 to be with Burroughs
while he was writing *Naked Lunch*.

Robert Frank was another important friend during Kerouac's years in New York. Here, below the renowned photographer's name and probably his telephone number, is a drawing of a bearded, long-haired man. Kerouac and Frank collaborated on at least two occasions: Kerouac wrote the introduction to the American edition of Frank's photography book *The Americans* in 1959, and in the same year, Frank, with Alfred Leslie, filmed the experimental short *Pull My Daisy*, a screen adaptation of the third act of Kerouac's play *Beat Generation*, featuring Jack as the off-screen narrator.

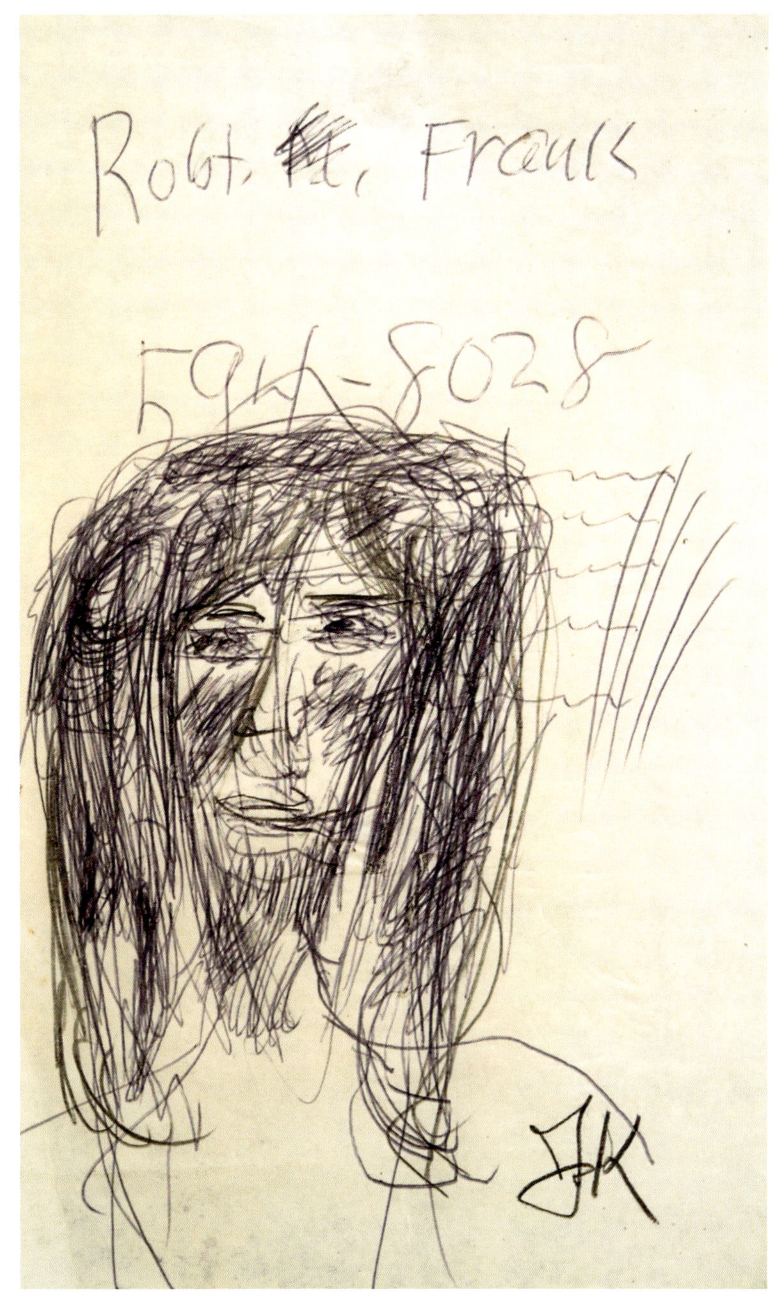

It is inconceivable that Dody Muller would not make her appearance among the portraits in this first section, and in fact, she can be recognized in this portrait. Widow of the Expressionist painter Jan Muller and an artist in her own right, Dody introduced Kerouac to the Expressionist scene in New York, beginning in 1959.

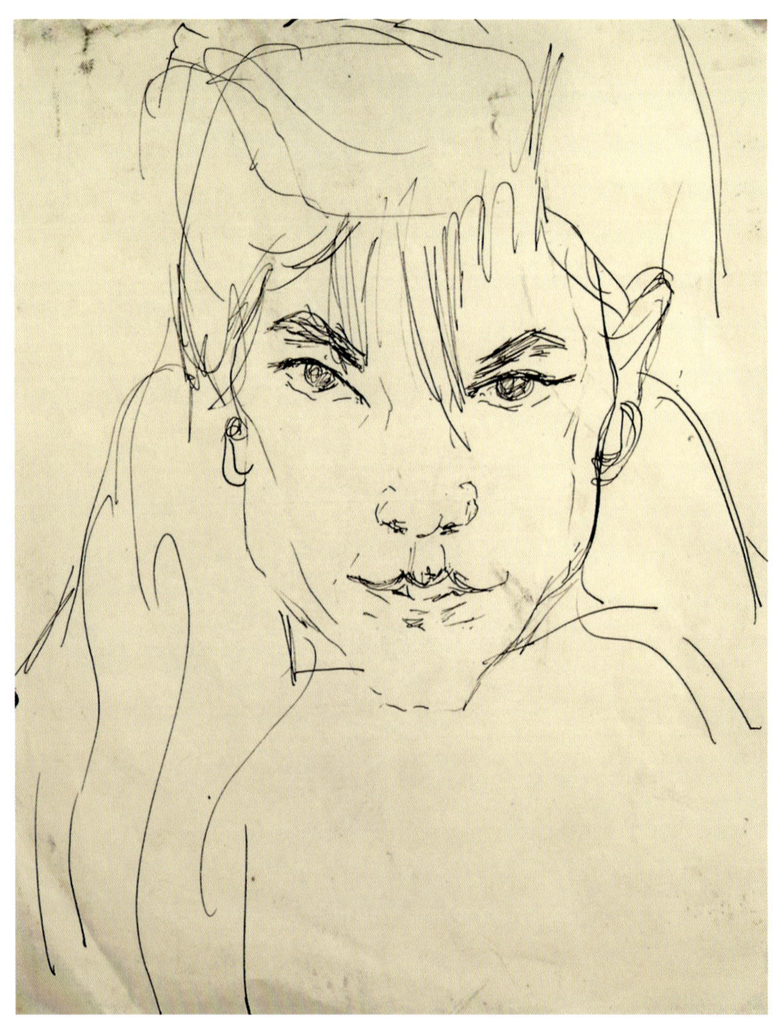

According to a
reconstruction by
Stefania Benini, this
portrait may depict
Leo-Alcide Kerouac,
Jack's father, who died
the year that appears
on the drawing, 1946.
The name "Stanley"
at the bottom,
however, is of dubious
attribution.

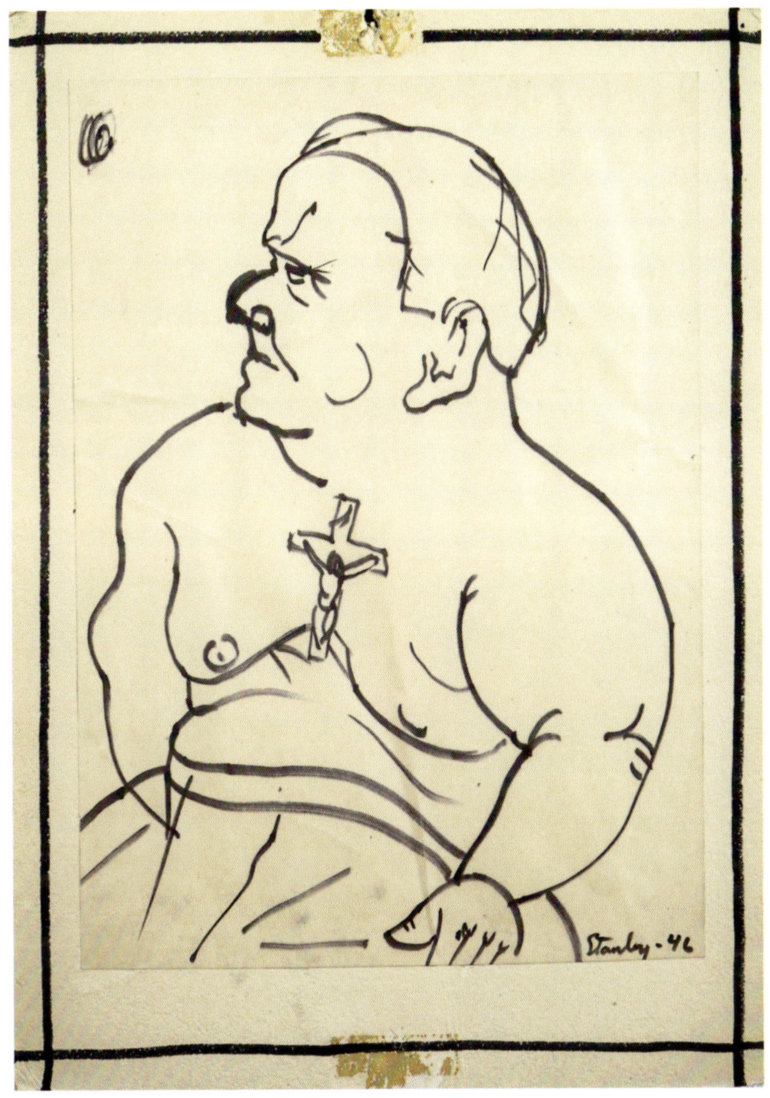

11 *Untitled*, n.d.,
marker on cardboard, 34 x 25 cm

Visions of Jack

Following an analysis of Kerouac's sacred imagery by Stefania Benini, this section presents a series of drawings with explicit references to religion, specifically to Catholicism, which in fact appear in a significant part of the author's art. The graphic works also help cast a new light on Kerouac's more mystical and hermetic writings, suggesting new reflections on his private biographical and psychological world. The drawings and paintings touch upon issues that resurface periodically in the artist's work, that is, the themes of visions, pain and the Cross, and a Beat syncretism that overlays and fuses Christianity and Buddhism. (A.C.)

"Visions of Jack": Sacred imagery
in Kerouac's writing and painting

Stefania Benini

[...] I went one afternoon to the church of my childhood (one of them), Ste. Jeanne d'Arc in Lowell, Mass., and suddenly with tears in my eyes I had a vision of what I must have really meant with "beat" anyhow when I heard the holy silence in the church (I was the only one in there, it was five P.M., dogs were barking outside, children yelling, the fall leaves, the candles were flickering alone just for me), the vision of the word Beat as being to mean beatific.[1]

We begin this exploration of some examples of the sacred imagery in Kerouac's work with two quotes that illustrate what Mircea Eliade – and Pier Paolo Pasolini – would define as "hierophanies," that is, apparitions of the sacred.

The first, above, describes a Catholic setting, a church interior, and the perception of a sacred silence heard against a background of profane noises, which leads to a revelation of the holy essence of the word "beat": not "beat" as "beat up," but as "beatific." The second quote, here below, describes a sensory overload, an overpowering synesthesia that embraces sight, hearing, smell, breath and emotions tinged with the sadness of twilight hour in Jack's childhood neighborhood. Kerouac equates this revelation with a birth:

The day I was born, there was snow on the ground and the descending sun colored westwise windows with an old red melancholia, as of dream. I was walking home with my sled, aged six. Suddenly, I stopped in my tracks and stared, standing quietly on the sidewalk in Centralville. "What is this," I asked myself, noticing the sudden swoop of a sad moment as it flew across our rooftops. "What is this strange thing I see?" In that manner, I was born into the world, February 1929, just before supper. [...] The whisp of winter's dusk caught hold of me – for the first time in my little life I was puzzled by the sound of children's voices, the smell of snow at sunset, the vapors which puffed from my mouth with every icy exhalation, and above all that fleeting old sadness which hung tenderly over the crimson houses of Centralville.[2]

Speaking of the sacred in Kerouac, in both his literary and figurative work, necessarily involves the concept of the vision, beginning with his vision of reality, of writing, and of a sensitive and all-encompassing perception that reached the extreme of an "outlaw of the sensorium."[3] In Kerouac, the silence in the Lowell church and the experience of the sounds and snow in his old neighborhood produce visionary resonances and sudden *satori* – illuminations and realizations of absolute truths.

The theme of the vision helps explain the author's omnivorous gaze and his immersive perception of reality, which posits the visceral relationship with the world at the heart of his writing and painting, and the body as the main setting for this relationship. With the help of alcohol, Benzedrine and other drugs, Kerouac stimulated his unusually receptive senses even further, venturing into "other" dimensions of consciousness. The term "vision" appears in the repertoire of titles chosen by Kerouac for some of his writings, from *Visions of Gerard* (1956, published in 1963) to *Visions of Cody* (1951–52, published in 1960), and also penetrates into the substance of his books, from *Book of Dreams* (1951–60, published in 1960) to *Book of Sketches* (1952–57, published in 2006). These "visions" are populated by imaginary Catholic or Buddhist figures who characterized the spiritual, literary and figurative path of the artist Kerouac in the 1950s and 1960s.

There is one such vision in his most famous novel, *On the Road* (1951, published in 1957), in which Dean Moriarty appears as an apocalyptic angel.

> Suddenly I had a vision of Dean, a burning shuddering frightful Angel, palpitating toward me across the road, approaching like a cloud, with enormous speed, pursuing me like the Shrouded Traveler on the plain, bearing down on me. I saw his huge face over the plains with the mad, bony purpose and the gleaming eyes; I saw his wings; I saw his old jalopy chariot with thousands of sparking flames shooting out from it; I saw the path it burned over the road; it even made its own road and went over the corn, through cities, destroying bridges, drying rivers. It came like wrath to the West.[4]

In a literary short circuit reminiscent of William Blake, the narrative flares into a visionary dimension where the symbol of the Shrouded Traveler alludes to life that presses down upon us or to death that impels us to live. The burning angel, Dean, is none other than one of the countless incarnations of an autobiographical "angel" – Jack's older brother Gerard, who died of rheumatic fever at the young age of ten, and who, according to the writer, was perhaps reincarnated in the person of Neal Cassady. Indeed, throughout all of his writings, Gerard represents the wound of the presence of death, a veritable death drive against which the writer struggled all his life, sign of a troubling attraction, a profound sense of guilt and a deep-seated fear. The figure of Gerard is conflated with that of the dying Christ, which Kerouac had known since he was a young boy in Lowell from the Pawtucket Street grotto, a holy site of the local French-Canadian Catholic community, where the twelve Stations of the Cross are displayed in glass showcases.[5] This childhood experience generated a series of symbols and characters in the artist's paintings: angels, Christs and saints as iterations of that one figure and that one trauma. Let us consider a few examples.

The work *Untitled* (Fig. 24 verso), drawn in pencil on the back of a watercolor, shows two angels and the Holy Ghost floating on high, near a house. For Kerouac, the presence of angels is as strong and obsessive as it was for Paul Klee, another twentieth century painter. Rather than the Angelus Novus that inspired Walter Benjamin, however, Kerouac's angelic figures are coming from the world of his childhood, and a constant presence in the archetypical scene of the crucifixion or in urban landscapes. Angels also appear in Kerouac's title choices, from *Old Angel Midnight* (1956–59; published in 1973) to *Desolation Angels* (published in 1965). Indeed, for the artist, the presence of angels is integrally connected to writing:

Jack's angel, as an agent of the Holy Ghost, is ever-present. He guides Jack's pen, form his words, and like Jacob, Jack must wrestle to keep from going over the 'edges of language where the babble of the subconscious begins.[6]

Kerouac's "spontaneous" writing springs from a metaphysical, transcendent source. In this regard, it is telling that he experienced an epiphany at the Louvre upon seeing Rembrandt's *Saint Matthew and the Angel*. As he rhapsodized in a letter to Ed White, "St. Matthew being Inspired by the Angel is a MIRACLE, the rough stroke so much so, the drip of red paint in the angel's lower lip making it so angelic and his own rough ends ready to write the Gospel (as I will be visited). [...] Also miraculous is the veil [of] mistaken angel smoke on Tobiah's departing angel's left arm."[7]

The constellation of painting, writing and angelic presence could not be more complete. Angels also figure in other paintings and drawings by Kerouac, where there is a sort of depiction of Supper at Emmaus (Fig. 14), for instance. Three figures sit at a table placed frontally as in the painting of the same name by Rembrandt, with one standing on the right and a blood-red angelic presence, a Holy Ghost that appears as if in flames over the head, sketched rapidly with a few red strokes, of a figure who could be Christ. Another angel can be seen in the drawing of the angel leaving the family of Tobias (*Untitled*, Fig. 13). With rapid, decisive strokes of the pen and the sanctifying presence of a bluish-white watercolor wash filling the silhouette of the angel/Holy Ghost, Kerouac reinterprets Rembrandt's archetype in his own style, bringing together many citations, from the table of the Supper at Emmaus to the angel leaving Tobias' family (Fig. 12). A fish appears on the table as a symbol of Christ while a watercolor area creates a sacred space around Tobias, highlighted and vibrating inside his stylized halo, whose radiating pen lines anticipate the configuration of Keith Haring's *Radiant Child*.

The work *Untitled* (Fig. 12) essentially repeats the same composition as the previous drawing, with three people sitting at a table. This time, however, one is a nun holding up a cross and the person with a halo at the other end of the table represents Jack's older brother, as signaled by the presence of the nun – probably a nun from Gerard's school. Gerard, too, is portrayed like *Radiant Child*: notice the white aura that surrounds him and is echoed in the white blotches of the winged image of the Holy Ghost.

Other angels are present in the scene of the Crucifixion or the Pietà, Jack's archetypical scene *par excellence*. We know from a letter to Ginsberg that Kerouac was obsessed by the Crucifixion and the silhouette of Calvary in the last years of his life.

> As Jack grew older, in despair and lacking the means to calm his mind and let go of the suffering, he tended more and more to grasp at the Cross. And so, in his later years, he made many paintings of the Cross, of cardinals, popes, of Christ crucified, of Mary [and pietas]; seeing himself on the Cross, and finally conceiving of himself as being crucified. He was undergoing crucifixion in the mortification of his body as he drank.[8]

Kerouac's typical Pietà depicts the crucified Christ, angels or the Holy Ghost floating in the sky, and devout women at the foot of the Cross, especially the

Virgin Mary but also Mary Magdalene, while Judas hangs from the gallows in the distance. The entire scene takes place below a horizon with the urban skyline of Jerusalem/New York/Lowell.

The Pietà from 1958 (*Untitled*, Fig. 16) is particularly interesting. The Cross with the letters INRI is drawn with an expressionist flair, almost sliced by the vertiginously diagonal line of the horizon, with a stormy night sky above evoked by rapid, dense pen strokes. The Holy Ghost floats on the right and Judah hangs in the background, while the group of devout women in the foreground are drawn as fingers of a hand. This detail is actually an autobiographical reference: as a child, Jack's mother affectionately called him *Ti Pousse*, which means "little thumb" in Joual, and here, a few fingers are anthropomorphized with faces (the most obvious one is the Madonna).

The next Pietà (*Untitled*, Fig. 17) is a very detailed pencil drawing with two angelic presences (a Renaissance putto and an angel that seems to have Burroughs's face), a crowd of figures at the foot of the cross, among whom we see the Virgin Mary and Mary Magdalene, her head drooping and her long hair hanging down. Strangely, the body of Christ is not depicted in either of these two crucifixions; in fact, we will see that Kerouac often painted an empty Cross or just the face of Christ, the *Ecce Homo*. Rarely in the writer's figurative work do we find Christ portrayed on the Cross in all His physicality. It could be said that, in his representations of sacred Christian themes, Kerouac conformed to time-honored genres, such as the Pietà, *Ecce Homo* (the Holy Face), Golgotha (with the crucified Christ clearly visible), and the Sacred Heart, with distinct reference to sacred imagery from classical painting traditions as well as from popular devotion.

Returning to the Pietà (Fig. 17), we again find a face on the horizon under a stormy sky marked by a dense area of pencil lines suggesting night time, and the outline of the gallows where the lifeless body of Judas hangs. The obsessive proliferation of this figure in Kerouac's Pietàs is directly related to the personal trauma he experienced with his brother's death. In a letter to Neal Cassady dated January 9, 1951, Kerouac explains the autobiographical significance of Judas, with reference to a famous painting by Titian depicting the moment that Jesus is betrayed by Judas (Venice, Scuola Grande di San Rocco).

> Did you ever see the great Titian portrait or picture of Jesus and Judas? The scene takes place right after the Last Supper. "There is one among you who will betray me," Jesus has said, and the disciple sadly shakes their heads. From among them steps forth Judas, a tanned and muscular man, feverish for gold, trembling in his boots, to deny in Christ's face that he could ever betray him. [...] Have you ever seen my hand and wrist when it hangs out of a half-rolled sleeve? It's the same Judas wrist... of physical strength [...], the same sweaty muscular greedy wrist [...]. I gaze at the hand of Christ in its delicate dovelike gesture [...]. I think of Gerard. Judas is me, Jesus is Gerard. What have I gone and done; and what hath God wrought?
>
> I never asked to be Judas and I'm sure that Judas never did [...]. But if I hadn't been born then how could I have betrayed Gerard; for I betrayed him merely by living when he died. He was an angel, I was mortal; what he could have brought to the world, I destroyed by my mere presence; because if I had not lived, Gerard would have lived. Isn't it mad, that I

sense this now, and sensed it as a child, and all of it completely devoid of rational meaning; all of it merely a "sense" and a hidden conviction, and a fear, and perhaps a hope, and a thousand-and-one-mysteries.[9]

Gerard died when Jack was four years old. His death had catastrophic consequences on the writer's entire life – on his inner turmoil and his relationship with his family, especially with the *Mater dolorosa*, *Mémère* Gabrielle. Jack's memory of his brother is fragmentary, complex and contradictory. In a letter to his sister Nin in 1945, he confessed:

> Now all I remember about Gerard, for instance, is his slapping me on the face, despite all the stories Mom and Pop tell me of his kindness to me. The psychoanalyst [*probably Burroughs*] figured that I hated Gerard, and he hated me [...] and that I wished he were dead, and he died. So I felt that I had killed him, and ever since [...] I have been subconsciously punishing myself and failing at everything.[10]

In his figurative work, Kerouac elaborates this primal scene of his sense of guilt through the motifs of the angel and the Crucifixion. It is also played out in his writing: his 1956 novel *Visions of Gerard* is effectively a hagiography of his older brother, portrayed as the incarnation of a tenderness that is simultaneously Franciscan and Buddhist. Gerard has visions (he dreams that he is taken up to Heaven by the Virgin Mary in a wagon pulled by two lambs) and is venerated like a saint by the nuns at the St. Louis de France Catholic school that Gerard attended. The book about his brother represents Jack's most emotionally charged work, and the one most indicative of his religious syncretism, comprising the Buddhism he discovered in libraries and the semi-Jansenist French-Canadian Catholicism he inherited from his mother.

We find Judas once again in a pencil sketch of the *Last Supper* (not included here), which somewhat recalls the painting of Tobias. Here again a table with a fish on it appears in the lower part of the drawing; Christ leans his hand on the table at the same time as the disciple who will betray him, seen in profile versus Jesus' frontal portrayal. The group of apostles is represented with expressionistic traits (like those in Edvard Munch's *The Scream*), whereas Jesus has almost no distinct features except a halo that distinguishes him from the mass of faces in the group. The background is charged with dynamism by diagonal lines that follow the trajectory of Judas' arm, adding dramatic tension to the moment of betrayal.

The figure of Christ is present not only in Kerouac's Pietàs, but also in his portrayals of the *Ecce Homo*, a long-established pictorial tradition that began with Antonello da Messina. In a sense, Kerouac introduces it in his description in *Visions of Cody*, a passage that seems to anticipate and interpret in words his pencil and pen portraits such as *Untitled* (Fig. 9). The portrait of America – poor, entirely dispossessed, racked by hunger and the desperation of the *fellaheen* – is envisioned almost like the tormented face of one of Kerouac's Christs:

> America, the word, the sound is the sound of my unhappiness, the pronunciation of my beat and stupid grief. [...] America is being wanted by the police, pursued across Kentucky and Ohio, sleeping with the stock-

yard rats and howling tin shingles of gloomy hideaway silos… It is where
Cody Pomeray learned that people aren't good, they want to be bad –
[…] America made bones of a young boy's face and took dark paints and
made hollows around his eyes, and made his cheeks sink in pallid paste
and grew furrows on a marble front and transformed the eager wishfulness
into the thicklipped silent wisdom of saying nothing, not even to yourself
in the middle of the goddamn night. […] America's a lonely crockashit.[11]

The vision of the Cross and of Christ crucified remains with Kerouac through to
the harshest and most difficult text of his literary corpus, *Big Sur* (1962), where
the Cross appears to the protagonist Jack Duluoz in the midst of an attack of
delirium tremens:

> Suddenly, as clear as anything I ever saw in my life, I see the Cross… I
> see the Cross, it's silent, it stays a long time, my heart goes out to it, my
> whole body fades away to it, I hold out my arms to be taken away to it,
> by God I am being taken away my body starts dying and swooning out to
> the Cross standing in the luminous area of the darkness. I start to scream
> because I know I'm dying but I don't want to scare […] anybody with my
> death scream and just let myself go into death and the Cross […] – "I am
> with you, Jesus, for always, thank you."[12]

It can be argued that the Cross is emblematic of Kerouac's overall conception
of life, which he saw increasingly over the years as defined by suffering. He also
nurtured this conception in his Buddhist "digression," between 1953 and 1957.

In addition to Christs, Kerouac includes numerous saints in his paintings,
mingling the sanctity of Christianity with that of Eastern religions in his own personal, original syncretism. One telling example is the oil painting *Untitled* (Fig.
30). The scene shows a mystic sitting in contemplation of the Calvary on the dis-
tant horizon. The woman's long, reddish hair is reminiscent of Mary Magdalene
– particularly the Magdalenes of Caravaggio and Titian – who is represented
here as a hermit in the forest, contemplating the scene of the Crucifixion. The
mystic sits in lotus position, adding a Buddhist touch to the Christian content
of the painting. She is surrounded by an aura of orange light, while the Calvary
in the other half of the composition is lit with yellow light contrasting with the
green tones of the outline of the hill. To the right at the same height stands
another tree, perhaps an allusion to the tree of Buddha's vision, although it has
the shape of a cypress, a tree associated with death.

Other figures of saints, male and female, alternate throughout the corpus
of Kerouac's sketches, identified by auras or halos in watercolors or white or
yellow oil paint, as in Figs. 23, 36, 56, 59, 60, and 69.

Finally, one last Christian "genre" expressed in his paintings and drawings
is that of the Virgin and Child, as seen in *Untitled* (Fig. 19) and *Untitled* (Fig. 72).
In both cases, the Virgin's face is drawn with dramatic, tormented lines, which
may be related to the unfortunate story of Kerouac's disputed fatherhood. It
is possible that this trauma drove him to "inflict" a distortion on the image of
the Virgin Mary as a correlate of the persecutory image of his ex-wife, Joan
Haverty, with their daughter Jan, whom Kerouac refused to recognize as his
child for almost nine years.[13]

The presence of essentially Christian "genres" of religious representation in Kerouac's pictorial and graphic work is echoed frequently in his literary production, where it is expressed through the theme of the vision, specifically visions of symbolic angelic or Christological figures and of the Cross. The complexity of Kerouac's spiritual quest and his syncretism of Buddhism and Catholicism are nonetheless consistent with a vision of existence as suffering and martyrdom. The centrality of the Incarnation motif, emphasized by the ever-present symbolism of the Cross, seems entirely natural to poetics based on a paroxysmal sensoriality, reeling between sensuality and ecstasy, and on a visceral struggle with writing, with the synesthesia and hierophanic approach to reality that characterized Kerouac's experience.

As he wrote in *Big Sur*:

If I don't write what actually I see happening in this unhappy globe which is rounded by the contours of my deathskull I think I'll have been sent on earth by poor God for nothing.[14]

Kerouac's end, the writer's painful path towards atonement for his inner conflicts through an irreversible alcoholism, confirms the essential pathos of the writing and painting of this artist from Lowell, forever struggling to find a balance between an ecstatic vision of existence – the awe of enlightenment – and the perception of daily life as a *via crucis*.[15] Through a difficult process mirroring the cultural fluctuations of the period, shifting between Abstraction and Figurative art, Swing and Bebop, French-Canadian Christianity and global Buddhism, Kerouac's writing, painting, senses and aesthetic sensibility made this alcoholic yet visionary, consummate intellectual a towering figure of the America of the 1950s.

[1] J. Kerouac, *Scrivere bop. Lezioni di scrittura creativa* (Milan: Mondadori, 1996), p. 68.
[2] *My Sad Sunset Birth*, typescript,1941, [1] p. s.n.; Kerouac Archive, box 32, folder 3, qtd. in I. Gewirtz, *Beatific Soul. Jack Kerouac on the Road* (New York-London: The New York Public Library in association with Scala Publishers, 2007), pp. 149–50.
[3] "An outlaw of the sensorium," definition by Michael McClure in the 1986 documentary *What Happened to Kerouac?*, directed by Richard Lerner and Lewis MacAdams.
[4] J. Kerouac, *On the Road* (New York: Viking Press, 1957), p. 259.
[5] S. Turner, *Jack Kerouac. The Angelheaded Hipster* (London: Viking, 1996), p. 33.
[6] E. Adler, *Departed Angels. Jack Kerouac, The Lost Paintings* (New York: Thunder's Mouth Press, 2004), p. 180.
[7] Ibid., p. 139.
[8] A. Ginsberg, "Kerouac's Ethic," in *Un Homme Grand: Jack Kerouac at the Crossroads of Many Cultures*, Ed. P. Anctil, et al. (Ottawa: McGill-Queen's University Press, 1990), p. 56.
[9] J. Kerouac, *Selected Letters 1940-1956*, Ed. A. Charters (New York: Penguin Books, 1995), pp. 281–82.
[10] Kerouac Archive, Box 74, folder 3, qtd. in I. Gewirtz, *Beatific Soul. Jack Kerouac on the Road*, p. 37.
[11] J. Kerouac, *Visions of Cody* (New York: McGraw Hill, 1972), pp. 90–91.
[12] J. Kerouac, *Big Sur* (New York: Farrar, Strauss and Cudahy, 1962), pp. 204–05.
[13] Adler, *Departed Angels*, p. 234.
[14] Kerouac, *Big Sur*, p. 167.
[15] Compare B. Giamo, *Kerouac, the Word and the Way. Prose Artist as Spiritual Quester* (Carbondale (IL): Southern Illinois University Press, 2000). Also worthy of consideration is this analysis by James Fisher: "The Cross remained primarily a sign of contradiction for Kerouac, a personal cross he shouldered in the depths of loneliness and alcoholic despair. It did not really provide him with a way back into the world. He continued to reflexively associate Catholicism with sadness, withdrawal, and resignation to suffering." J.T. Fisher, *The Catholic Counterculture in America, 1933-1962* (Chapel Hill: The University of North Carolina Press, 1989), p. 242.

12 *Untitled* (Tobias' Family + The Angel),
n.d., watercolor, acrylic, marker and glue
on paper, 34.5 x 41.5 cm

82

The work seems to overlap the events related to
the life of Kerouac's older brother, Gerard, who
died of rheumatic fever at only nine years old
in 1926, with that of Tobias, a Biblical character
from the Old Testament. Guided in his travels by
the healer Archangel Rafael, Tobias intermingles
with the image of the sick brother suffering on
his death bed. From a broader historical point
of view, *Visions of Gerard* and the overlapping
of Gerard and the salvific figure can be seen
in relation to the powerful impact on Catholic
communities around the world of the visions
of Fatima in 1918 and the subsequent painful
deaths of two Portuguese shepherdesses in 1919
and 1920.

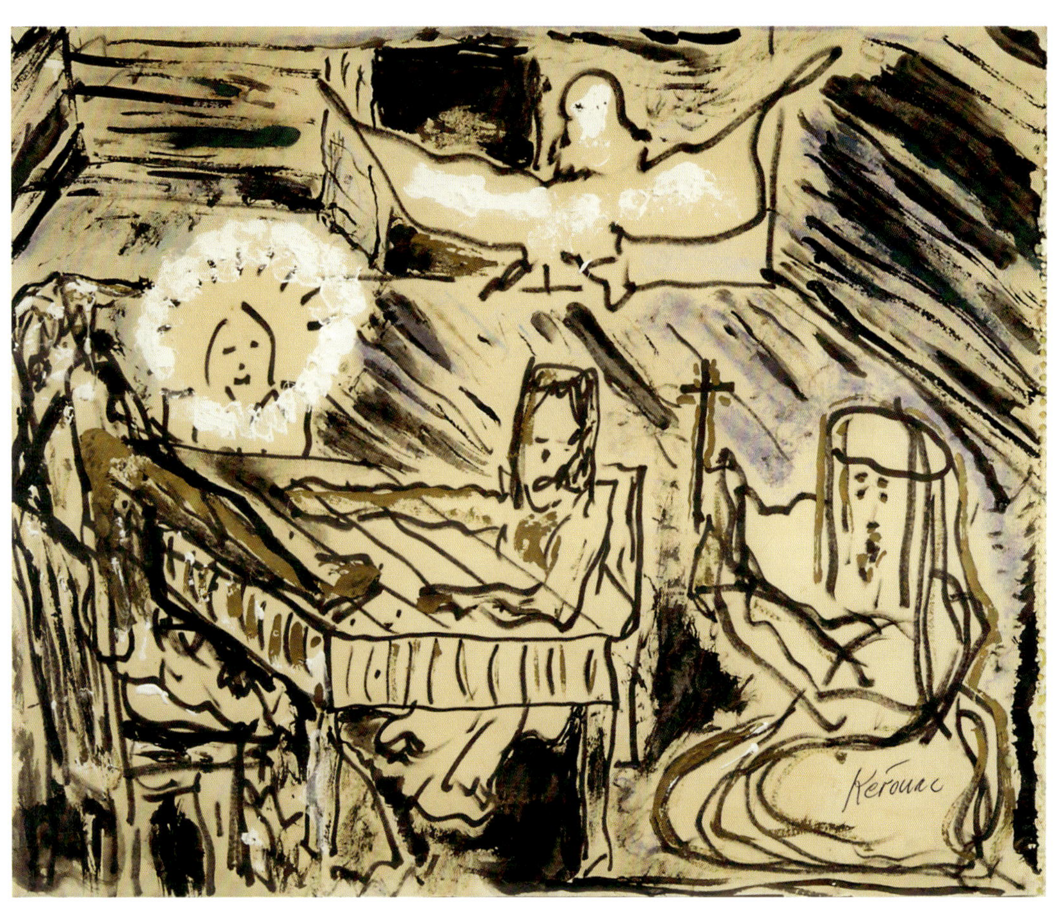
Kerouac

13 *Untitled*, n.d.,
watercolor, marker and glue on paper,
28 x 22 cm

The scene of this work is closely related to the previous one, but its specific Biblical iconography makes it more easily comprehensible. We see Tobias at a table with the fish that the Archangel Rafael had him capture in order to heal the sick and cure his father's blindness. In the distance, we see the figure of the angel who, after finally revealing himself, leaves the house. The subject re-proposes the theme of sanctity, of the arduous relationship between illness and cure, and introduces the figure of the angel in flight, defined by Ed Adler as the "departed angel," a constant presence in Kerouac's sacred imagery.

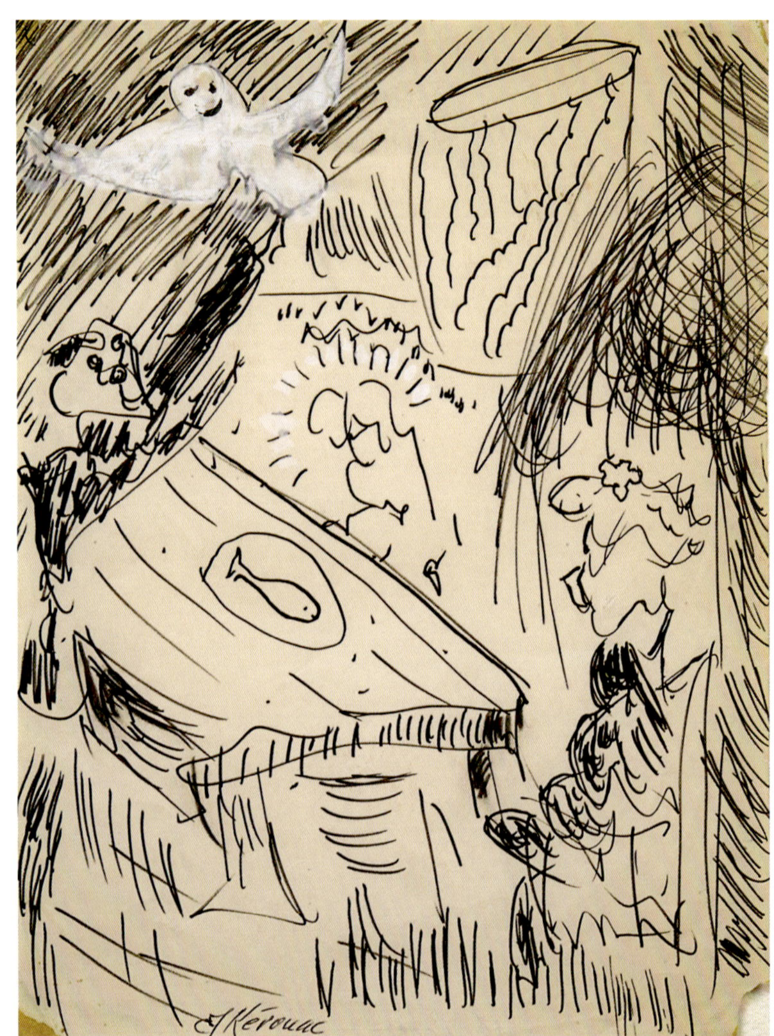

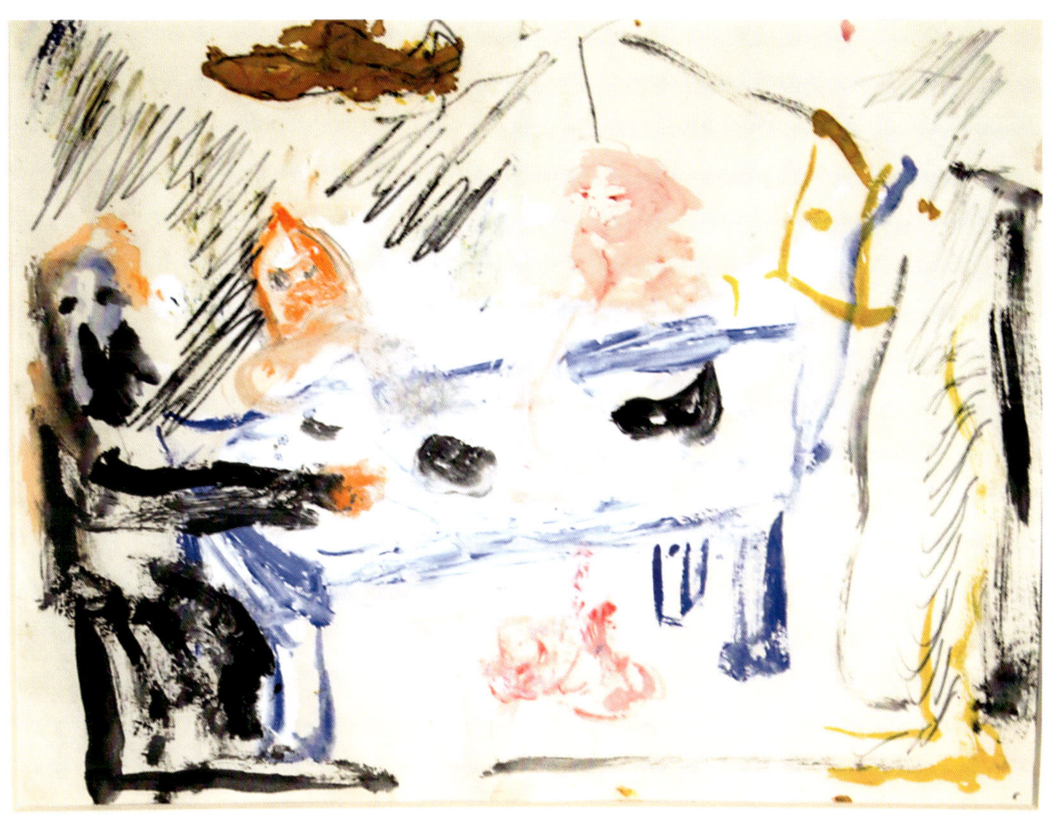

Here is another domestic scene with a series of
figures around a table and an angel in the upper
part of the page. As Benini notes, the subject is
a citation of the iconography of the Supper in
Emmaus (Gospel According to Luke 24:13–32).
In this subject, as in that of Tobias, the theme of
the vision and a *post mortem* apparition is key,
making it consistent with the most far-reaching
and dramatic reflections emerging from Kerouac's
works, beginning with *Visions of Gerard*.

These crucifixions are quite analogous. They belong to a series of works with religious themes of which Kerouac spoke on several occasions in conversations with Twardowicz when he was living in Northport. Looking at their composition, the Cross creates a powerful centrality and verticality in the various works, and all three share the detail of Judas hanging. The dramatic quality of the subject is echoed in other drawings with sacred themes, such as the figure of a saint obsessively covered in crosses (Fig. 18) or the tremulous Virgin and Child (Fig. 19).

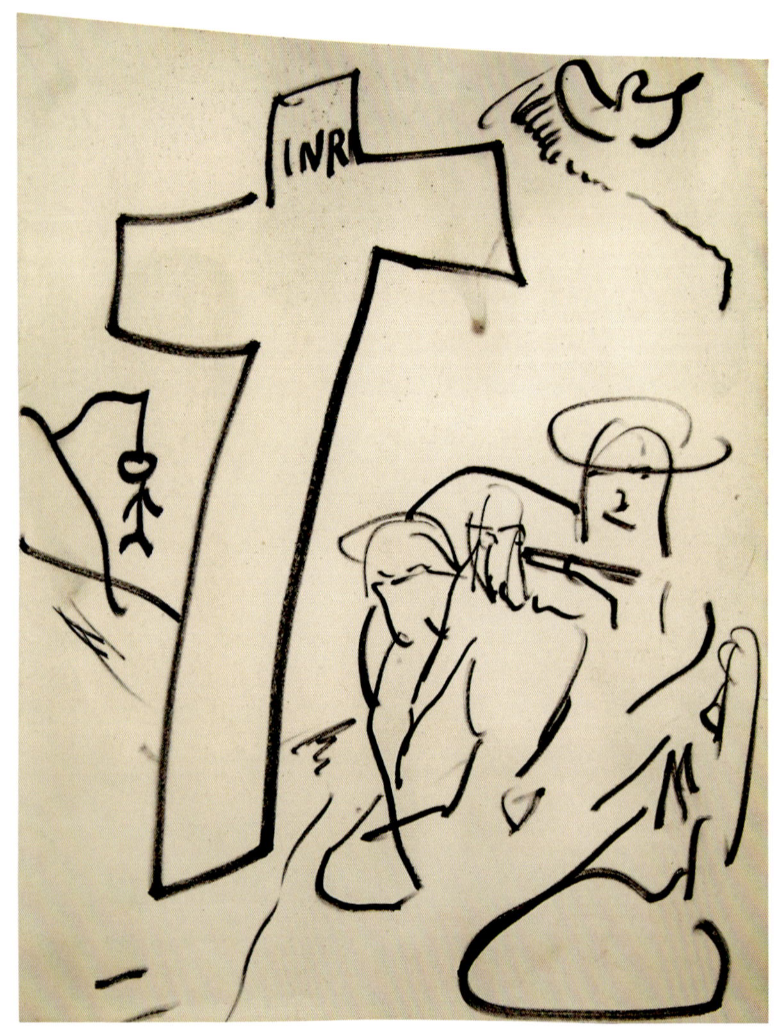

16 *Untitled*, 1958,
pencil on paper,
30 x 22.5 cm

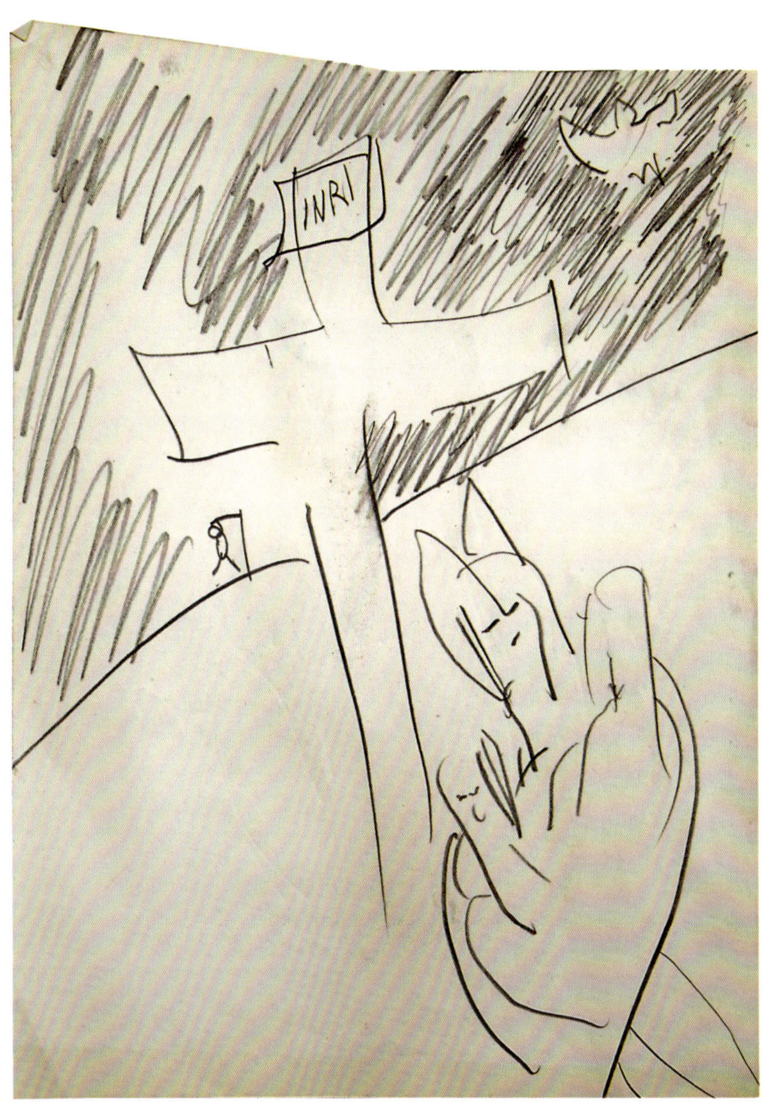

17 *Untitled*, n.d.,
pencil on paper,
21 x 27.7 cm

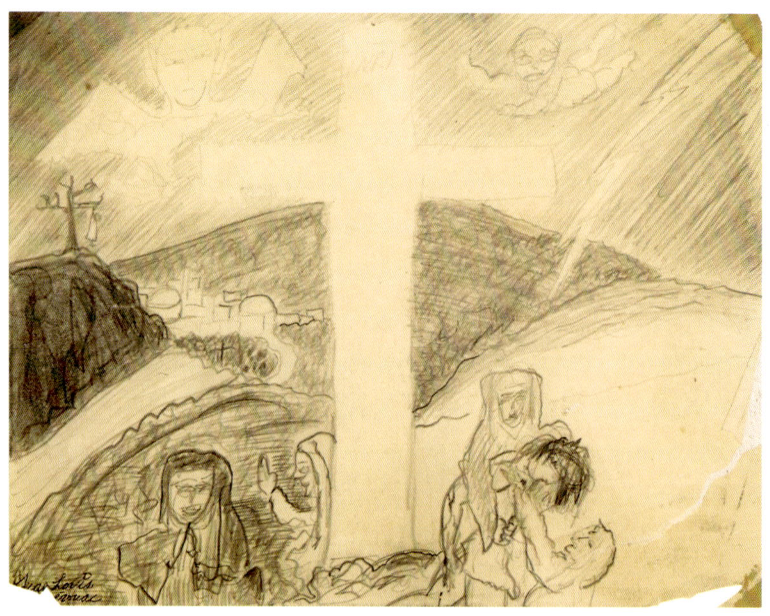

18 *Untitled*, n.d.,
marker on paper,
30 x 22.5 cm

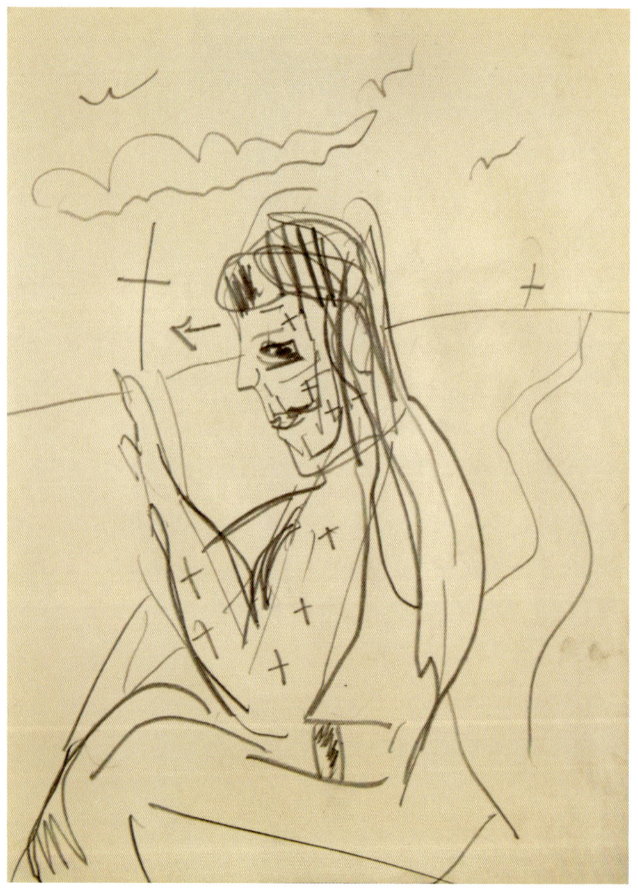

19 *Untitled*, n.d.,
pencil on paper,
30 x 22.5 cm

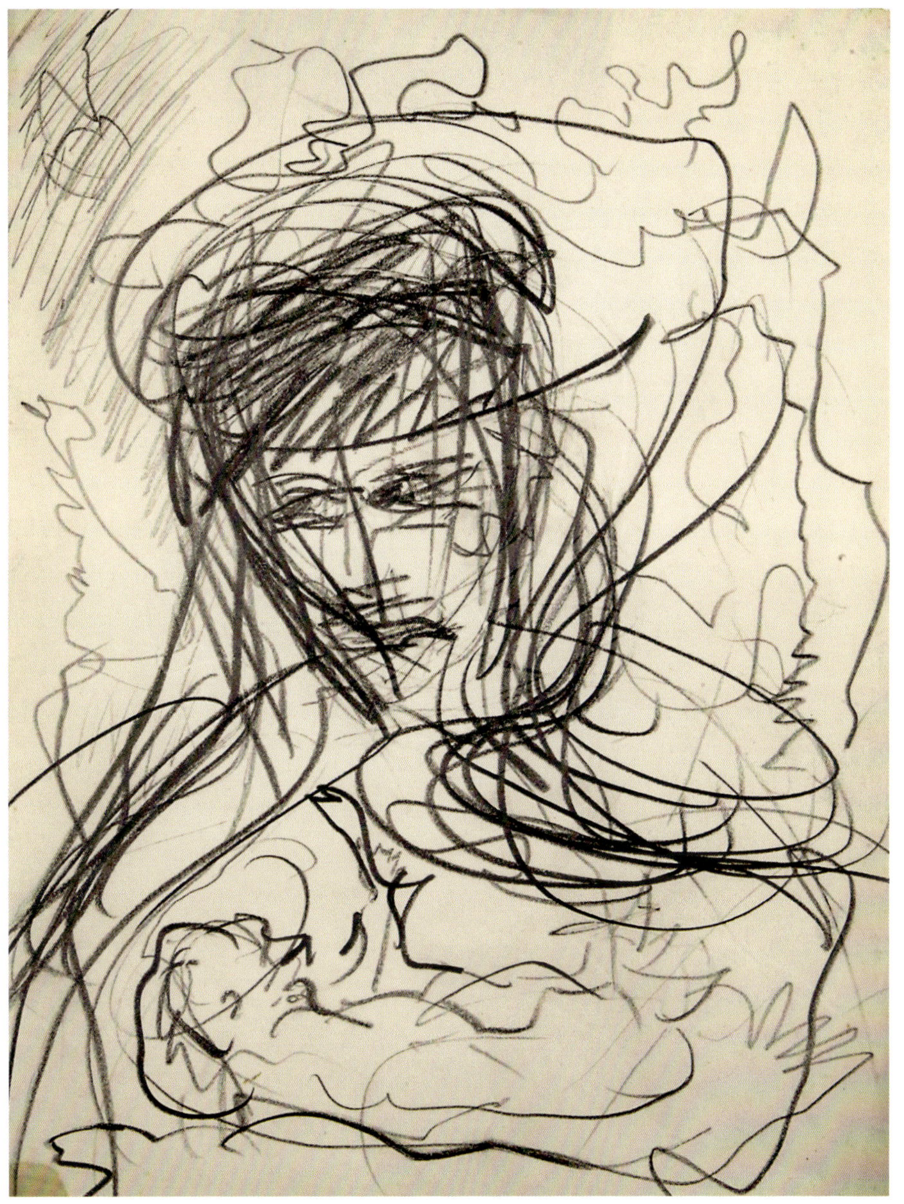

20 *Untitled*, n.d.,
marker on paper,
23.5 x 17.5 cm

21 *Untitled*, n.d.,
marker on paper,
28 x 21.5 cm

These figures refer
specifically to the
previously mentioned
religious syncretism
typical of Kerouac's
poetics in the 1960s.
In fact, the figures
simultaneously present
elements associated
with Buddhism, such as
the yoga lotus position,
and others associated
with Christianity
suggestive of a Nativity
scene (Fig. 21). The
end result is impressive
– a Beat icon that mixes
the cultures of the East
and the West.

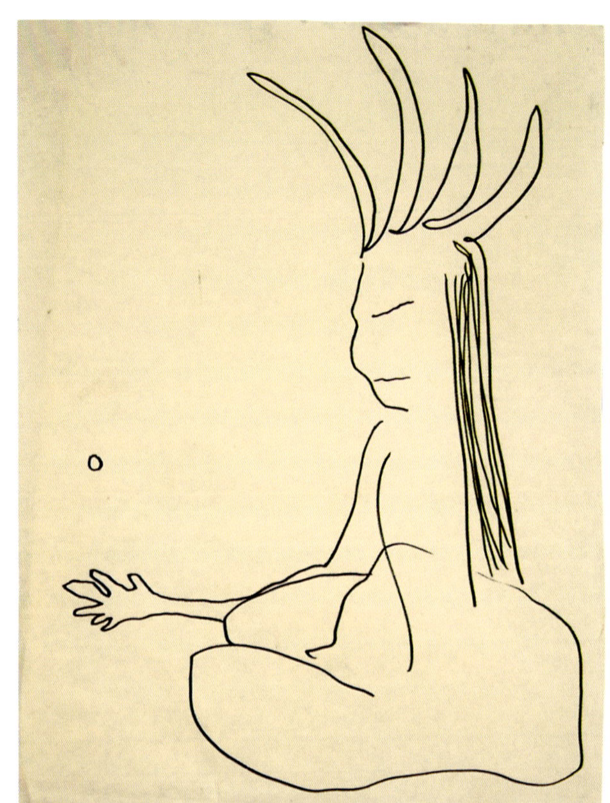

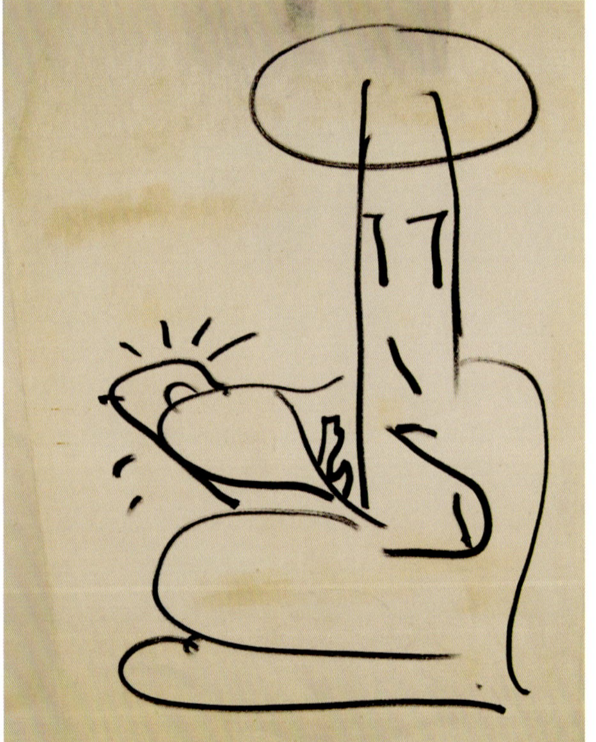

91

There is a certain exotic and esoteric interest in these visionary subjects, in which an angelic figure, penciled in on the right, seems to dialogue with the mysterious figures with incandescent auras. Kerouac returns here to the visionary theme of angelic figures immersed in an unfathomable landscape, inspired by his mystical, psychotropic trips.

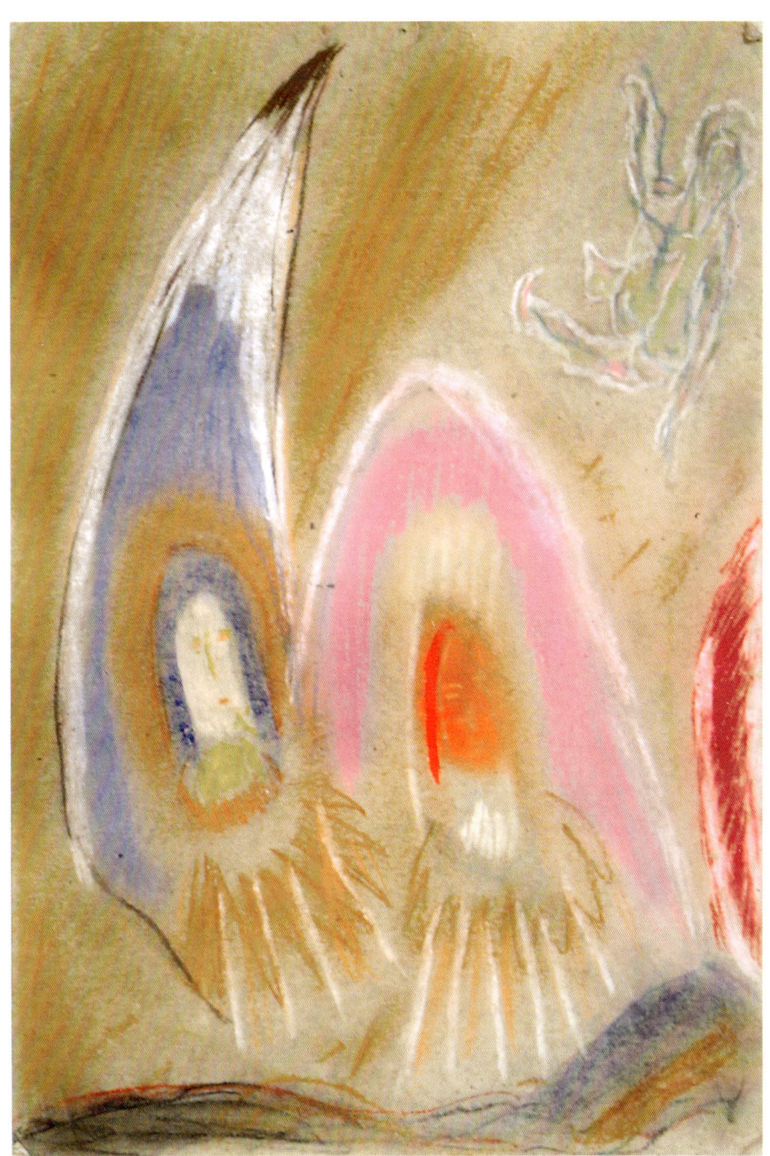

92

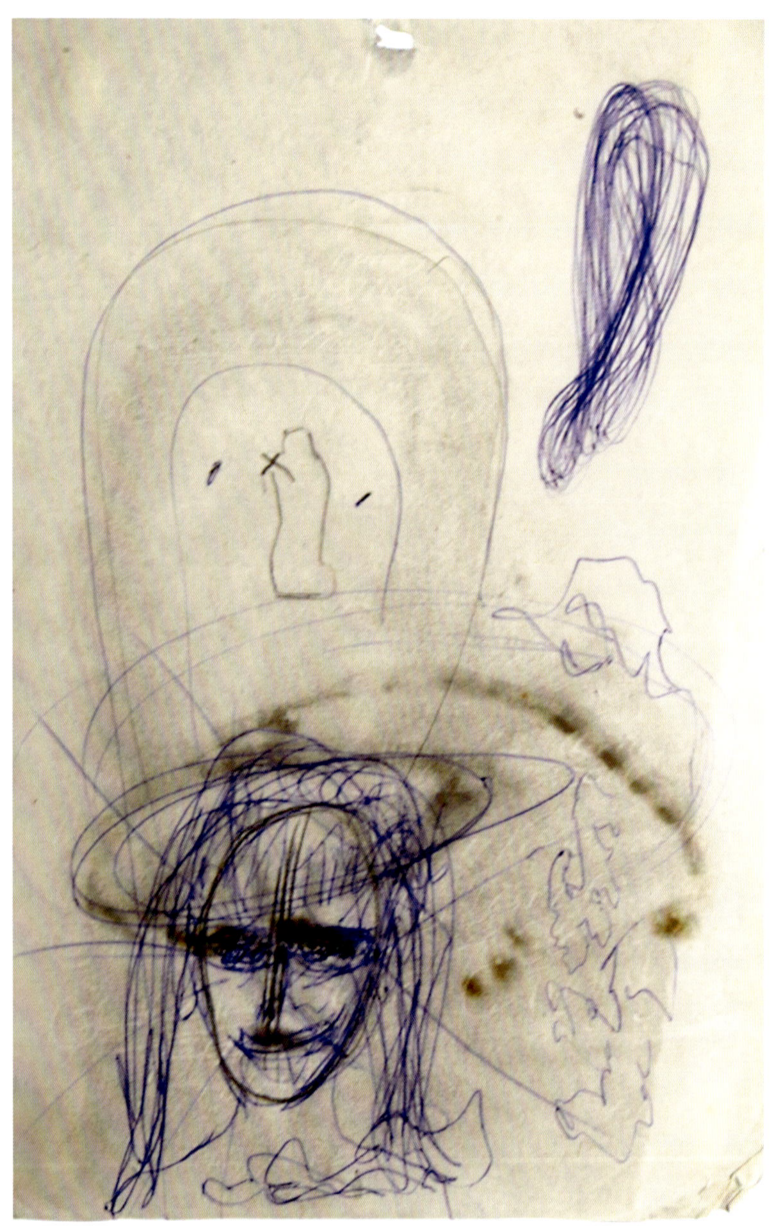

24 *Untitled*, n.d.,
pencil on paper,
30 x 23 cm,
recto and verso

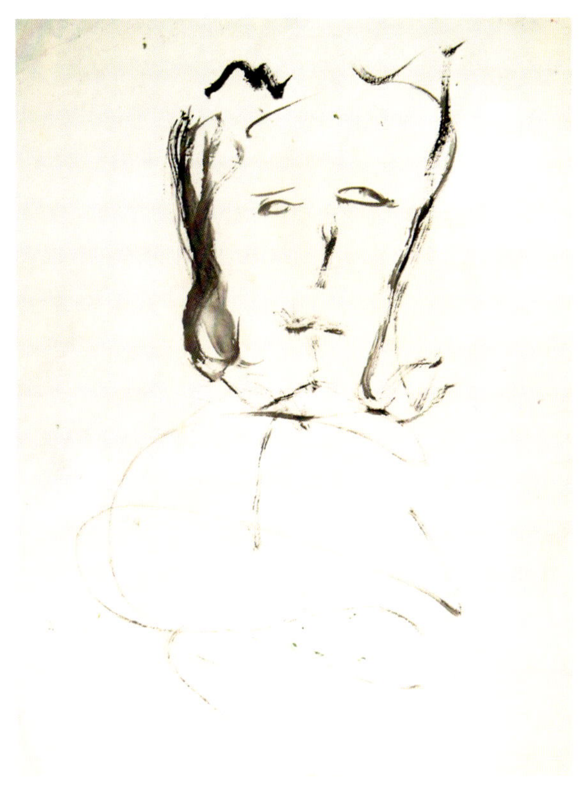

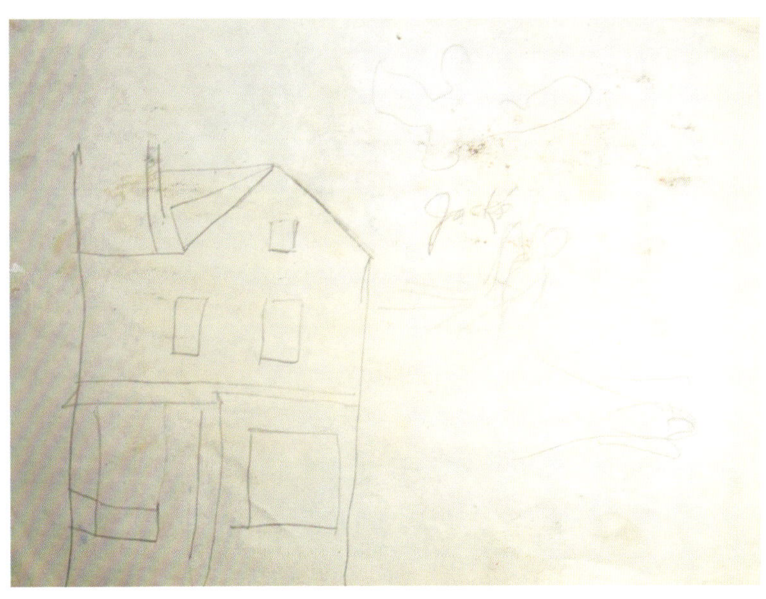

Beat Painting

As Allen Ginsberg pointed out in the introduction to the book edited by Anne Waldman, *The Beat Book. Writing from the Beat Generation* (1996), the term "beat" has at least three possible explanations: "beat" as "subterranean" or "hidden"; or, as they used to say around Times Square in the early 1950s, "Man, I'm beat" to mean "broke," "worn out," "exhausted" but at the same time "wide open" and "receptive"; or, finally, as Kerouac himself explained in 1959 "beat" as "beatific," that is, "angelic" or "blessed." This section brings together images, paintings and notes from this world where art is "the manifestation of the exploration of the structure of consciousness" (Ginsberg), simultaneously rarefied and mundane, comprising both the everyday and the urge towards the infinite. Featured in this section are Kerouac's companions – Corso, Cassady, Ginsberg, Burroughs, and others – fellow travelers in a movement defined by Jean-Jacque Lebel as "rhizomatic," like a constellation, as well as places and images of their dramas, explorations and trips, including Times Square, Cedar Tavern in the Village, California, and Mexico. (A.C.)

Is the word holy?
On Kerouac's Voice in *Pull My Daisy*

Enrico Camporesi

The expression "unwind the tape" is certainly apropos in a discussion of Jack Kerouac, whose typewritten text, *On the Road,* unscrolls like a Torah, literally opening out like an analog road. Written in 1951 but only described in detail later by Kerouac,[1] this text is an artifact of stratified mythology, often subject to imprecisions that magnify its reputation. The actual material substance itself remains controversial (many still claim that it was a telex roll when in fact it was tracing paper),[2] and the entire event of the writing is enveloped in an almost impenetrable aura. Allegedly, it was written in a single creative burst over twenty-one days, with neither commas nor periods (when actually there are undeniable traces of punctuation). It matters little that the scroll of *On the Road* is only one of the multiple configurations of the novel during its gestation: its form is symbolic, and it is only the beginning of a series of transformations and passages from one roll to another.

For example, in 1952, when he was working on the third chapter of *Visions of Cody*, Kerouac substituted, conceptually (and temporarily), the roll of paper with a tape recorder: the title of the chapter is, appropriately enough, "Frisco: The Tape" (recorded in five nights with Neal Cassady).[3] The length of the work and the means at their disposal reinforce the impression of naturalness that would remain such a defining feature of most of Kerouac's novels (beginning after *The Town and the City*, 1950).

Moving beyond Kerouac's written work, the myth of spontaneity is also used effectively with another type of "tape," that is, film, in *Pull My Daisy* (Robert Frank and Alfred Leslie, 1959). Such is the rhetoric of many of the film's defenders, including the "flaming, prophetic John the Baptist of New American Cinema," Jonas Mekas.[4] In a survey of the New York scene for *Sight and Sound* in 1959, Mekas described *Pull My Daisy* as a free improvisation of a scene from a play by Kerouac that was never actually performed. Like *Shadows* (John Cassavetes, 1959), he claimed, it was filmed without a script.[5] Referring specifically to Kerouac's commentary, which was added after the fact to the silent film, Mekas explained, "During the recording of the commentary, Kerouac spoke the lines of each actor without any preparation or a previous viewing of the film – he just went on, as the images went by, in a sort of drunken trance; and his commentary has the immediacy and magic of such an improvisation."[6]

Kerouac did not write; he simply spoke (at least according to Mekas). But then what happened to the third act – a written act, that is – of *Beat Generation*, the 1957 script that the author expressly adapted for *Pull My Daisy*? And how can we explain the spoken performance that impressed Mekas so much? In the absence of other elements, it is difficult not to accept it as a genuinely mystical improvisation, with no concession to repetition or testing. Actually, the sound is not the result of some kind of inexplicable and spontaneous trance, as Mekas's comments would seem to suggest. In that case, the viewer's amazement at the brilliant synchronization of sound and image could be compared to the dismay caused by the miracle of the *Pentecost* (*Acts* 2, 4–11). This is not, however, a very convincing explanation.

While it is true there is a bishop (played by Richard Bellamy) in *Pull My Daisy* and that the film deals with questions about the nature of the sacred (Allen Ginsberg asks the bishop: "Are holy flowers holy? Is the world holy? Is glasses holy? Is time holy?"), that is still not enough. In fact, the surprising effect stems from a complex interaction between the restitution of the moving images (filmed by Frank and Leslie) and Kerouac's words. Ironically, the most relevant description of the process is embedded in a verbose, complicated response offered by Alfred Leslie himself to a question from Jack Sargeant, whose most salient points are worth including here.

The film does in fact originate from a tape – a magnetic tape, that is, not a 16mm film. Kerouac had the habit of recording himself reading passages he had written, often accompanied by the radio left on as background music. Alfred Leslie, who had read the script of *Beat Generation*, was not convinced that it could be turned into a film. During a visit to the writer, however, Leslie and Robert Frank had a virtual epiphany when they heard the tape with Kerouac's voice. Straight away, Leslie began to conceive of a film adaptation of the text made by working from the spoken configuration of the script, not from the written script itself. Only that voice could guide the film. Leslie realized, "You can't act out Kerouac's characters, because they're all poetry... They're not independent people, independent characters. Each person he writes about is another aspect of himself."[7]

In fact, Kerouac does not act in *Pull My Daisy*; he only figures in the film through his voice, permeating almost the entire verbal and sound texture. To allow him to improvise, Leslie organized work sessions at Kerouac's home. Using a portable 16mm projector, Leslie and Frank showed him the film so he could know the material he would be working with – the script turned into film awaiting sound.[8] Seated as a viewer, Kerouac would speak to the recorder, and then stop and rewind it to listen to what he had said. The setup was crude and cumbersome; it took time for Kerouac to feel at ease. Nonetheless, through these first analogical gymnastics, the writer slowly discovered the brilliant timing, rhythm and pace for the improvisation that would become the soundtrack of the final version of *Pull My Daisy*.

The film proceeds from the domestic setting to a more professional one. Leslie rented an actual recording studio, one owned by Jerry Newman no less, the famed "bootlegger" of jazz concerts (and who switched from 78 rpm to magnetic tape recording). Adapting his particular method of filming to the sound recording, Leslie, who always shot scenes three times, chose to do the same with Kerouac's improvisations in the studio. The spatial arrangement also had three parts: the film was projected while David Amram improvised the music in one booth and Kerouac recorded his voice in the other.

Leslie specifically told Newman not to cut anything once Kerouac began speaking – to never turn off the tape recorder from the moment the writer began to comment on and dub the images. Later Leslie offered a practical explanation with a sort of rugged eloquence, saying: "What I needed was every fucking sound that he made."[9] Thus there is no form of authorial respect in his statement, only total attention called to the most instinctive elements of the spoken word.

On second thought, this approach could certainly not have shocked Jerry Newman. Kerouac had gone to the back of Newman's Esoteric Records store (75 Greenwich Avenue) to hear the clarinetist Milton Mezzrow (he mentions this explicitly in a 1951 letter to Neal Cassady)[10] and must have been quite aware of Newman's clandestine recordings of jazz concerts. It seems that the sound engineer's irresistible urge to record aroused an amused wariness among the Village musicians. When they would tell him personal anecdotes, they found it opportune to insist not have that machine on, undoubtedly fearing that he would preserve their confidential stories forever, just as he did with their music.[11]

And yet, setting aside the gossip, there is definitely one thing that Leslie did want to preserve, perhaps inspired by Jerry Newman, and that was all the moments when the word does not *signify*. Later, Kerouac despairingly referred to these moments in another tape, the one for *Visions of Cody* (with Neal Cassady), guilty of having retained all the "*ahs* and the *ohs* and the *ahums*," all the hesitations, stuttering and accidents of speech.[12] Perhaps he missed the typewriter used for *On the Road*, and the orthogonal organization of the page (even if "stretched," elongated to the dimensions of the roll of paper).

Nonetheless, the other tape, the magnetic one, produced several stunning moments. It is again Leslie who describes them. One in particular might pass unnoticed but has a special poignancy. At one point between two recording sessions, Kerouac lit up a cigarette and, seeing the smoke rise, sang under his breath, "Up you go little smoke, up you go, up you go." Leslie ingeniously synchronized the little song with the moment when Milo (Larry Rivers) picks up his son (Pablo Frank) as smoke rises from an ashtray on the nearby table.

There may be no image more apt than this evanescent smoke to signify the fleeting presence of the spoken word. "All sensation takes place in time," Walter Ong wrote much later, "but sound has a special relationship to time unlike that of the other fields that register in human sensation. Sound exists only when it is going out of existence. It is not simply perishable but essentially evanescent, and it is sensed as evanescent. When I pronounce the word 'permanence', by the time I get the 'nence', the 'perma' is gone, and has to be gone."[13] *(Up you go little smoke...).*

Indeed, Jesuit father Walter Ong, famed exegete of the epistemological gap between orality and literacy, can provide a final hypothesis, a speculative fiction, for this discussion of *Pull My Daisy*. His research on Ramus and the paradigm shift from the art of discourse to the art of reason was published in 1958.[14] What if Ong himself had been the "bishop" who visited Alfred Leslie's studio on 4th Avenue in New York in early 1959? Allen Ginsberg (with Kerouac's voice) would surely have plied him with questions, adding to his series "Is the word holy?" And now, the only thing left to do is rewind the tape.

[1] See in particular the interview with Al Aronowitz (*New York Post*, March 10, 1959).

[2] See I. Gewirtz, *Beatific Soul. Jack Kerouac on the Road* (New York: Scala Books, 2007), p. 109.

[3] See T. Hunt, *Kerouac's Crooked Road. The Development of a Fiction* (Carbondale – Edwardsville: Southern Illinois University Press, 1981), p. 137. On this point, see also the essay by P.A. Michaud, "Odds and Ends," in *Beat Generation. New York, San Francisco, Paris*, exhibition catalog (Paris: Centre Pompidou, 2016), p. 38.

[4] A. Arbasino, "New American Cinema," *America Amore* (Milan: Adelphi, 2011), p. 585. In April 1960, in his magazine *Film Culture*, Mekas awarded *Pull My Daisy* with the second Independent Film Award, specifically for the "immediacy" of the film. (The first had been assigned in January 1959 to the first version of *Shadows* by John Cassavetes.) See P. Adams Sitney (ed.), *Film Culture Reader*, first ed. 1970 (New York: Cooper Square Press, 2000), p. 424.

[5] J. Mekas, "New York Letter: Towards a Spontaneous Cinema," *Sight and Sound*, vol. 28, no. 3, Summer 1959, p. 120.

[6] Mekas, "New York Letter: Towards a Spontaneous Cinema."

[7] Alfred Leslie, qtd. in B. Allan, "The Making (and Unmaking) of *Pull My Daisy*," *Film History*, vol. 2, no. 3 (September-October 1988), p. 191.

[8] Information on the making of the film was taken from J. Sargeant, "An Interview with Alfred Leslie," in *Naked Lens: Beat Cinema*, first ed. 1997 (Berkeley: Soft Skull, 2008), pp. 38–40.

[9] Sargeant, *Naked Lens*, p. 39.

[10] See B. Morgan, *The Beat Generation in New York: A Walking Tour of Jack Kerouac's City*, (San Francisco: City Lights Books, 1997), pp. 67–68.

[11] B. Fox, "Live Recording's Golden Age," *New Scientist*, December 20–27, 1984, p. 53.

[12] T. Berrigan, "Jack Kerouac. The Art of Fiction no. 41," *The Paris Review*, no. 43, Summer 1968, pp. 67–68. Ted Berrigan began the interview stating, classically, "Well, I'm no tape-recorder man, Jack. I'm just a big talker, like you."

[13] W.J. Ong, *Orality and Literacy*, first ed. 1982 (London: Routledge, 2013), pp. 31–32.

[14] See W.J. Ong, *Ramus, Method, and the Decay of Dialogue. From the Art of Discourse to the Art of Reason* (Cambridge: Harvard University Press, 1958).

Jack, His Jeans, and the "Anti-Fashion" of the Beat Generation

Virginia Hill

"He was wearing a suit of some thick fabric, maybe tweed, obviously bought readymade. Maybe his mother bought it and he never even checked the size. His shirt was typical American working class, and his shiny shoes with rounded toes didn't match at all; they looked like they were made of plastic."[1]

This was how Fernanda Pivano described Jack Kerouac when he came to visit Milan in 1966. She could not reconcile his careless, sad, almost squalid sartorial look with her expectations of this famous man. His books were literary powerhouses selling like hotcakes; he was invited to speak all over the place; magazines and newspapers around the globe were writing about him. Why then did he not take care of his appearance, of the way he dressed?

While they may have shared a vision and a culture, the first Beat writers did not share any particular look. Some preferred jeans, others slacks; almost all of them wore cotton shirts, generally somewhat wrinkled and left partly open, revealing the classic white T-shirt underneath. Their shoes were of various types, from white sneakers to canvas espadrilles to ankle leather boots. Other than that, they wore shapeless wool sweaters, oversized wool coats, most likely bought second-hand, and hardly any leather jackets, which were simply too expensive, while Ginsberg wore a parka (an item bought in "army surplus" stores).[2] One is struck, while looking at the photographs, by their neglect of their appearance, not shabby exactly, simply thoughtless. "Extremely normal" may be an appropriate way to define it. Was this perhaps an ideological choice? A visible rejection of the sartorial conventions of the era? Or a subconscious desire to look poor in order to grant authenticity to their much-criticized careers as writers uncontaminated by the mainstream culture? The only one to have a strong sense of style was William Burroughs, who wore suits almost all his adult life. All in all, their appearance was in marked contrast with the image of America of the 1950s on show in the contemporary media.

The austerity of the war was over. There were jobs, and fashion stores were springing up everywhere. One could even buy "wash and wear" men's clothing made with the new synthetic fibers of the DuPont corporation, clothes that were stylish yet easy to keep in good shape, with no dry cleaning or ironing needed. In other words, there was no longer any excuse not to dress fashionably, or at least dress well. Not to do so was an insult, an offense to the establishment.

The Beat "anti-fashion" or "non-fashion" began as a natural reaction to the imposition of the standardized, predictable look typical of American consumer society. The Beats were young people united by their disregard for the mass culture in which they were growing up and by their search for new forms of cultural expression in poetry, music and art. They lived the true reality, that of the American metropolis with its multi-racial neighborhoods, and not the fake version appearing on billboards. When measured against the fashion canons of the era, their way of dressing was basically off the chart. Obviously, the Beats were no model customers browsing the teen sections in department stores or high-end tailors; they simply put on some clothes every day. They put on gym shoes outside the gym because they were comfortable; they put on jeans – the historic Levi's (not yet transformed into a fetish or fashion statement) – not because they identified ideologically with miners or dockworkers, but because they identified with the object itself. They chose comfortable cuts and resistant materials that adjusted to the body's shape over time, the fabric fading and softening after each wash. Jeans were the anti-fashion object *par excellence* at that time: anonymous, timeless, an object that became personalized on the body and never went out of style because it was not part of the Fashion System. Young Beat women felt sufficiently emancipated to blur sartorial gender boundaries; for example, oversized men's shirts became a must-wear item, especially with a super-sensual pencil skirt. In *Subculture: The Meaning of Style* from 1979, Dick Hebdige[3] describes the tension generated by the added meaning attached to these clothes worn out of context. What had been ordinary, innocuous items suddenly became elements in a "practice of resistance through style." Girls dressing this way knew they were calling attention to themselves, just as they knew that their late-night presence in Village bookstores or night clubs frequented by black musicians would provoke harsh criticism. In the early 1950s, however, Beat girls did not consider themselves style icons, though they became so for future generations, who revered them as the original true rebels.

The first Beat generation – Jack and his friends – probably thought little about fashion. They were young intellectuals discovering the world, discovering life. In their vision, filtered through alcohol, marijuana and too many cigarettes, clothes had a function for daily life but did not need to be analyzed, deciphered or codified. That intellectual exercise would begin later.

And then came the beatniks. They were a different breed from the very beginning. They had a more studied, intentionally anti-conformist look, with their all-black clothes, their sandals, and long beards on the boys. But as Kerouac said with obvious disdain, they came afterward, like the bohemians who were next in line. They cultivated their look but produced nothing, no literature or serious writing. Like most authentic subcultures, the first Beat generation lost its identity once it was recognized, criticized, and then "normalized" by the mass media, all in the space of a single decade.

[1] F. Pivano, *C'era una Volta un Beat* (Milan: Frassinelli, 2003), p. 80.
[2] Towards the beginning of the short film *Pull My Daisy* from 1959, Kerouac can be heard commenting on the arrival of his friends, "Allen Ginsberg comes in wearing a parka."
[3] D. Hebdige, *Subculture: The Meaning of Style* (London: Routledge, 1979).

Ettore Sottsass,
(from the left) Lawrence Ferlinghetti,
Allen Ginsberg, Bob Dylan,
Peter and Julius Orlovsky,
San Francisco USA 1965

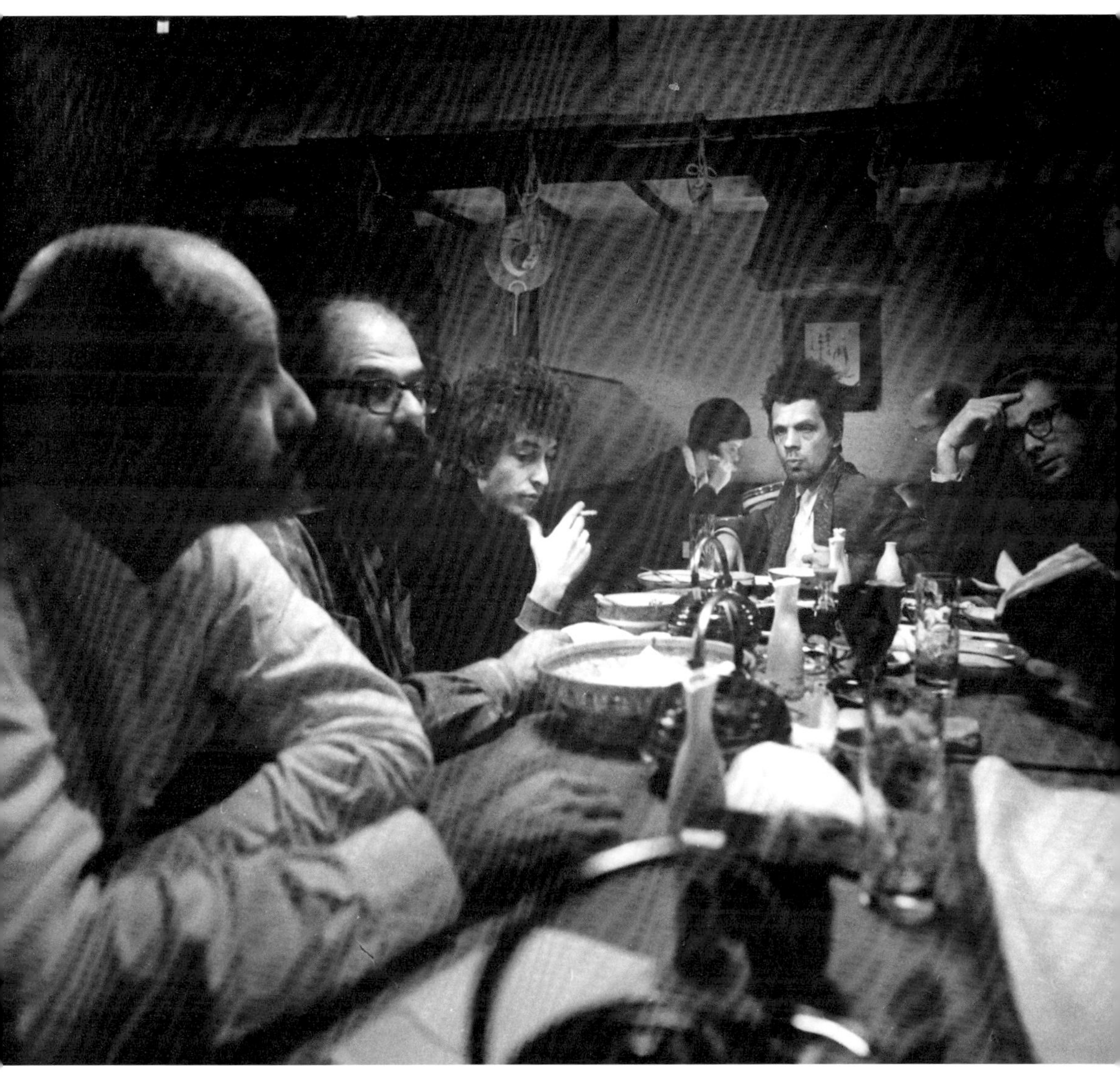

103

This is one of the most enigmatic works of
Kerouac's entire corpus, depicting "simply" a blue-
green ball and the imprint of a hand without a
thumb. The work has two possible interpretations,
but it is surely one of the masterpieces of the
exhibition, synthesizing, in painting, the concept
of spontaneous prose generated from notes and
the free flow of words and images that Kerouac
applied in his writing. The first interpretation is
based on the back of the painting, where Kerouac
himself wrote the word "Surrealisme."
As suggested by the *Beat Generation. New York,
San Francisco, Paris* exhibition at the Pompidou
Center in Paris, curated by Philippe-Alain Michaud,
this detail helps us appreciate the influence of
French culture on Kerouac, (as also stressed by
Sandrina Bandera and Franco Buffoni), who was
after all born into a French-Canadian family.
The painting can thus be seen as a surrealist
experiment, just like Man Ray's rayographs or Hans
Arp's collages. A second interpretation, which
does not exclude the first and was proposed
by Ed Adler in 2004, calls attention to the constant
presence in Kerouac's various *Choruses* of poetic
references to "balloons" and "blue moon" (in
Orizaba 210 Blues, for example). Also in *Doctor
Sax*, a novel full of Jack's childhood memories
in Lowell, he writes, "A vast perwigillar balloon
exploded over my head, it was a blue balloon that
had risen out of the blue powders in the forge,
and so suddenly everything was blue."

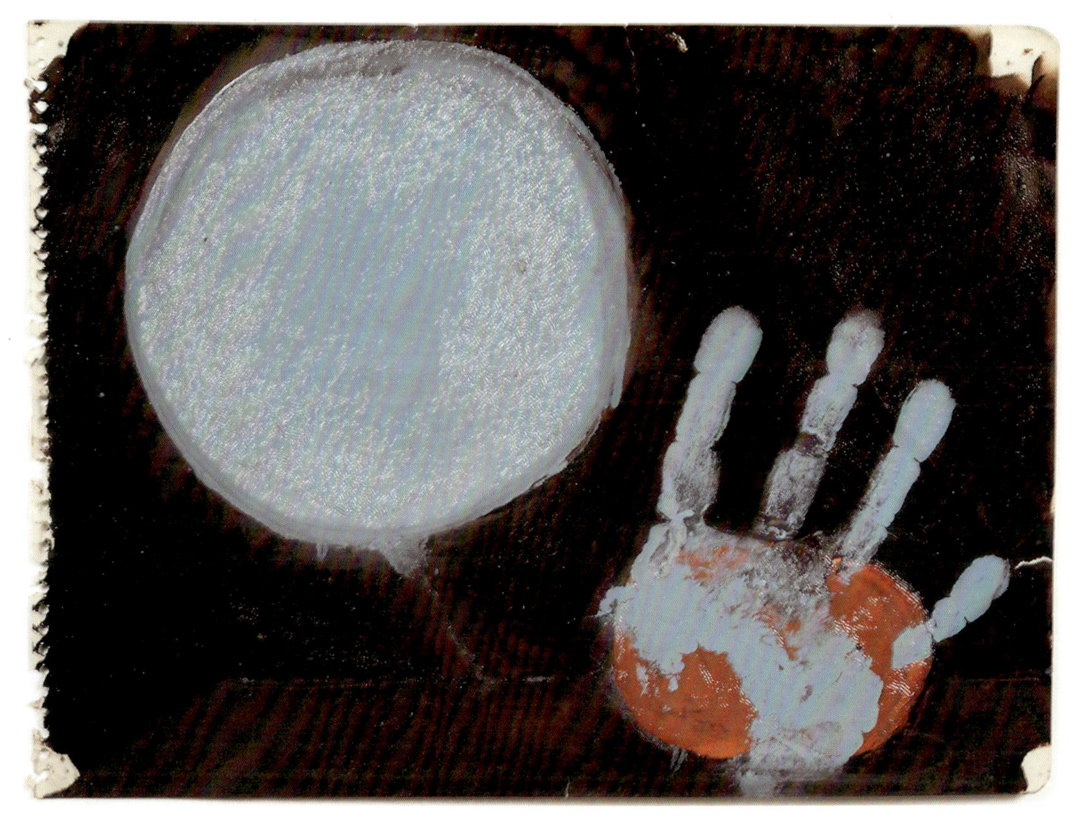

On the Road features many descriptions of natural settings, like the Louisiana plains or the jungle near Gregoria, Mexico, for example. In the book, the environment is no longer and not only presented as simply a surprising, exotic feature, but rather as a fact, an overwhelming context that consumes man, as Kerouac says, in a dense, dark, ancient way. These paintings reinterpret that ancestral, primitive dimension in the relationship between man and nature. The most striking characteristic is the expressionist treatment of the subject, still with a French influence, citing Matisse, Vuillard or Bonnard. The first of these images shows an exotic interior where a female figure lies with a guitar, a scene with classic Beat elements. In the next painting (Fig. 27), this dimension becomes more abstract, with thick, textured paint and figures (perhaps another female body) dissolved in the gestural quality of Kerouac's pictorial sign.

The third painting (Fig. 28) shows a subject immersed in nature, asleep in a field at night. Kerouac made reference to this work in his notes on January 27, 1959, saying he had painted "a blonde girl on the grass."

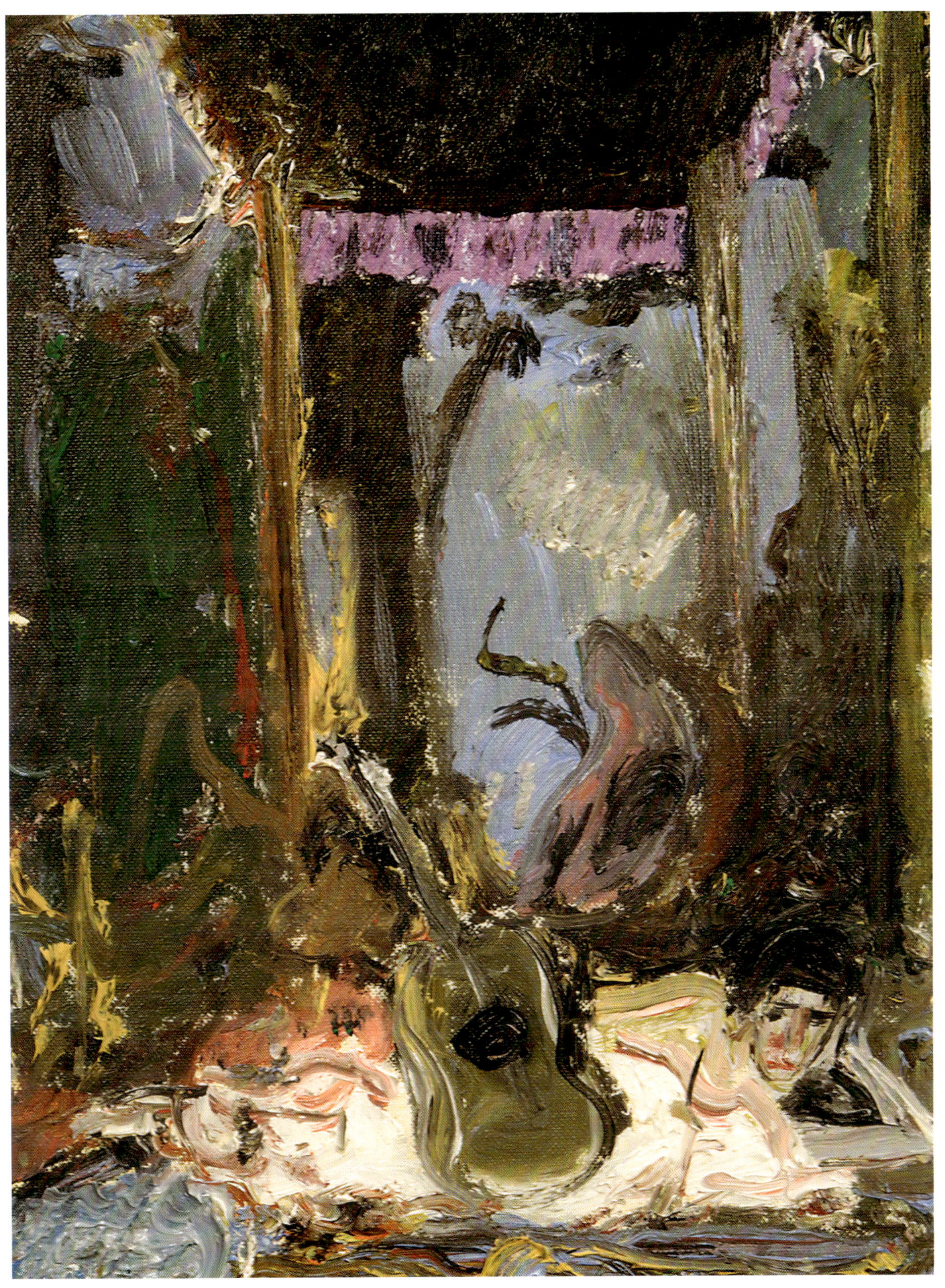

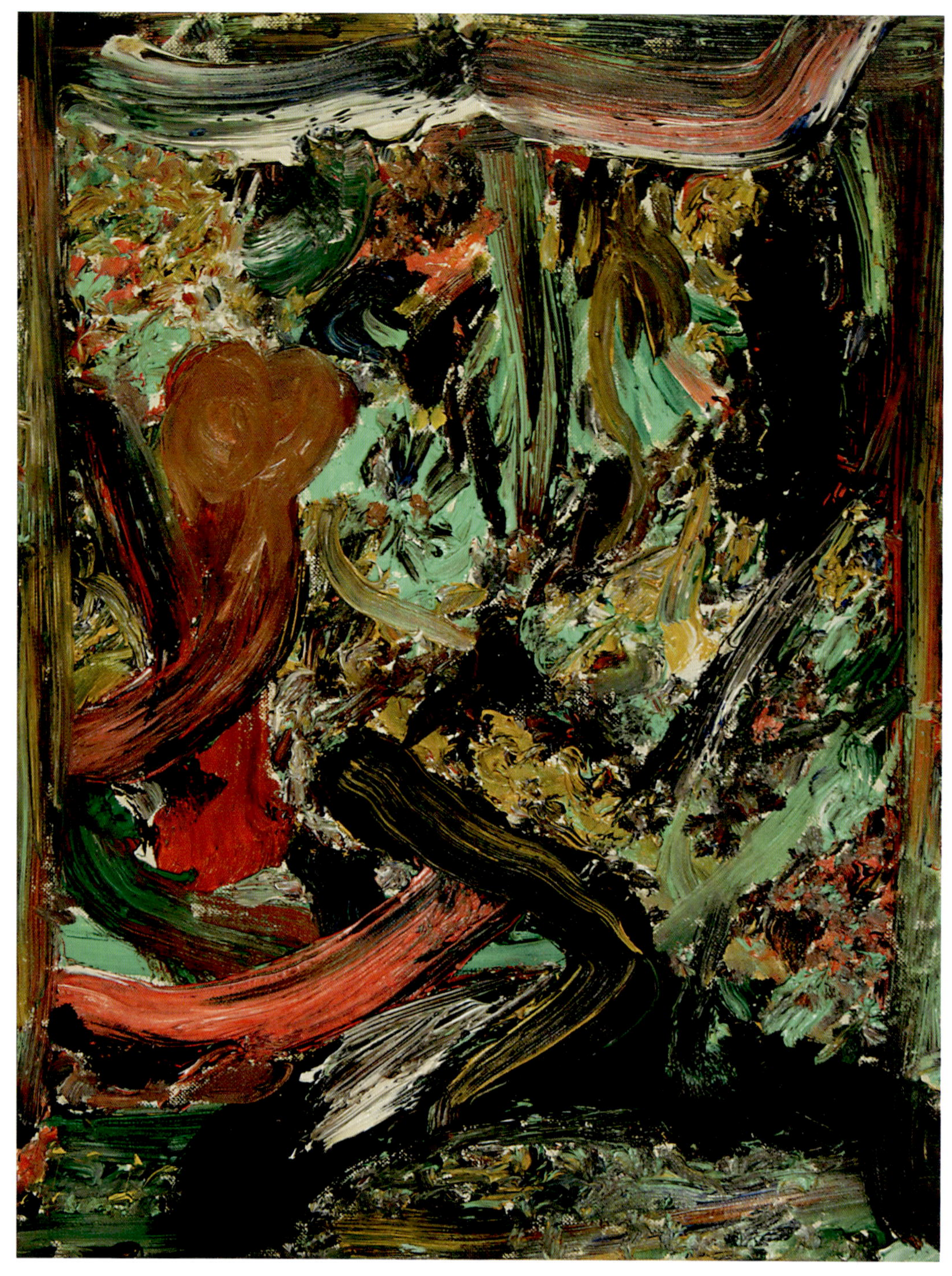

27 *Abstract I*, n.d.,
oil on canvas, 41 x 30 cm

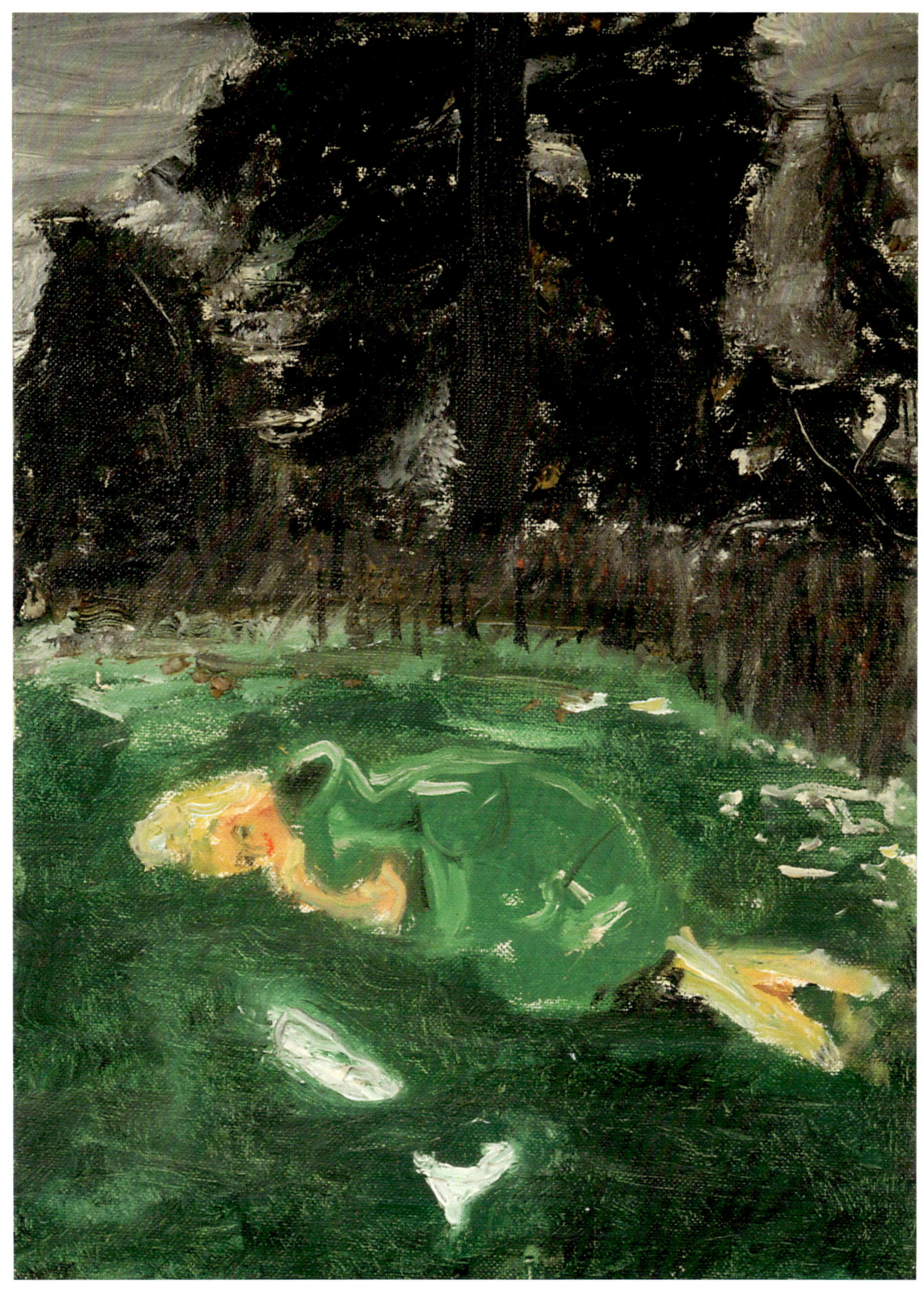

28 *Untitled*, n.d.,
oil on canvas, 30 x 22 cm

110

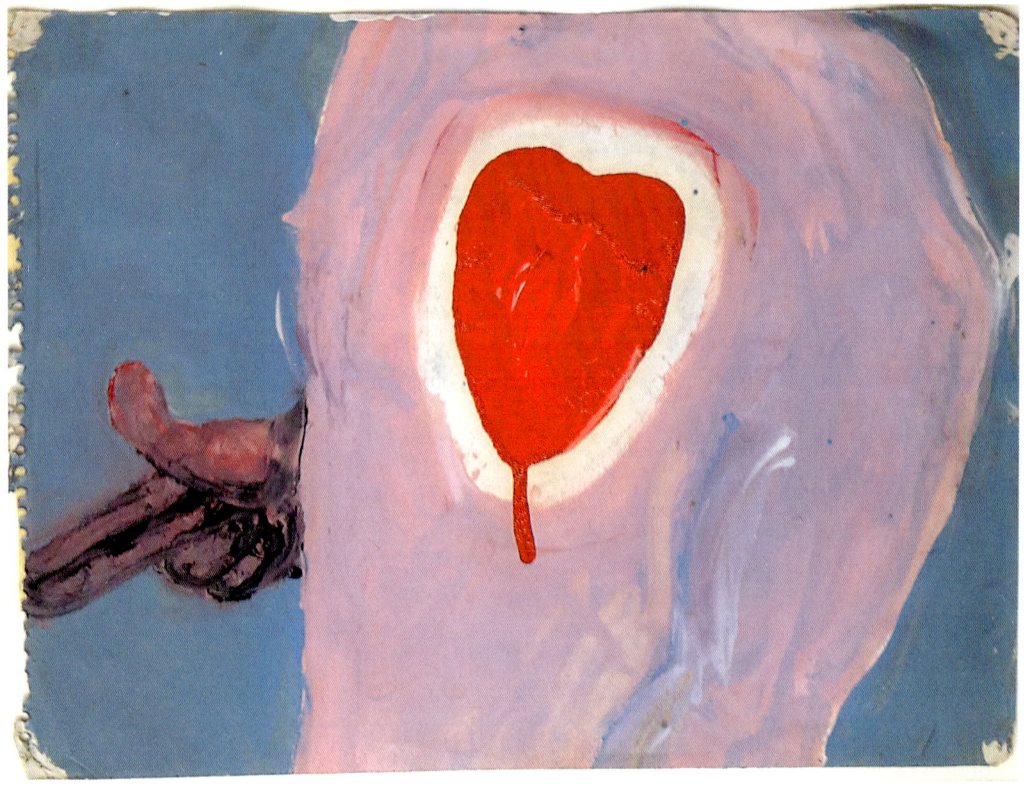

30 *Untitled*, n.d.,
oil on canvas,
22.5 x 30.4 cm

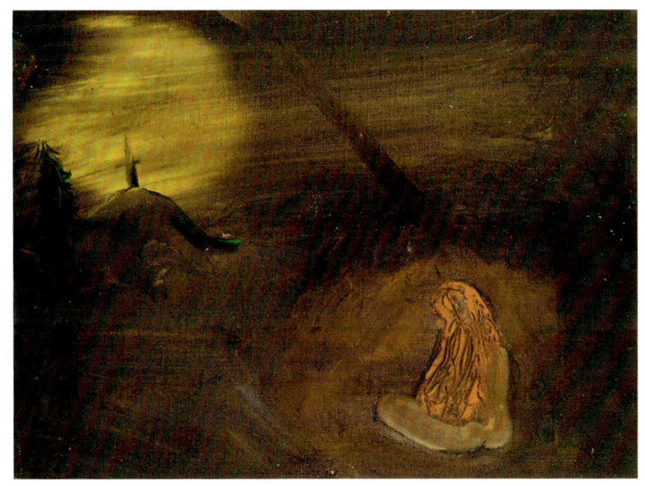

31 *Untitled*, n.d.,
oil on canvas, 40 x 29.5 cm

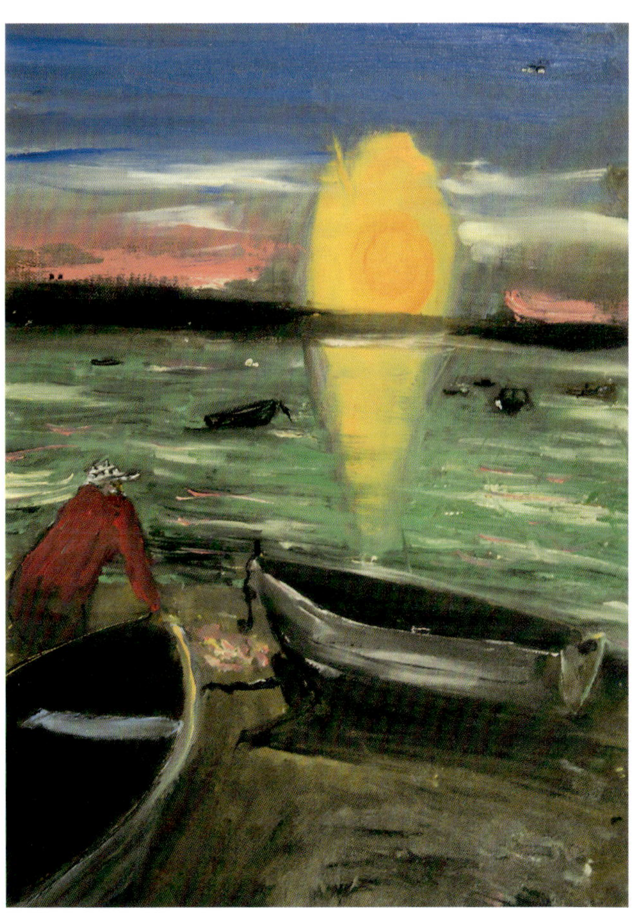

In Kerouac's notes from late January and early February 1959, he refers several times to the painting *Girl in White, Boy in Red* and to *Eagle*. Both works are painted with expressionist lines and renewed attention to color, visible in the contrast between the clothes of the two characters in the first painting and the contrast between the yellow background and the red eye in *Eagle*. We know from Kerouac's notes that the eye was the last element to be painted, just as it was in *The Silly Eye* (Fig. 6).

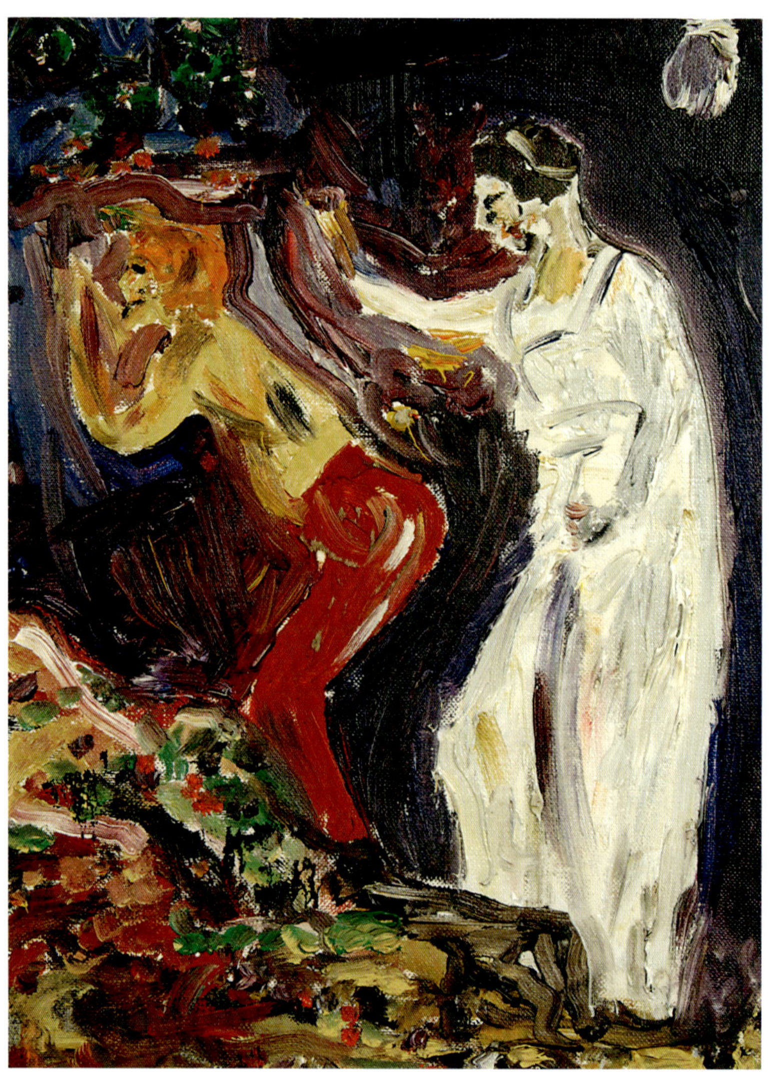

33 *Eagle*, 1959,
oil on canvas, 29 x 23 cm

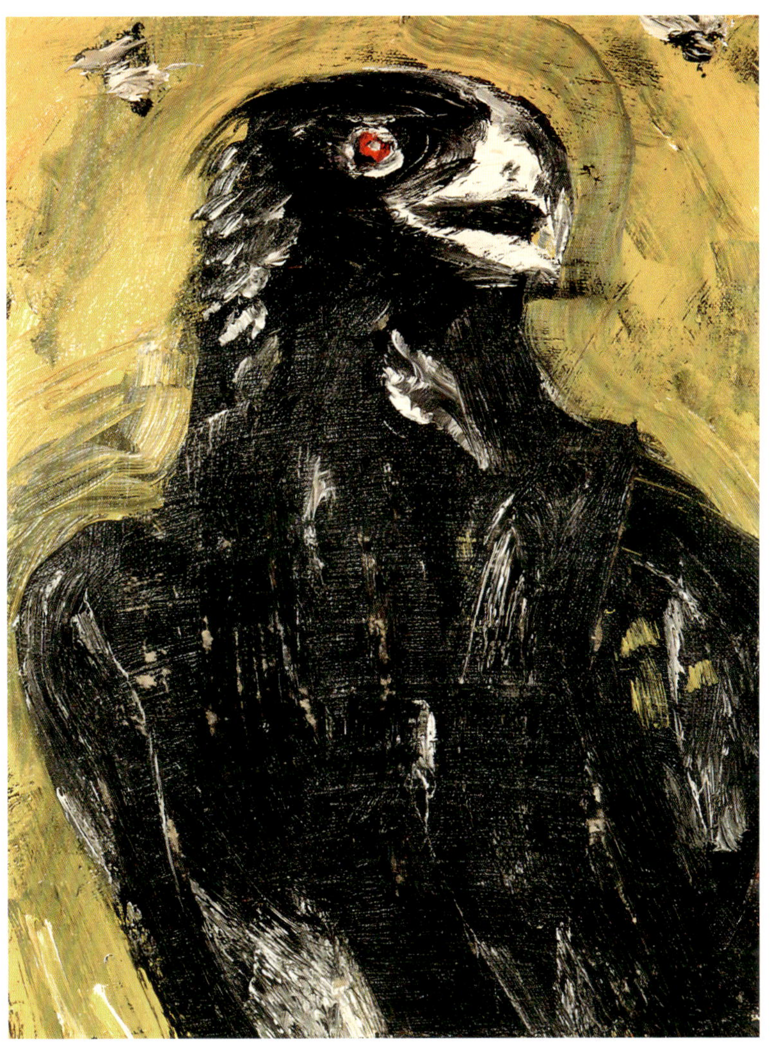

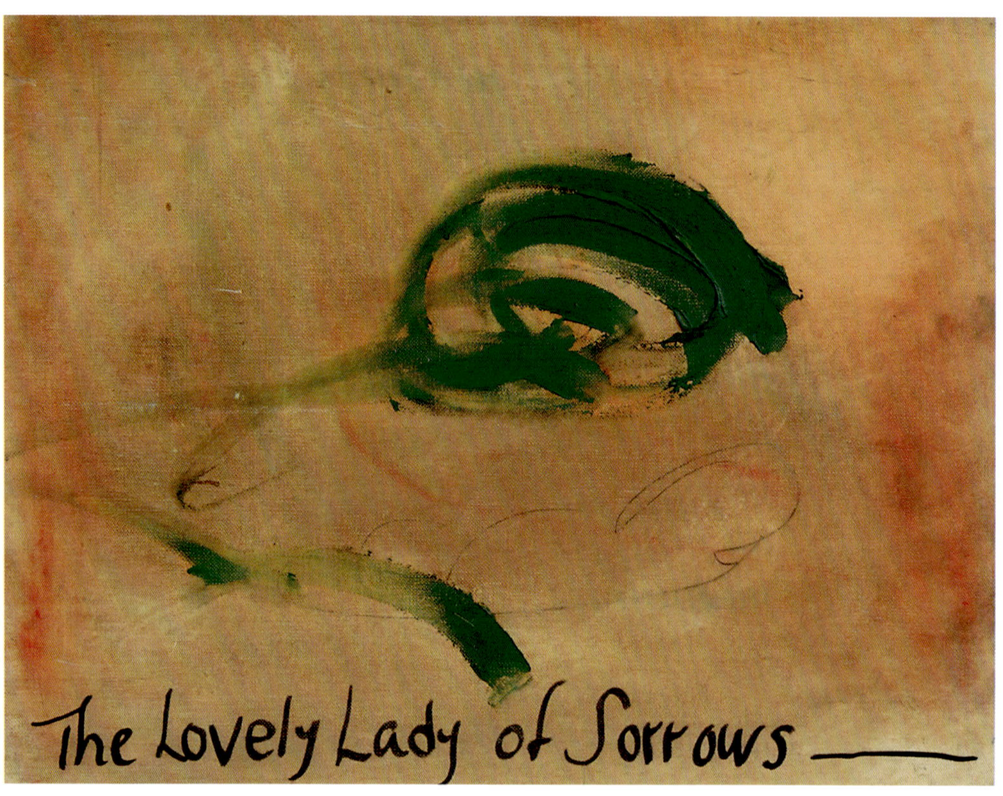

34 *The Lovely Lady of Sorrows*, n.d., mixed media on canvas 30.5 x 40 cm

While these two works are extremely diverse, they share an overall scheme that includes a synthetic, gestural pictorial element accompanied by a short text. The first text is a devotional reference to the Lady of Sorrows of Catholic tradition, who becomes "lovely" in Kerouac's interpretation. The second image clearly refers to the book *Doctor Sax*. Specifically, the phrase "Sax on the River" may refer to the dream at the opening of the book, a vision experienced in Lowell (the book specifies "on Moody Street, Pawtucketville, Lowell"), right along the Merrimack River that passes through the city.

35 *Sax on the River*, n.d.,
oil pastel on paper,
21.8 x 28.6 cm

115

SAX ON
THE RIVER

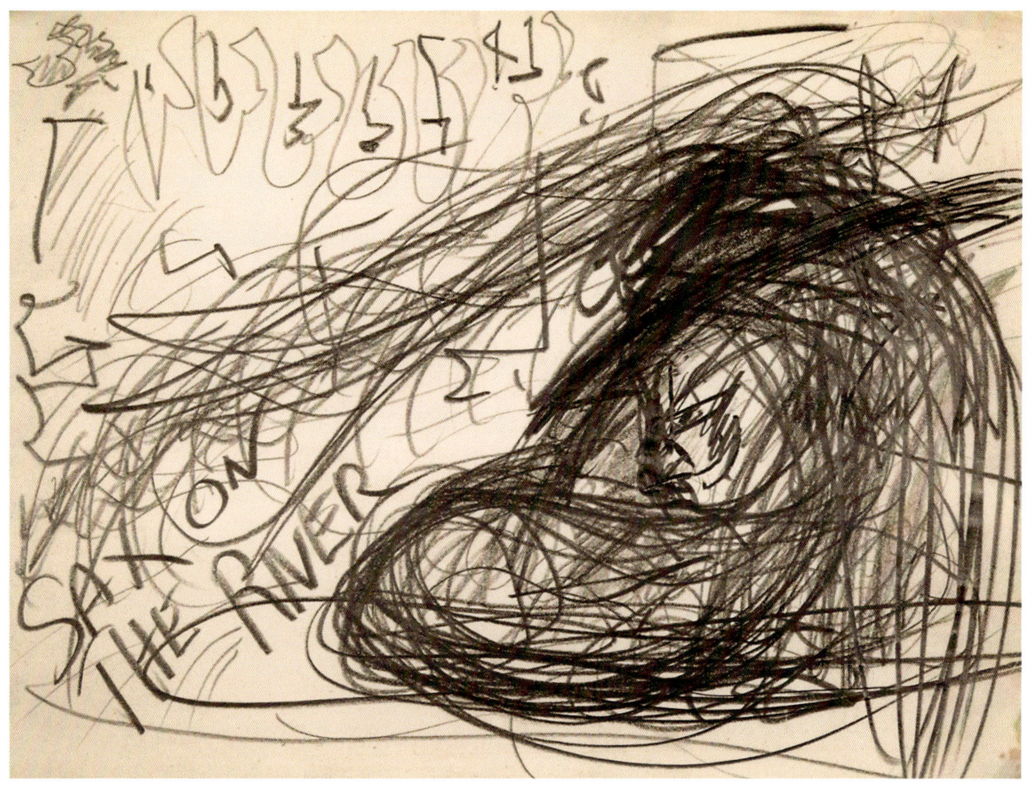

36 *The Spiral Drawing Tablet*, n.d.,
oil pastel, pen and glue on paper,
44 x 36 cm

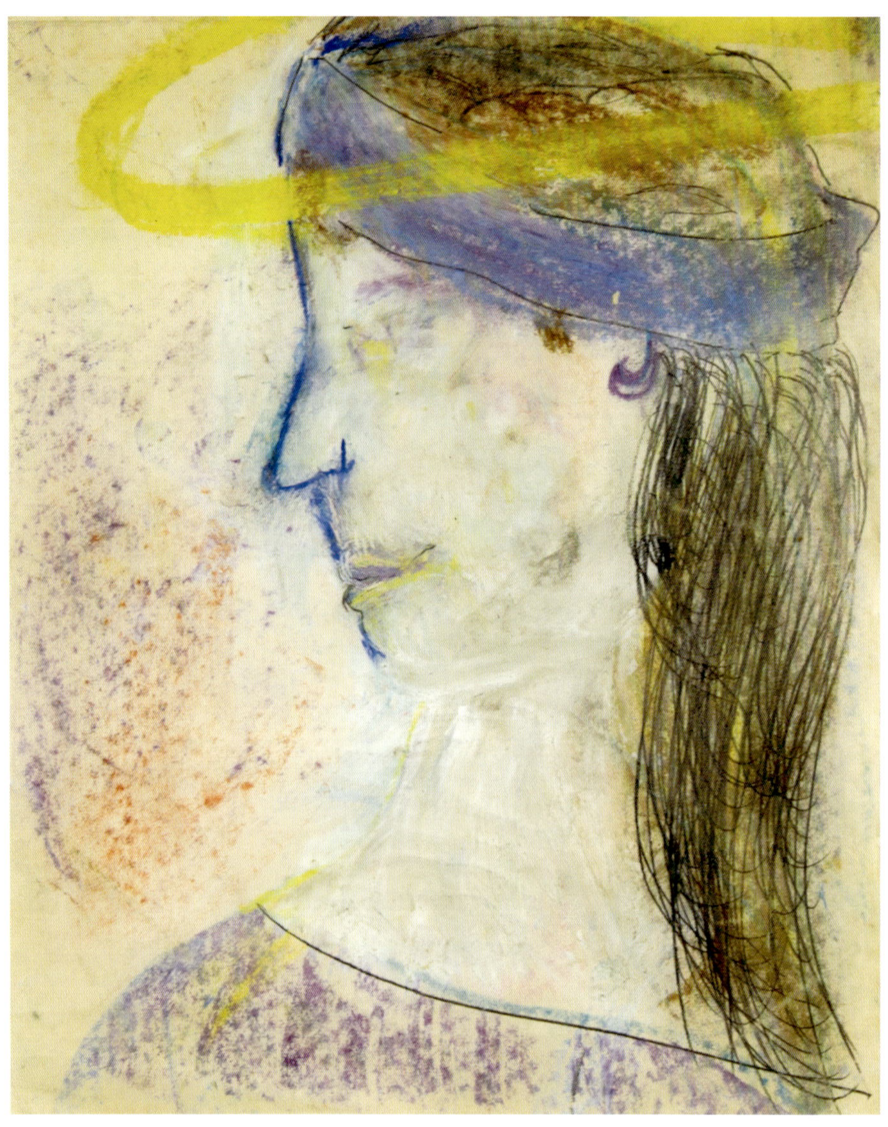

37 *The Spiral Drawing Tablet*, n.d.,
oil pastel on paper, 44 x 36 cm

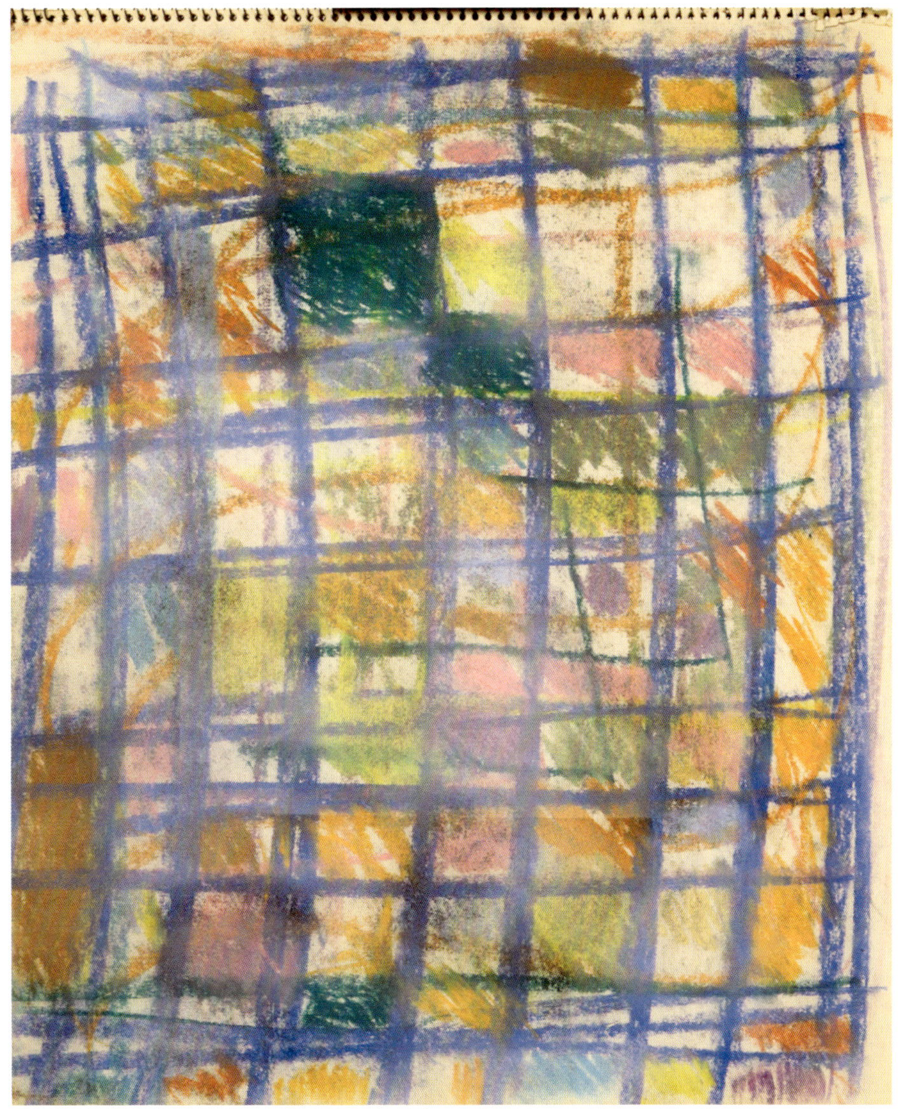

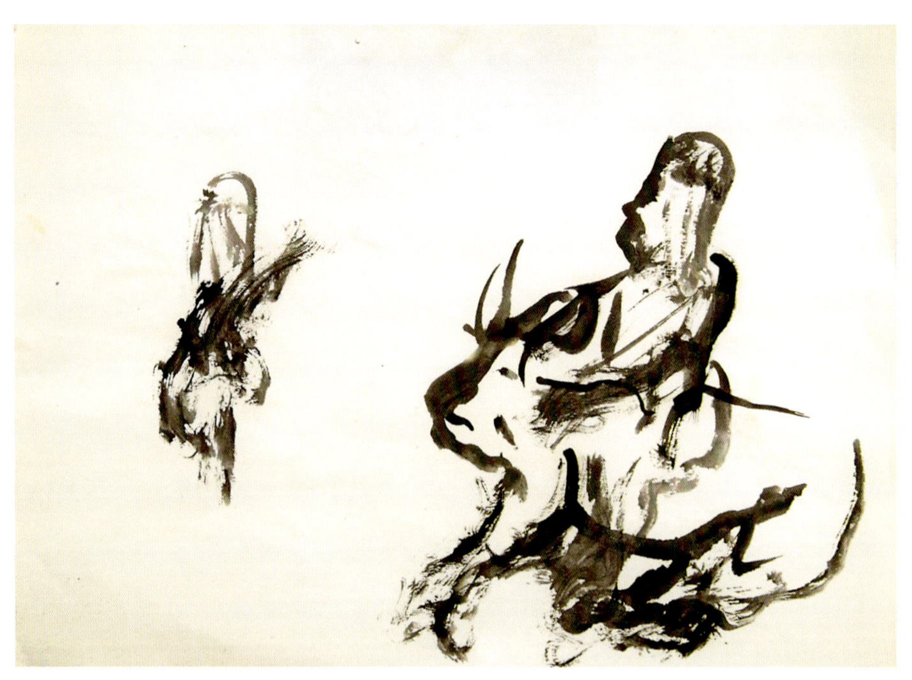

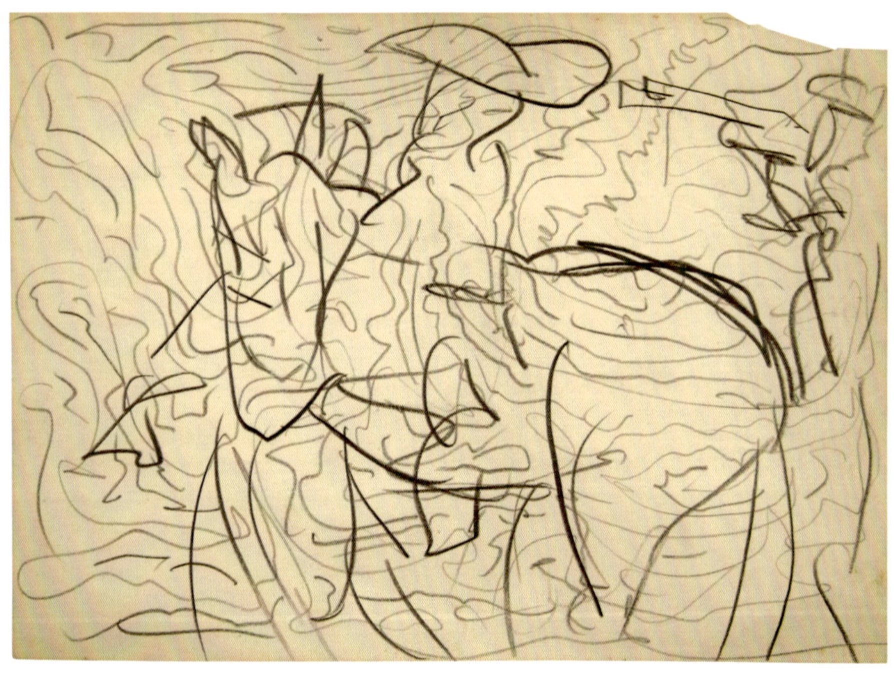

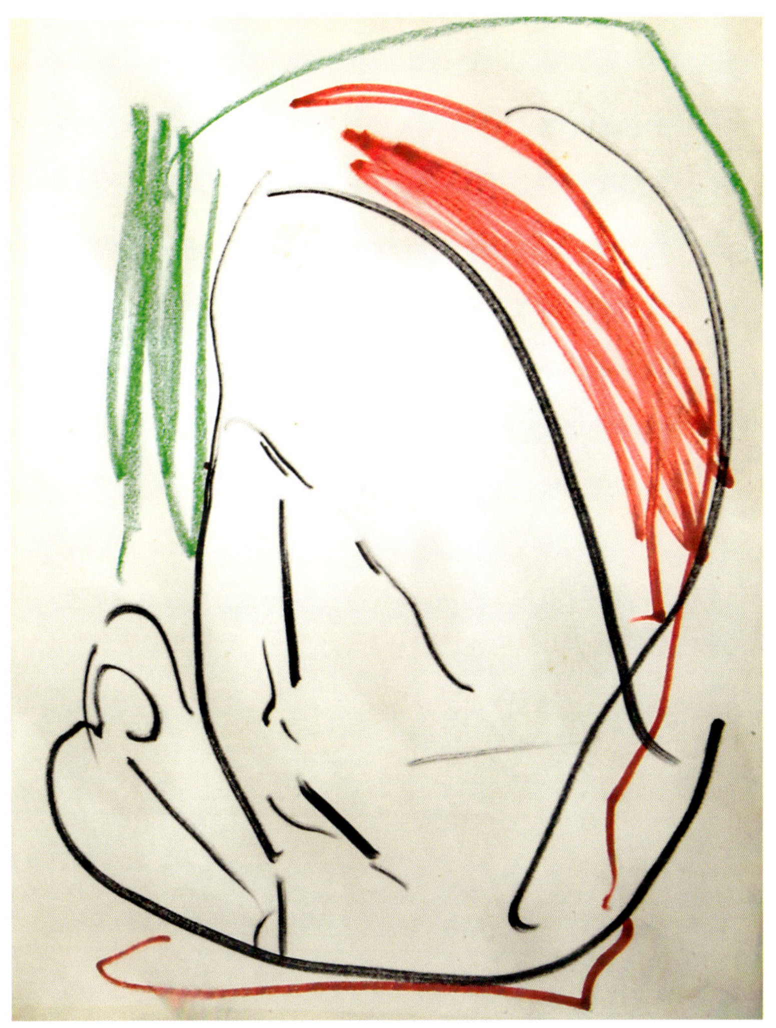

41 *Untitled*, n.d.,
oil and marker on paper,
14 x 8.5 cm

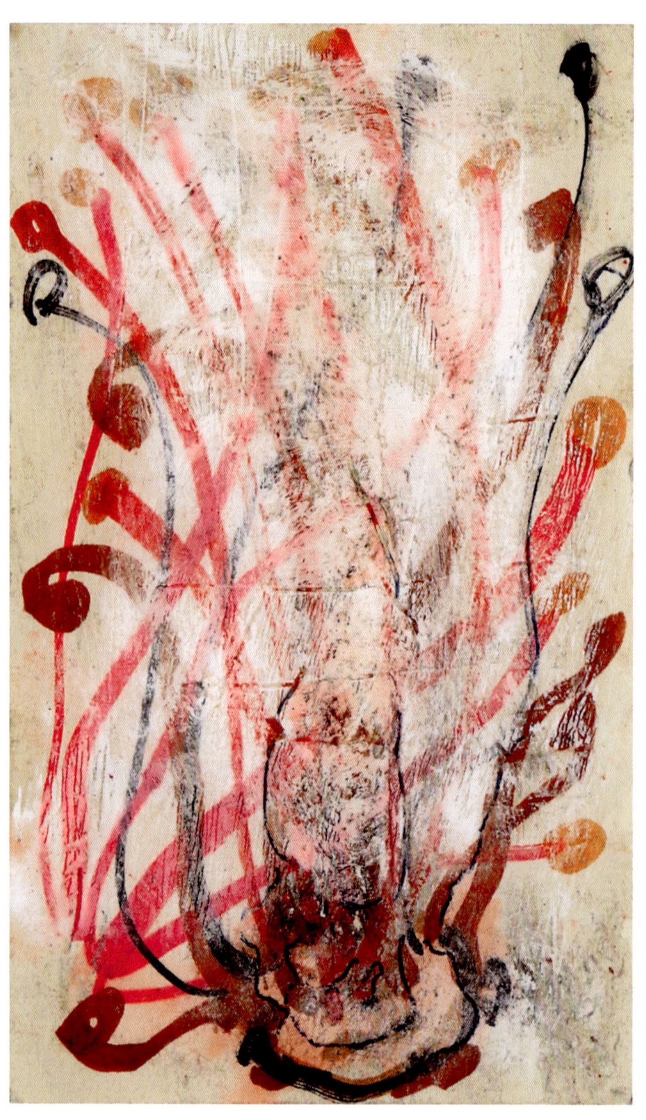

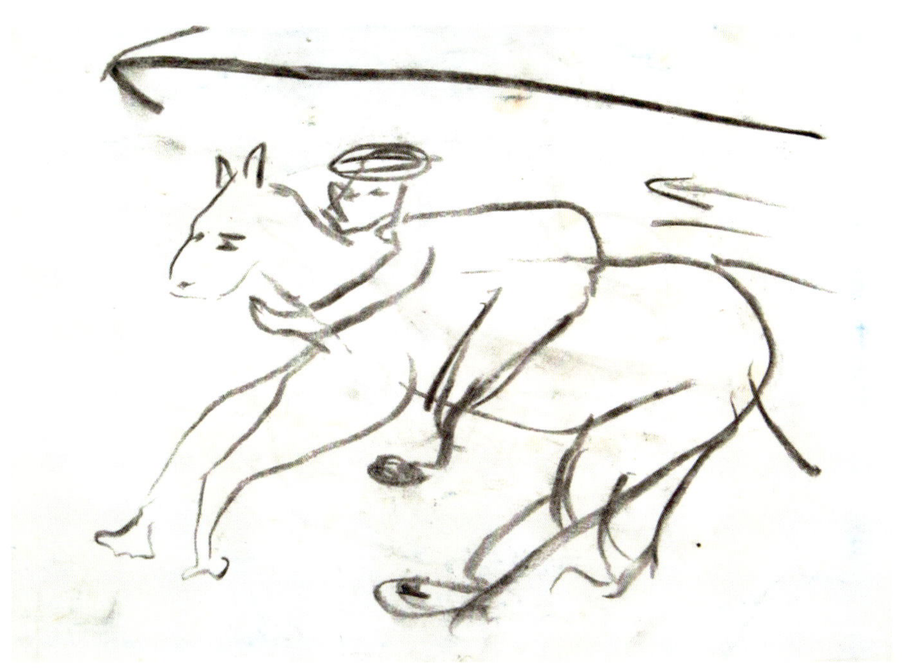

42 *Untitled*, n.d.,
pencil on paper,
23 x 30 cm,
recto and verso

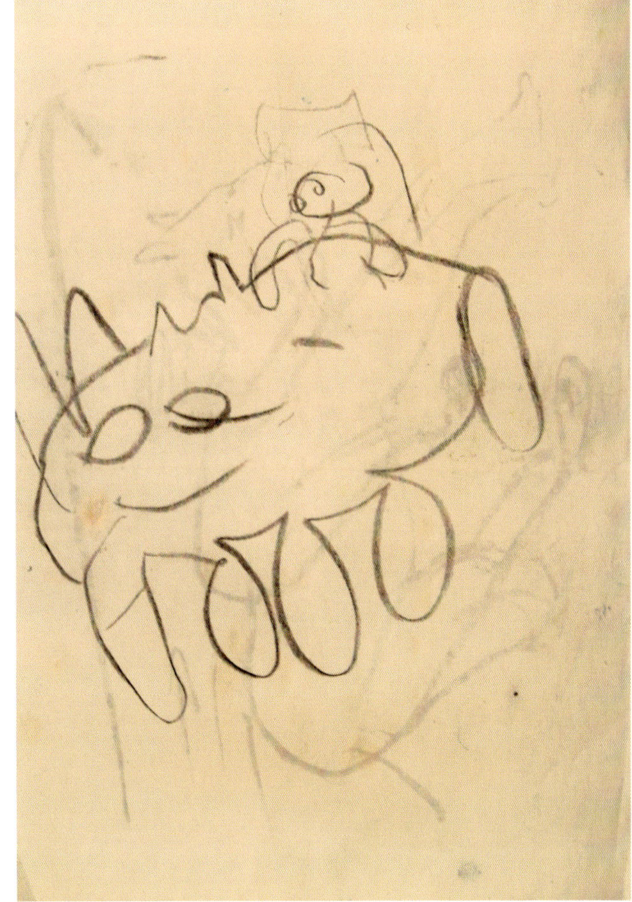

43 *Untitled*, n.d.,
oil pastel and pencil
on paper, 35.5 x 28 cm,
recto and verso

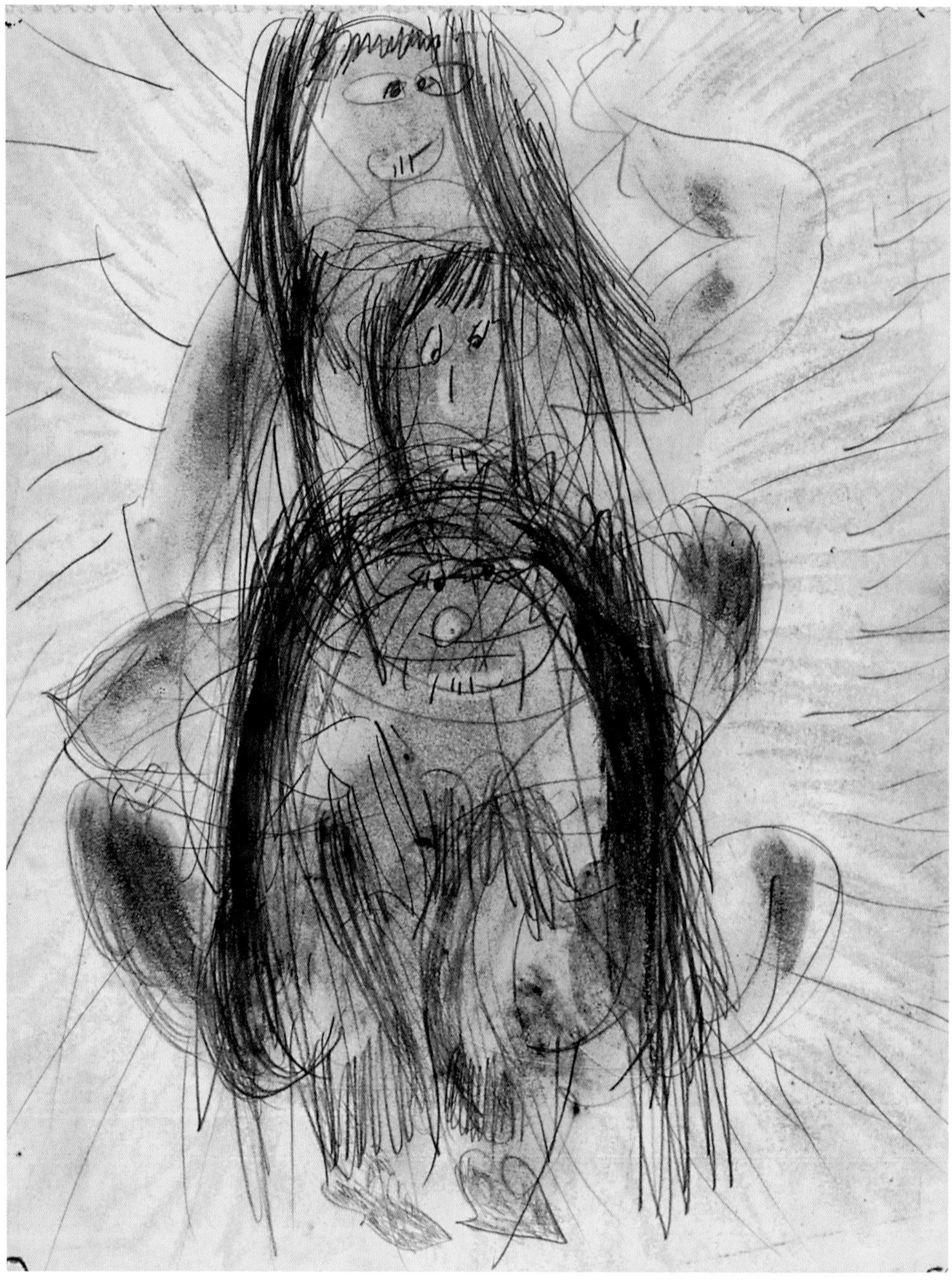

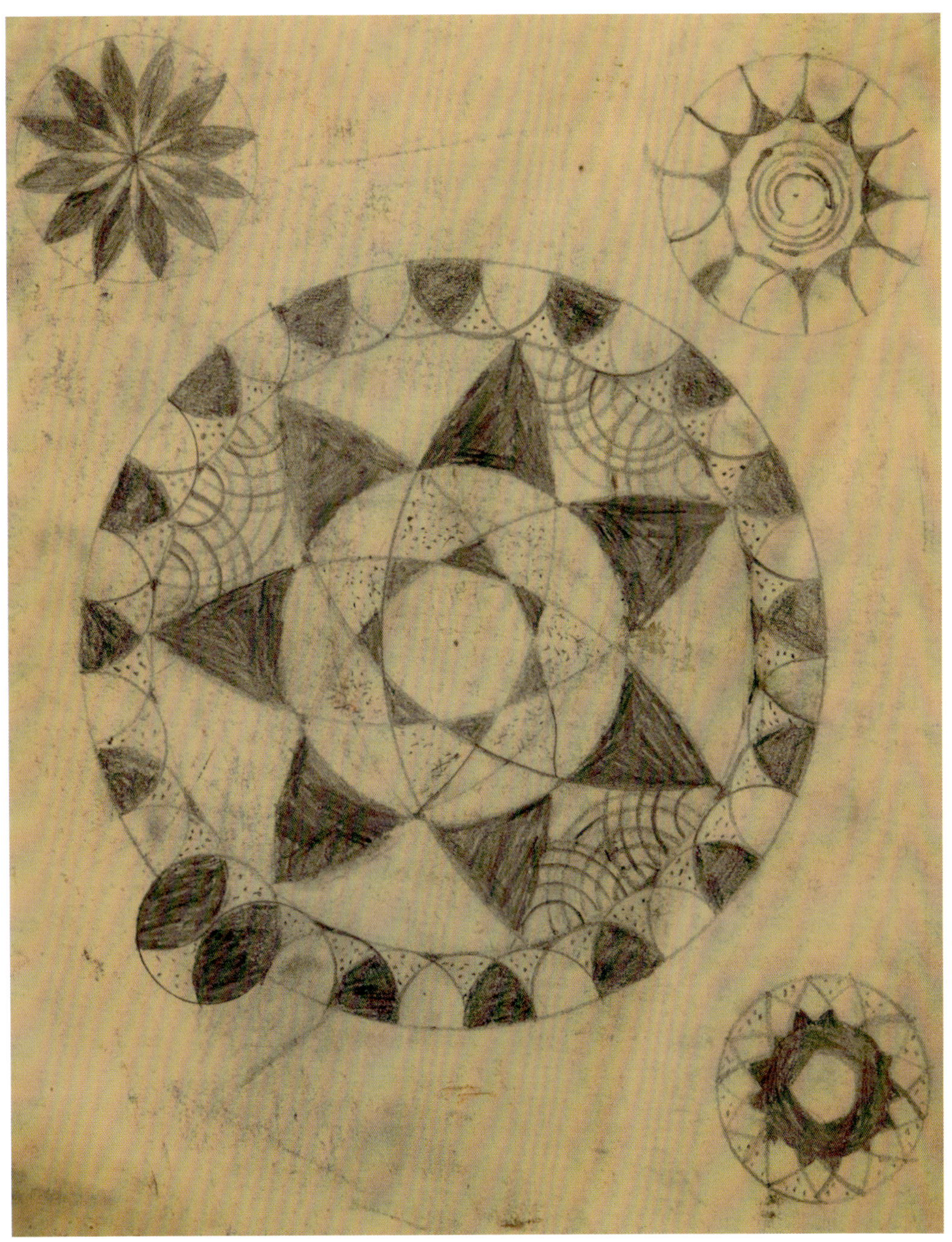

44 *Untitled*, n.d.,
pencil on paper,
24.5 x 17.2 cm

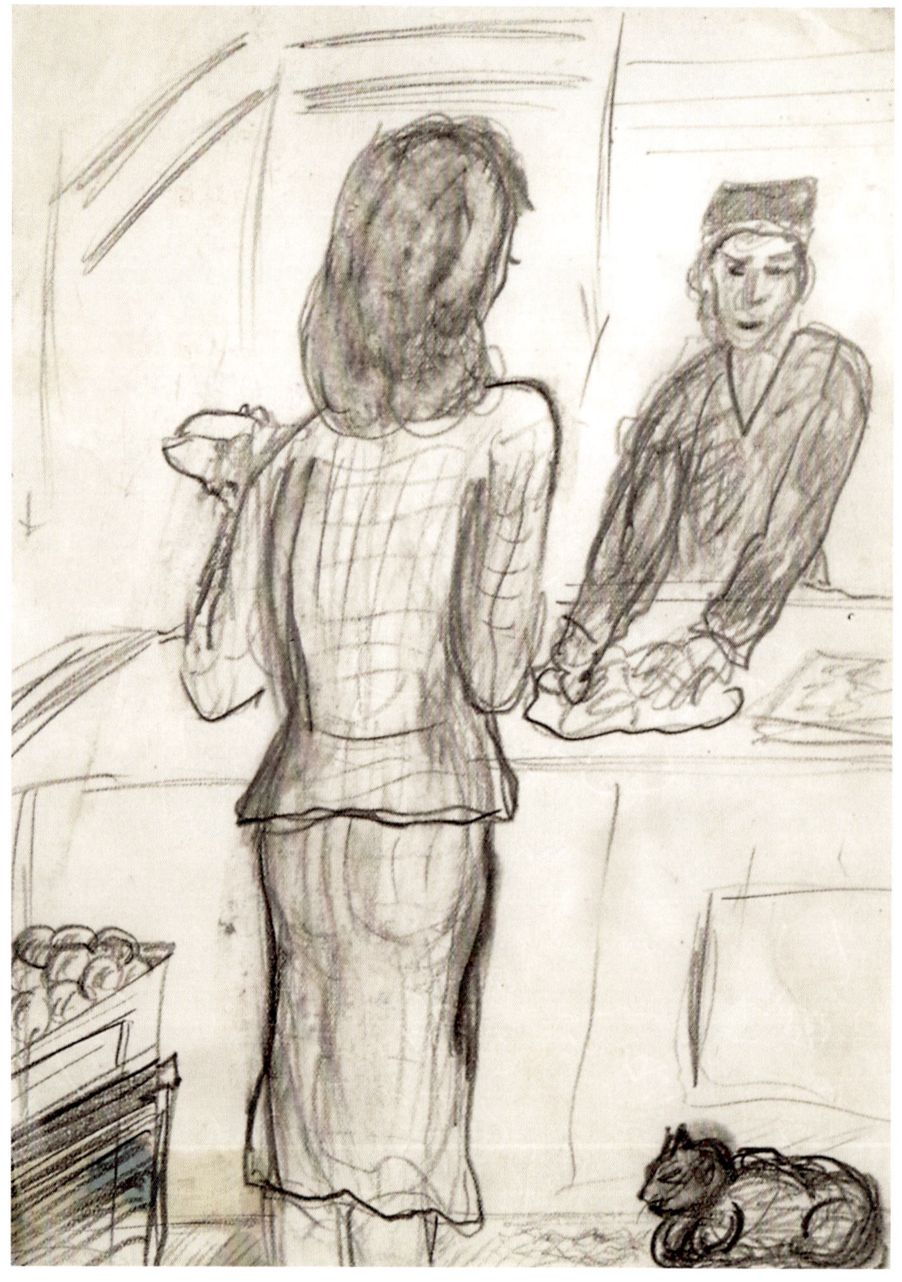

The small works on this and the next
two pages were drawn on the back
of a set of invitations to an exhibition
held on September 17, 1956 in
Berkeley, California, where Jack was
living as a guest of Beat poet Gary
Snyder. These examples of Kerouac's
graphic work from before he
encountered the New York School
show him beginning to complement
his literary work with graphic
experiments, drawn with a naïve
spontaneity not unlike illustration
or caricature.

45 *Untitled*, n.d.,
graphite and oil pastel
on cardboard,
12.5 x 10 cm

46 *Untitled*, n.d.,
graphite and oil pastel
on cardboard,
12.5 x 10 cm

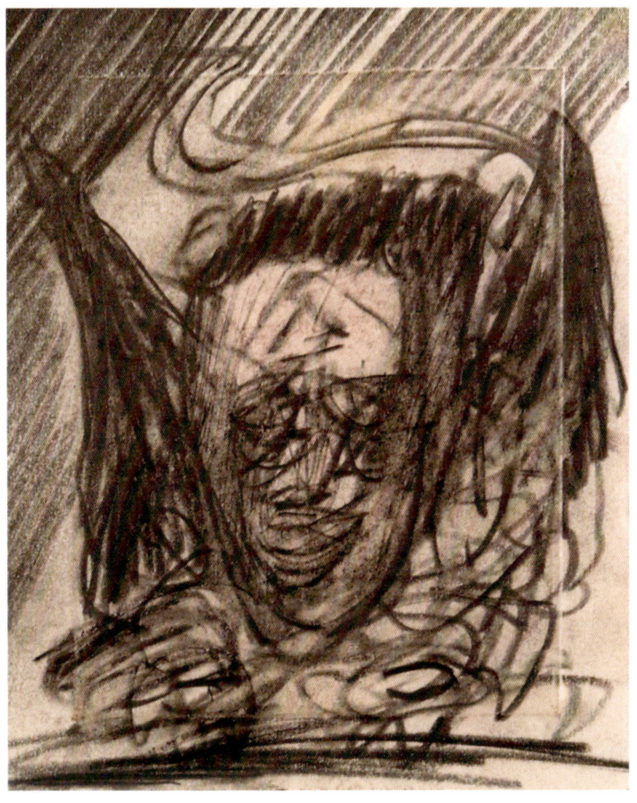

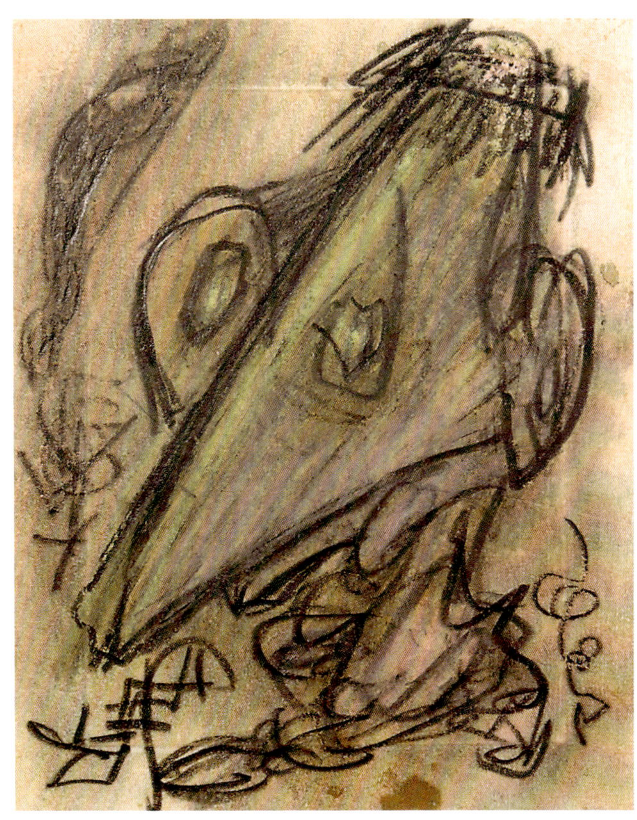

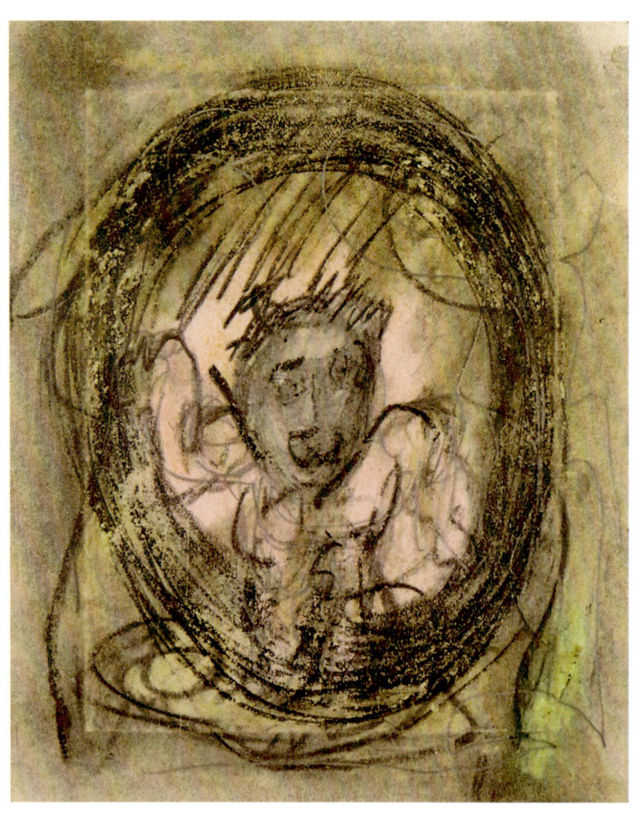

47 *Untitled*, n.d.,
marker and oil pastel
on cardboard,
12.5 x 10 cm

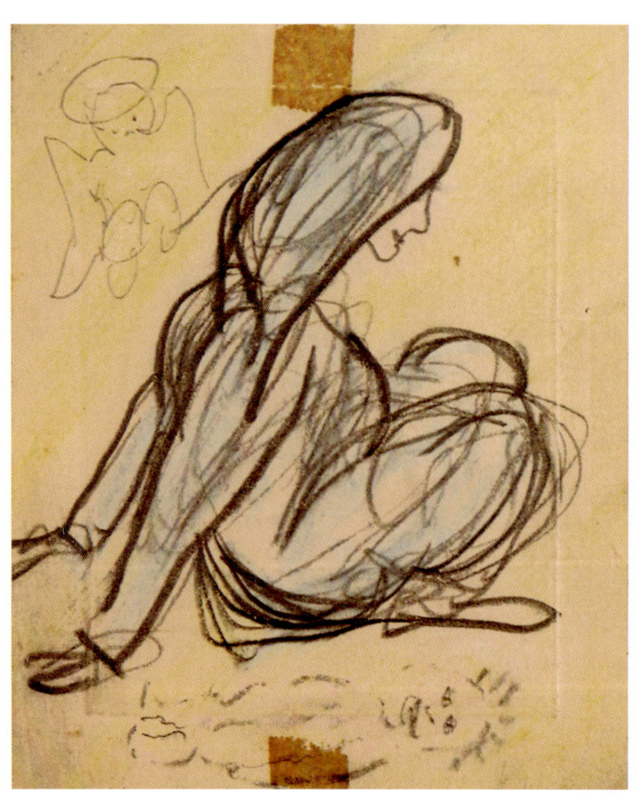

48 *Untitled*, n.d.,
graphite and oil pastel
on cardboard,
12.5 x 10 cm

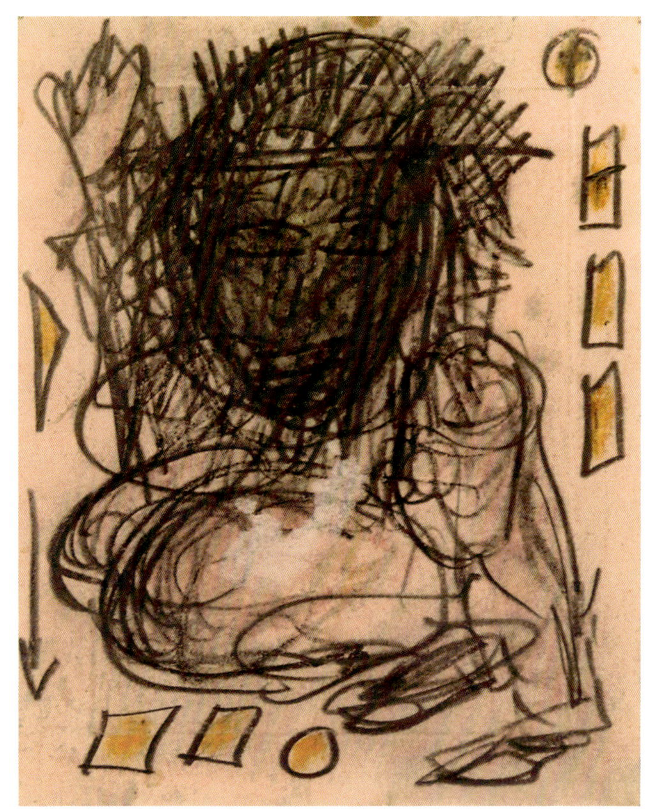

49 *Untitled*, n.d.,
graphite and oil pastel
on cardboard,
12.5 x 10 cm

50 *Untitled*, n.d.,
marker on cardboard,
12.5 x 10 cm

51 *Untitled*, n.d.,
graphite and oil pastel
on cardboard,
12.5 x 10 cm

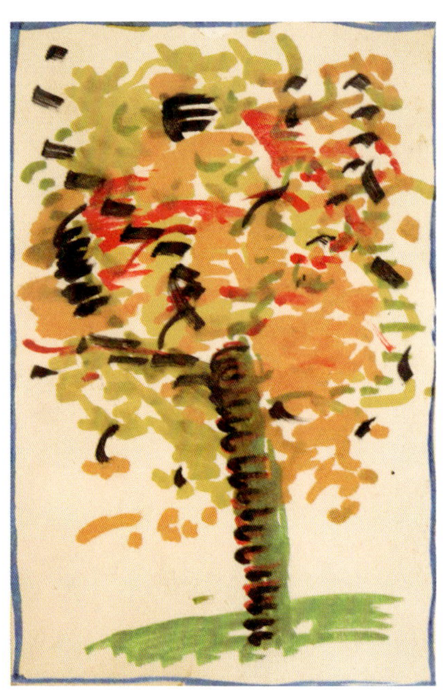

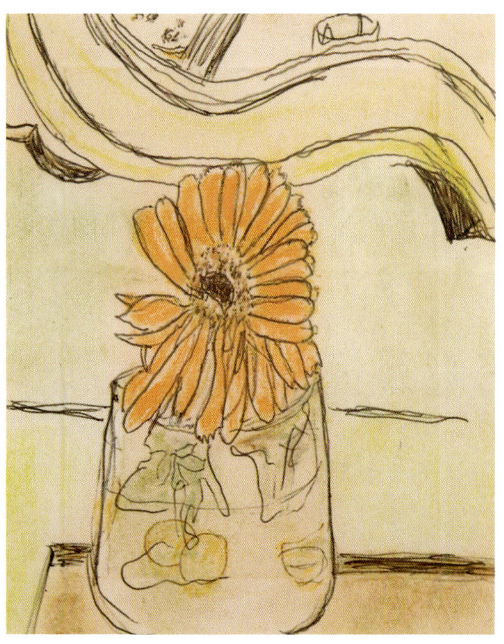

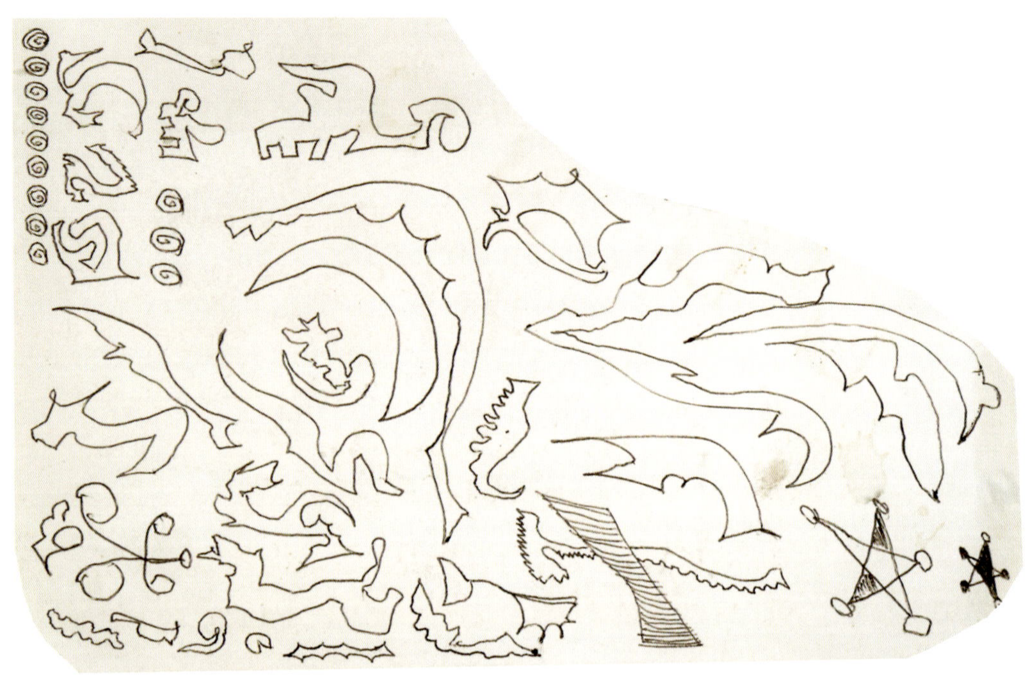

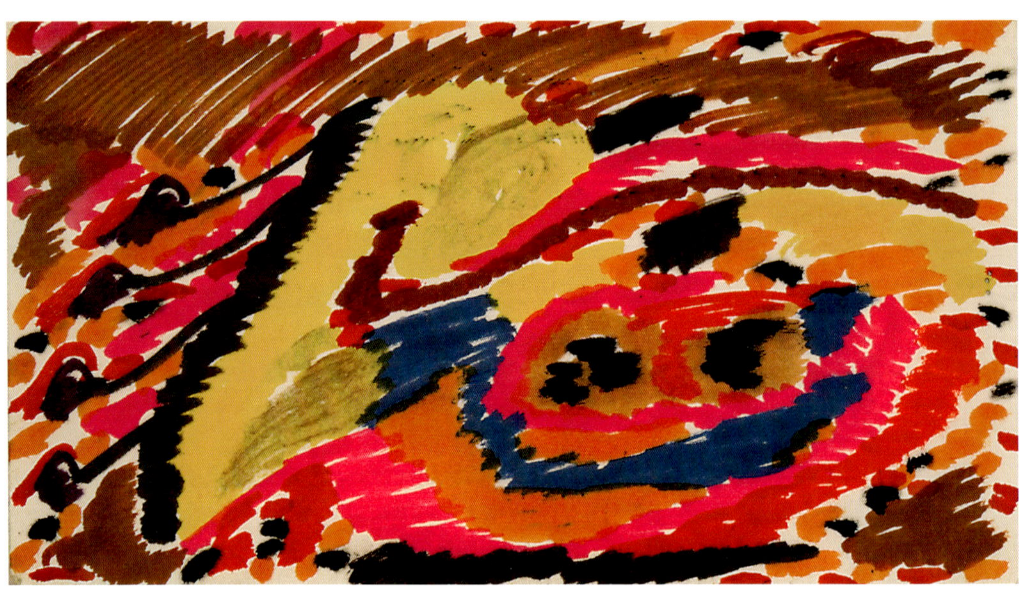

52 *Untitled*, n.d.,
marker on paper,
13 x 20 cm

53 *Untitled*, n.d.,
marker on paper,
9 x 16.5 cm

54 *Untitled*, n.d.,
pencil on paper,
23 x 30 cm

129

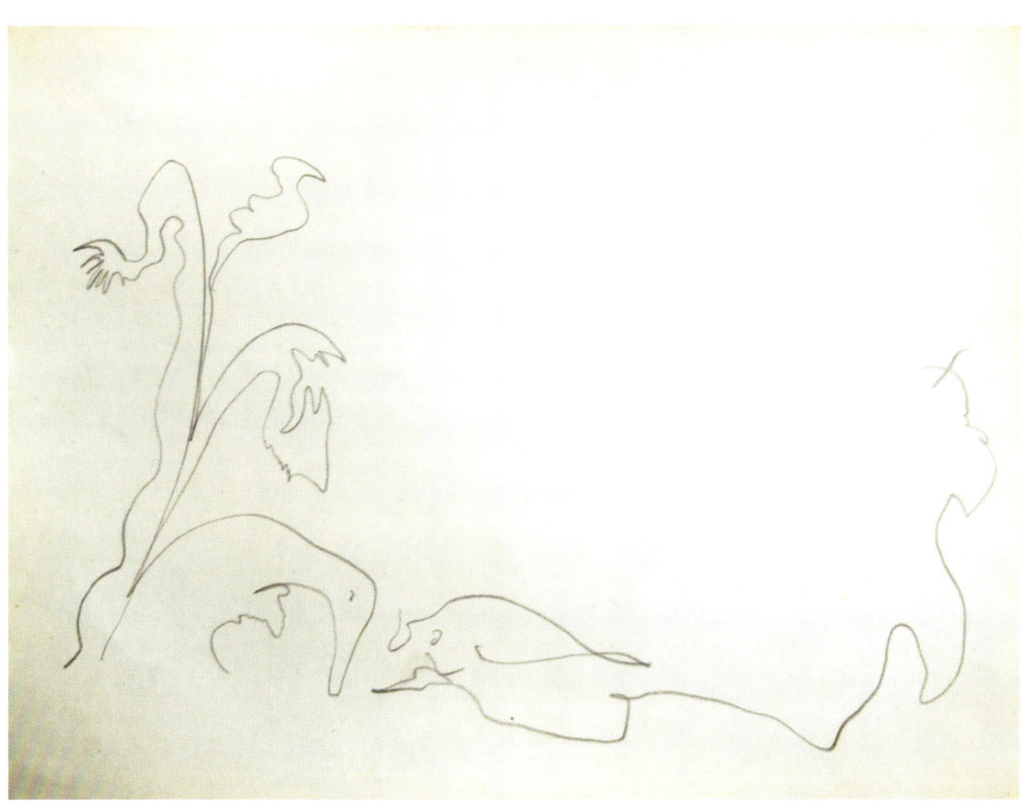

Abstract Expressionism

Speaking of "creative force," Isaac Gewirtz (*Beatific Soul. Jack Kerouac on the Road*, 2007) quotes an entry from Kerouac's diary dated January 27, 1959, where he wrote, "USE BRUSH SPONTANEOUSLY without drawing: without long pause or delay; without erasing… pile it on. […]. PAINT WHAT YOU SEE IN FRONT OF YOU 'NO FICTION'. STOP WHEN YOU WANT TO IMPROVE – IT'S DONE." This veritable poetic manifesto helps explain the selection of paintings that concludes this catalog documenting the change in Kerouac's pictorial language during the second half of the 1950s. This transformation coincides with his move to Northport, NY and his association and friendships with painter Stanley Twardowicz, his neighbor, with Dody Muller and with numerous artists of the so-called New York School. As noted by Francesco Tedeschi, the affinities between improvisation and artistic production, and the resulting overlapping of art and life, are absolutely fundamental to Kerouac's poetics, in both his literary and his visual works, especially those presented in this chapter. A comparison of different works also reveals the author's intention to pursue his artistic career professionally, within a perspective that was neither impromptu nor secondary to his literary production. In fact, in a letter written on October 10, 1956 from Mexico City to his friend Allen Ginsberg, Jack explains, "Only good thing is I started to paint – I use housepaint mixed with glue. I use brush and fingertip both, in a few years I can be topflight painter if I want – maybe then I can sell paintings and buy a piano and compose music too – for life is a bore." (A.C.)

Exercises in Improvisation with Word, Sound, and Image

About Jack Kerouac's painting and its relationship
to other sectors of artistic production

Francesco Tedeschi

The only people for me are the mad ones, the ones who are mad to live, mad to talk, mad to be saved, desirous of everything at the same time, the ones who never yawn or say a commonplace thing, but burn, burn, burn like fabulous yellow roman candles exploding like spiders across the stars and in the middle you see the blue centerlight pop and everybody goes "Awww!"

Jack Kerouac, *On the Road,* Penguin Press, 2003, p. 5

Improvisation is the guiding principle underlying all of Jack Kerouac's creations, and not only his writing. A study of his pictorial production, in fact, confirms that it too manifests a total correspondence between action and result, as occurs in action intended to superimpose art on life (and vice versa).

There is no doubt that many of Kerouac's readers are seduced and thrilled by his electric vitality, his extraordinary ability to take the energy generated by his need to exteriorize the pressure of his inner life and make it explode in an instant. What emerges from his art is a picture of a personality based on dynamism, on the immediate expression of his way of being and feeling, and on a profound hunger for and love of life. This is clearly communicated in some of the finest passages in *On the Road*, like the famous one quoted at the beginning of this article, as well as in his other writings.

At the same time, examining Kerouac's work in light of his life story, which is integrated into so much of his writing, gives all-too-clear evidence of how that dynamism can turn self-destructive – a development seen in other artists as well, whose extreme vitality drove them to operate with such intensity of gestures, urges and emotions that they simply burned themselves out. In this regard, one can consider the correspondence between the characters in *On the Road* and their existential vicissitudes with other real-life famed characters of the era, such as Jackson Pollock, Charlie Parker or even James Dean, to name three who in some ways can be likened to Kerouac – three distinct personalities and lives, each sacrificed in his own way. Excesses of alcohol, drugs, and other manifestations of self-destructive energy led to the sudden death of Charlie Parker (at the age of thirty-four, in March 1955), James Dean (twenty-four, in September 1955) and Jackson Pollock (forty-four, in August 1956), the first due to heroin and the other two to different types of car accidents. At the time when these three great artists died, Jack Kerouac had still not achieved any widespread notoriety; indeed, *On the Road* was not published until September 1957. Nonetheless, he, and they, were interpreters of those immediate post-WWII years, invading the new epoch with an energy that renewed and transformed cultural models from the inside out, challenging the old moral and formal conventions until they came tumbling down. Kerouac's painting can be analyzed within this framework, considering its connection to his writing as well as to the painting that defined that entire epoch. Nor can the distinct relationship with music be ignored, and indeed Kerouac himself pointed out specific correspondences.

Various critics, especially American ones, have gone so far as to identify specific points of contact between Kerouac, jazz and action painting.[1] In fact, the aesthetic and existential correspondences between Kerouac, Pollock and Parker – and to others as well, especially jazz musicians, as confirmed by specific references in Kerouac's writings[2] – justify such a dialogue, a starting point in a relationship or exchange between the arts, driven further by the heat of a period of such important shifts in the modes of expression.

This type of interaction may be explained by the original impulse towards transformation inherent in the very attitude towards creation as an act that is simultaneously generative and definitive. To comprehend these relationships, it is useful to turn to an analysis formulated only a few years after their conception by Harold Rosenberg. The American art critic outlined the characteristics of what he termed "action painting," which expressed a unique connection between the artist's inner being and the act that generates the work. As he wrote: "A painting that is an act is inseparable from the biography of the artist. The painting itself is a 'moment' in the adulterated mixture of his life – where 'moment' means, in one case, the actual minutes taken up with spotting the canvas or, in another, the entire duration of a lucid drama conducted in sign language. The act-painting is of the same metaphysical substance as the artist's existence. The new painting has broken down every distinction between art and life."[3]

This definition of the painting of American artists who rose to fame in the 1940s was largely accepted and incorporated into critical explanations with vast resonance. Not all critics shared it, however. In particular, when it came to de-fining American action painting and its creators, there is a clear and well-known divergence between Rosenberg's existential interpretation and the formalist one by Clement Greenberg. Nonetheless, Rosenberg's is useful to identify points of contact that could seem to relate exclusively to biographical correspondences if their linguistic elaborations are not explored. Obviously, there are certain cases and situations in which the two domains cannot be separated, when the fusion between creative acts and biography is considered to be – and perhaps is – complete. It could be theorized, however, that the new capacity to generate paintings formally through direct action – as exemplified best of all by Pollock – was sufficient to renovate pictorial language, producing a new "style." This is not unlike what Charlie Parker accomplished through his ability to restruc-ture the relationship between composition and improvisation to create bebop. Analogously, Kerouac's spontaneous writing can be viewed as the invention or direct reinvention of writing as a living act, corresponding more to the process of becoming than to past experience. This correspondence is even stronger in Kerouac than in the illustrious predecessors, including Joyce, surrealist au-tomatism, and Marinetti's anti-normative lyricism.[4] Employing improvisation, a method that relies on the indistinguishable relationship between the creative process and the formal result, they all seem to share an intention to reinvent the language of their chosen media. This change took place first and foremost in the individual artist's attitude towards his particular means of expression, which had to be introjected in order to be pertinent to his life, to the goal of an immediate representation of his deeper being, in an overlapping of living and acting. In a well-known remark of *My Painting*, for example, Pollock stated that he feels himself fully when he is *in* his painting.[5] Similarly, Charlie Parker often stressed the correspondence between his musical experimentation and his inner state. In an interview with Nat Hentoff, he explained that by repeating a passage and modifying its melodic lines, he was able to pull out musical forms that he carried inside himself. In two texts about his writing method written immediately after the publication of *On the Road*, Kerouac asserted that he was looking for an expressive form that would allow him "to remove literary, grammatical and syntactical inhibition" through the procedures of spontaneous prose, entirely unrestrained, a process analogous to how jazz musicians of the new generation breathed life into their instruments.[6]

For all three artists, the creative process involves a spoliation of external elements and conventions in order to recover the primary element, the basic linguistic principle for an unrestrained elaboration where word, image and sound flow from a source directly connected to the act of living.

The result, in each case, is a reconstitution of language through free gestural expression, with no apparent order, norm or mediation whatsoever. Symbolically, the procedures adopted by these artists, faithful always to their individual way of feeling and being, immediately call attention to the level of the subconscious that emerges, not because of any specific psychological or psychoanalytical probing but simply because it has become an operative part of daily living, whether the artist is aware of it or not. Their work becomes a "reflection," a mirror image of the condition of an ego-dominated chaotically by the need to assert itself through the existential dimension.[7] The subject of their work can thus be understood as the complex representation of an ego expressing itself and yet canceling itself out in the process, or, one could say that this expression of the ego oversteps the limits of the confession or story, which seems to be key to every form of experimentation unfettered by rational control.

In a consideration of the possible meaning of a pictorial and graphic production like Kerouac's, it may be useful to return to the theme of a connection between the various languages and the will to overcome the separation between the arts through the unity of art and life, which derives from his expansion from the domain of literature to that of music and figurative art. Hints at the explanation for this can be found in his primary art form, writing. As readers of his texts know, he inserts numerous references to jazz, viewed both as the subject of attention and stories, and as a model for a condition of life and creation. There are fewer references to the world of painting, though Kerouac places Willem de Kooning, Franz Kline, Robert De Niro (the painter, father of the actor), Dody Muller and Al Leslie among the patrons at the 10th St. taverns in the chapter "New York Scenes" in *Lonesome Traveler*, and the Californian painter Robert LaVigne appears in *Desolation Angels* and in *Big Sur*. Regardless, we know that Kerouac turned to painting to translate as directly as possible the visions born from his experience of things and to give life to the images he had within.[8] Another passage from *Desolation Angels* is pertinent here:

One night we even got high on peyotl, the Chihuahuan Mexican cactus button that gives you visions after three preliminary hours of empty nausea [...] It was the day that Ben had received a set of Buddhist monk robes in the mail from Japan (from friend Jarry) and the day I was determined

to paint great pictures with my pitiful set of housepaints. [...] And there I
am kneeling in the grass in the half dark pouring enamel paint onto paper
and *blowing* on it till it blossoms out and mixes up, and's going to be a
great masterpiece until suddenly a poor little bug lands on it and gets
stuck – so I spend the last thirty minutes of twilight trying to extricate the
little bug from my sticky masterpiece without hurting it or pulling off a
leg, but no go...[9]

The insect stays stuck on the painting, like the cigarettes and other materials
that fall on the paintings on Pollock's studio floor, leaving Kerouac, however, with
the sensation of having debased nature in some way in the rush of his painting.
One can recognize here a profound affinity between Kerouac's way of acting on
the pictorial surface and the ways of Abstract Expressionism, using a gestural
action that frees itself from reference to the subject. This is not, however, the
answer to the collocation of his paintings, although in some cases they manifest
traits of extreme gestural automatism. While these considerations serve well
to introduce his more abstract creations, in his drawings and paintings one
senses his desire and need to plunge inside life, inside and beyond the visible,
to attach himself to the origins of spontaneous creation, to that emergence of
faces, forms, and sensations, all of which Kerouac experienced with greater
force and awareness after his trip to Europe in 1957, when he visited Provence,
the places frequented by Cézanne, and then Paris and the Louvre. What he
absorbed there and aspires to is "exact painting (not imitating) of nature,"[10]
something that manifests in the language of its times and its precise moment.
The relationship with the American and New York art scene is clear, linked to
the New York School in the broadest sense, where the powerful influence of
de Kooning pushed many artists more towards a more expressive production
than towards the "generative" one of Pollock or the more highly praised one of
Rothko and the color field paintings of Newman or Still. The artists with whom
Kerouac had the closest relationship can be identified, as Ed Adler has done,
by reconstructing his contacts with artists working in New York or San Francisco,
especially at the end of the 1950s, the period when Kerouac was most involved
in visual arts. Among them is Alfred Leslie, with whom Kerouac created *Pull My
Daisy*, the experimental film that can be seen as a unique slice of life, with its
urban, beat feel, after which Leslie continued with his cinematographic experiments in conjunction with painting. In any case, at the heart of these bonds
lies the unity of the experience of life and creation that makes it possible for a
variety of expressive means to fuse in a single active, inspired burst. Indeed,
what is so surprising about Kerouac is his ability to produce jewels out of the
apparent chaos of a life lived forever on the brink, within the complementarity
that he always chose to pursue, between moments of acute abandonment to
the flow of life and others of a genuinely ascetic withdrawal into himself. While
there are certain passages that touch one's soul and reveal the enlightenment
of the profound meaningfulness of even small and absurd things, it is the poetic intuitions of haikus, instantaneous moments shaped by a sort of suddenly
unchained wisdom, which generate the closest proximity of word, image and
sound. They are held together not because one part dominates another but
because one thing flows into another, like from writing to painting, in a spoliation
of the central theme from its surroundings.

Perhaps more than anything else, Kerouac sought in his creation to adhere to a rhythm, an inner rhythm, which outer things, daily events, and encounters have brought to the fore. In Kerouac and in the Beat Generation in general, one feels a distinct solidarity between word, image and sound, which in some cases Kerouac actively sought and produced.[11] Public readings, a format adopted especially by Ginsberg, were performed by Kerouac as an intimate dialogue with that "jazz of life" that he explored, for example, in his recordings with pianist Steve Allen, as well as in his interaction with David Amram, composer of the "soundtrack" for *Pull My Daisy*. In these experiments, the word becomes a form of music, just as the images in his paintings and drawings are one with the stream of consciousness of his writing, making it so difficult to separate them from the entirety of Kerouac's persona and work.

Indeed, the participation of these figurative works in the spontaneous generation of images evoking episodes from his childhood, visions of the figures both real and symbolic who populate his inner path, and allusions to the presences and places of his life and stories is integral to his personal journey: you could almost consider them a "soundtrack."

Appendix

Another variation on the theme can be elaborated around the continuation of this message within the fusion of "linguistic phonemes" found in the relationship between word, sound and image, but not only in the literature of the Beat Generation or the context of the 1960s when its impact had visible, immediate consequences. Poetry readings, conducted by Lawrence Ferlinghetti, William Burroughs or John Giorno, were another part of the ongoing experimentation in this sector. Participating in these readings, Kerouac tended to perform in his own introspective style. Giorno also launched the *Giorno Poetry System* project, creating, promoting and publishing albums featuring various forms of collaborations that flourished in the 1980s and 1990s, in which performers and other artists of the New York avant-garde, like Laurie Anderson and Glenn Branca, introduced original expressions of the continuity, more than contiguity, of word and music.

Clearly, the Beat Generation thrived in a tight rapport with the jazz of the 1940s and 1950s, and with the painting of the heyday of the New York School (not to mention the Pacific School, in which Richard Diebenkorn could be considered another Kerouac-like figure). However, profound correspondences continued to exist much later as well, in the rock music that came after the 1960s and 1970s.

There is no end to examples of the influence of Kerouac's work in cinema, art and music, in the United States and beyond, over the subsequent decades. Many of the great legendary rock musicians felt deeply connected to it, and indeed one can find countless links in the songs and music by American and international musicians. One need only consider how Bob Dylan adopted and developed ideas that derive from Kerouac's word experiments, beginning with his first poem/songs, and he continued after that as well to reveal the influence of Kerouac, taken from the references to American literature flowing through his works. Jim Morrison is another rock legend much indebted to Kerouac; his *An American Prayer*, for instance, is undoubtedly in keeping with the legacy of the Beat Generation, with its mesmerizing dialogue between word and music.

137

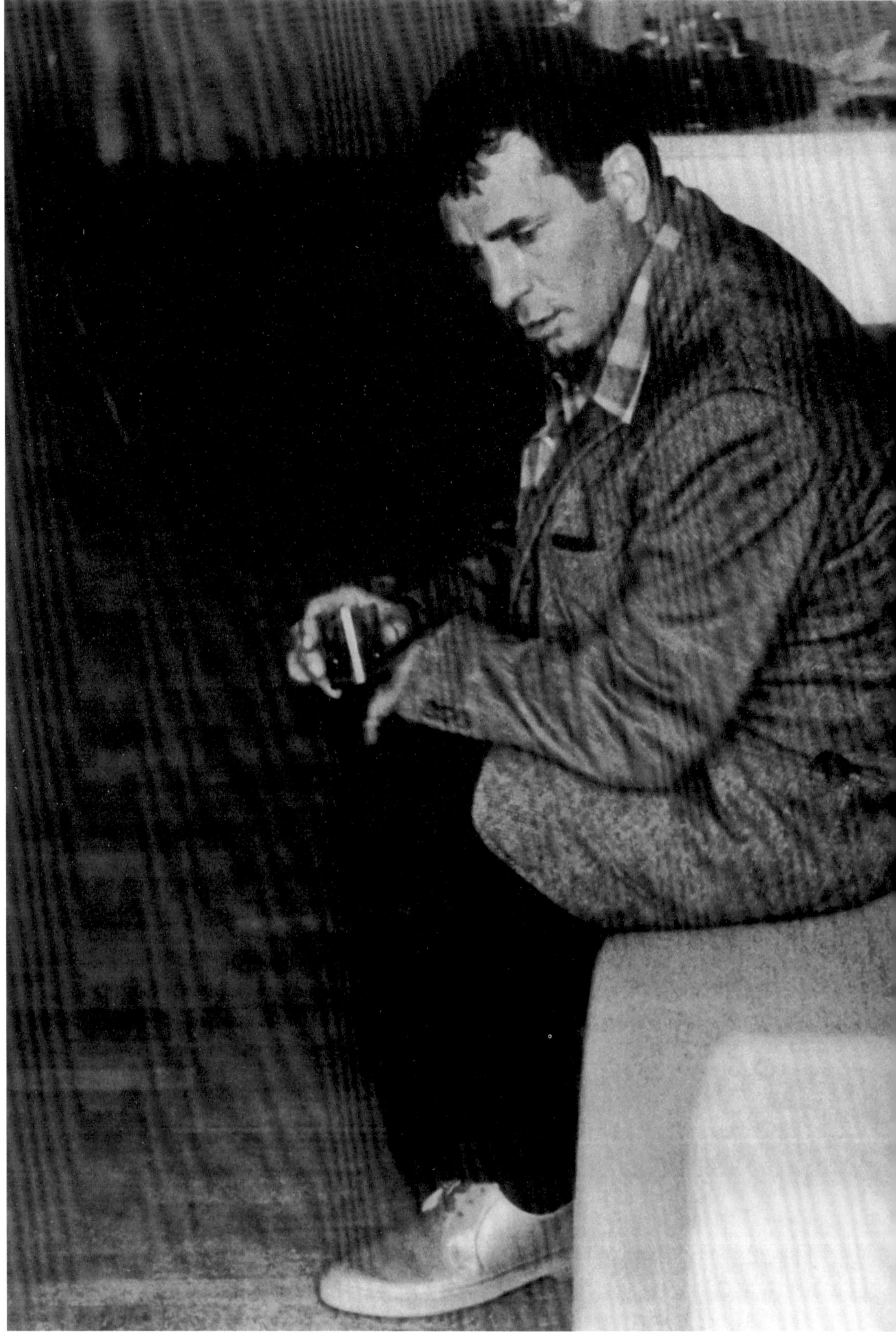

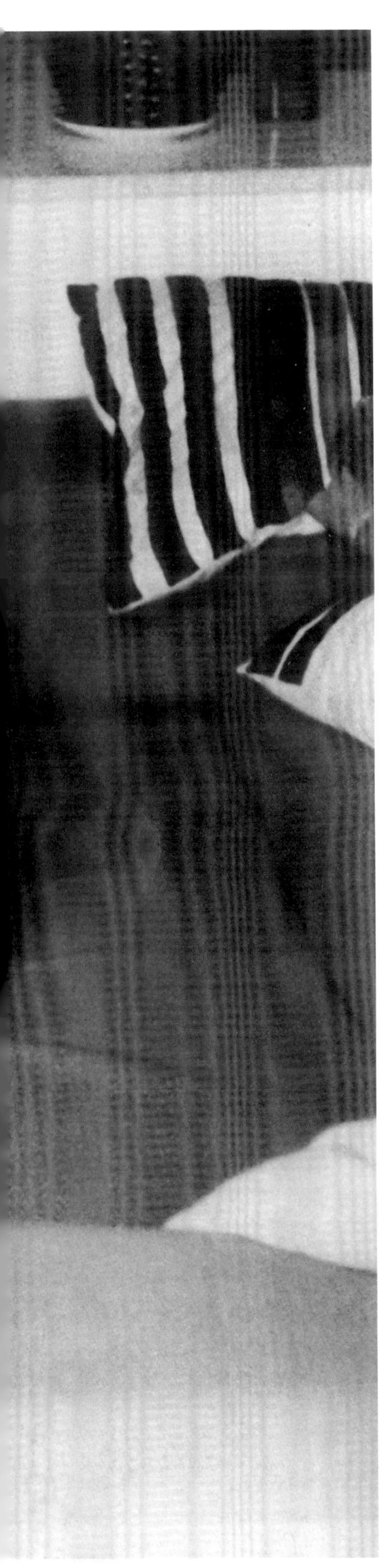

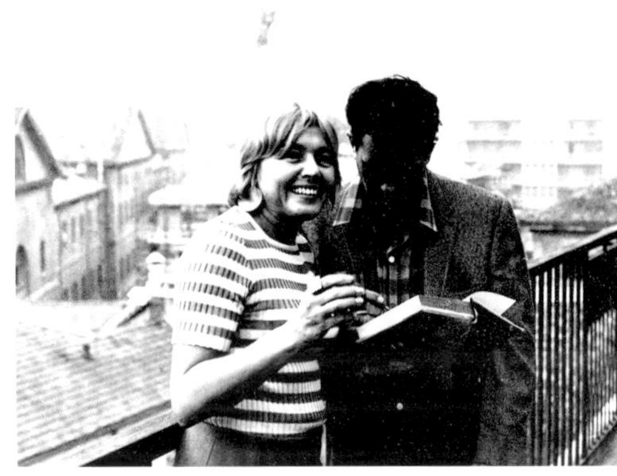

Ettore Sottsass, Fernanda
Pivano and Jack Kerouac,
Milan 1966

Ettore Sottsass,
Jack Kerouac, Milan 1966

The long-lasting influence of that period is demonstrated in two albums released a full eighteen years after the publication of *On the Road*: *Blood on the Tracks* by Bob Dylan and *Born to Run* by Bruce Springsteen. In different ways, these two albums confirm the modernity of Kerouac's message; in each case, the central theme of the narrative is a trip, which manages to represent the American spirit in a renewed, mature thrust towards the union of life and creation, in Springsteen, or towards the introspective solitude of the vagabond, in Dylan.

And there is so much more. Even after the period when young people's music was saturated with Beat Generation myths and dreams, Kerouac's message continued to be an object of attention, perhaps inadvertently, as in the song "The House Jack Kerouac Built" by the Australian group The Go Betweens. In other cases, an attempt was made to refashion it into a new total vision, as in *Beat*, a 1982 homage dedicated to the people and places of the Beat Generation by Robert Fripp's King Crimson. The most complex tribute of all was the album released in 1997, *Kerouac – Kicks Joy Darkness*, which unites excerpts of recordings of Kerouac himself with music and poetry by a number of influential rock musicians from the 1990s, including Michael Stipe, Joe Strummer, John Cale, Jim Carroll, Jeff Buckley, Patti Smith, and others. The performers join to render homage to this visionary man who nurtured multiple generations of rebels, dreamers, and seekers, helping to tear down the walls between different artistic expressions. In effect, Kerouac demonstrated that all of life is creation, a hunger for something unreachable and unstoppable that surges spontaneously from the encounter between the inwardness of feeling and the outwardness of the gestures of living.

[1] See T. Hunt, *Kerouac's Crooked Road. The Development of a Fiction* (Hamden (CT): Archon Books, 1981); L. Kart, "Jack Kerouac's 'Jazz America' or who was Roger Beloit?", *Review of Contemporary Fiction*, III, no. 2, Summer 1983, pp. 25–27; J. Burns, "Kerouac and Jazz," *The Review of Contemporary Fiction*, III, no. 2, Summer 1983, pp. 33–41; R. Snyder, *American Zeitgeist: Spontaneity in the Work of Jackson Pollock, Charlie Parker and Jack Kerouac* (Lincoln: University of Nebraska, 2006); S. Maffina, *The Role of Jack Kerouac's Identity in the Development of His Poetics* (Raleigh: Lulu. com, 2012).

[2] Which indicate great interest in a number of musicians, including Lester Young, Stan Getz, Lee Konitz, and Allen Eager, while Charlie Parker, in addition to being considered the pioneer of the most decisive shift in new jazz, figures as the subject of some of Kerouac's most inspired compositions in the final part of *Mexico City Blues*.

[3] H. Rosenberg, *The Tradition of the New* (New York: Horizon Press, 1959), p. 27.

[4] It has not been sufficiently noted that also in the Beat Generation's experiments, and quite distinctly in Kerouac's writing, one can find moments of direct or indirect affinity with Martinetti's "*paroliberista*" prose. This passage from *Desolation Angels* offers a clear example: "Sword etc., flat part of an oar or calamity, sudden vio-dashing young fellow, lent gust of wind, forcible stream of leaf, air, blare of a trumpet or horn, blamable deserving of Explosion as of gunpowder, blame, find fault with Blight; censure, imputation of a blatant Brawling noisy, Speak ill, blaze, Burn with a blameful meriting flame, send forth a flaming light, less without blame, innocent, torch, firebrand, stream of blamelessly blameless flame of light, bursting out, actness, worthy of blame, culblaze...", J. Kerouac, *Desolation Angels* (New York: Coward McCann, 1965), ch. 38.

[5] "If I'm in my painting, I'm not aware of what I'm doing. Only after a sort of 'get acquainted' period that I see what I have been about. I have no fears about making changes, destroying the image, etc., because the painting has a life of its own. I try to let it come through." J. Pollock, "My Painting," *Possibilities*, vol. 1, no. 1, New York (Winter 1947–48).

[6] "13. Remove literary, grammatical and syntactical inhibition," in J. Kerouac, "Belief & Technique for Modern Prose," *Evergreen Review*,

no. 5, Summer 1959, p. 57. In another earlier writing, he described his procedure as follows: "PROCEDURE Time being of the essence in the purity of speech, sketching language is undisturbed flow from the mind of personal secret idea-words, blowing (as per jazz musician) on subject of image...", J. Kerouac, "Essentials of Spontaneous Prose," *Evergreen Review*, no. 5, Summer 1958, pp. 72–73. For an exploration of the topic, see R. Weinreich, *The Spontaneous Poetics of Jack Kerouac. A Study of the Fiction* (Carbondale and Edwardsville: Southern Illinois Univ Press, 1987).

[7] According to the interpretation of American painting of the 1940s offered by Michael Leja, in relating the painting of Pollock and Abstract Expressionism to the culture of the period in the light of sociological theories that had adapted Rosenberg's analysis: "New York School art was involved in a broad cultural project – reconfiguring the individual (white heterosexual male) subject for a society whose dominant models of subjectivity were losing credibility. Narcissus was indeed in chaos, and these painters took that situation as thematic...", M. Leja, *Reframing Abstract Expressionism. Subjectivity and Painting in the 1940s* (New Haven/London: Yale University Press, 1993), p. 39.

[8] Again in the notes published in 1958 on his "spontaneous" prose, about the representation of a subject, he writes, "Begin not from preconceived idea of what to say about image but from jewel center of interest in subject of image at moment of writing..." This seems, by analogy, to suggest the possible acknowledgment of a visual source for his writing. In a note, published in Ed Adler's well-documented book about Kerouac's painting, from January 1959, Kerouac suggests a "spontaneous" use of the paint brush among the norms indicated to guide his painting ("without drawing: without long pause or delay, without erasing... pile it on"), confirming his idea of different arts all based on improvisation and spontaneity. See E. Adler, *Departed Angels. Jack Kerouac, The Lost Paintings* (New York: Thunder's Mouth Press, 2004), p. 142 and Fig. 3.

[9] Kerouac, *Desolation Angels*, III. 78.

[10] "HISTORY OF ART: from Egyptian & wall cavers to Meissonnier-Types [...] to exact painting (not imitating) of nature... So I will paint what I see, color and line, exactly FAST... Paint behind the holy blood...", J. Kerouac, letter to Ed White, April 28, 1957, in Adler, *Departed Angels*, p. 14.

[11] As regards this "solidarity," consider also Christophe Kihm's modern interpretation of the "synthesis" of the arts as "musical-plastic arrangements," deriving from a "continuity" in the concrete application of forms of composition and perception, regardless of disciplinary divisions, in a context increasingly tending to that type of unification. See C. Kihm, "Agencements musico-plastiques. Discours critiques et pratiques artistiques contemporaines," in *Sons & Lumières. Une histoire du son dans l'art du XXe siècle*, exhibition catalog (Paris: Centre Pompidou, 22 September 2004–03 January 2005), pp. 103–11.

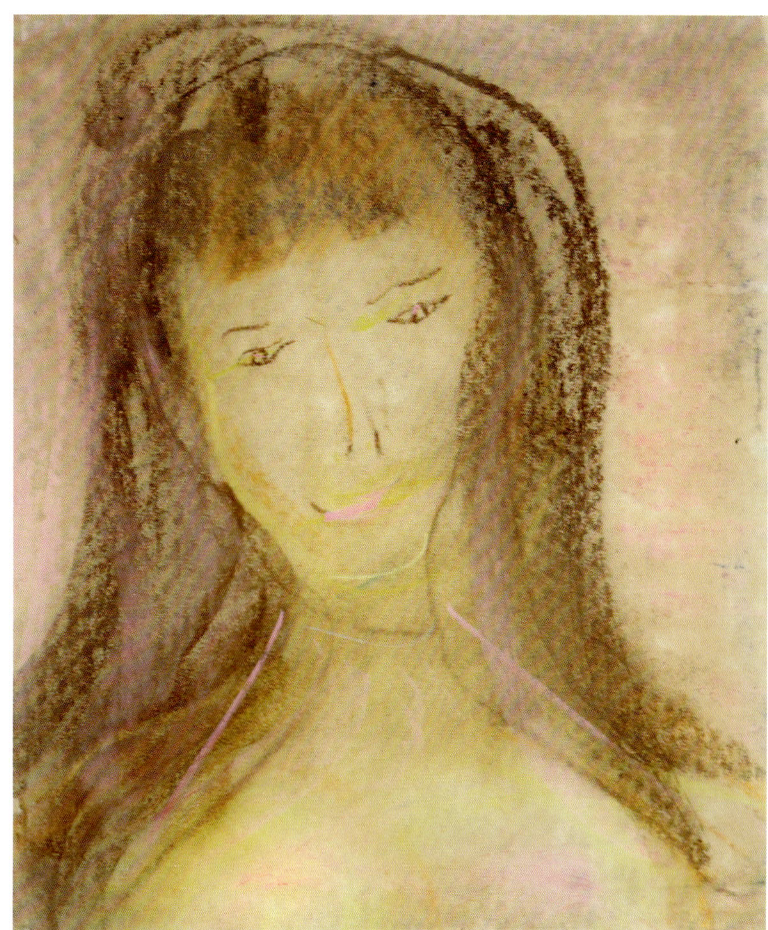

In a close parallel between writing and painting,
Kerouac's celebrated composition technique based
on notes is echoed in a slow and progressive
reworking and destructuring of reality. This process
can be well documented by comparing various
female portraits, whose subjects appear less
precisely described over time until their form
seems to melt into the color and a free gestuality.
Thus differences can be noted between angelic
figures still charged with religious references
(Fig. 55), subjects with an Expressionist character
and force (Fig. 63) or a compositional freedom
tending towards abstraction (Fig. 62).

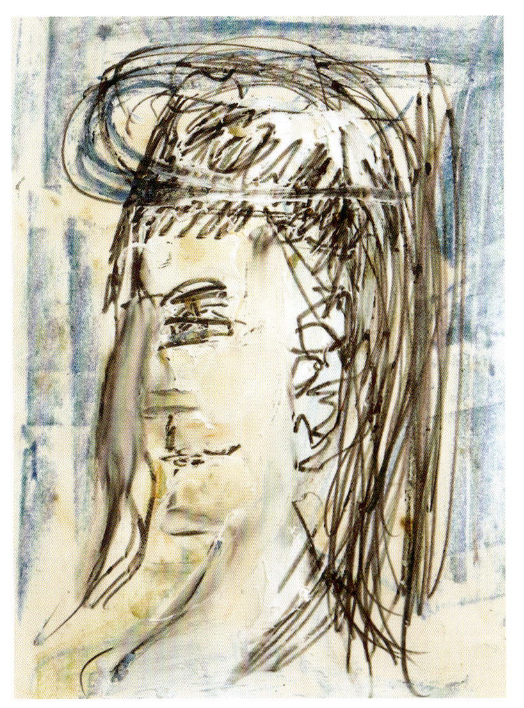
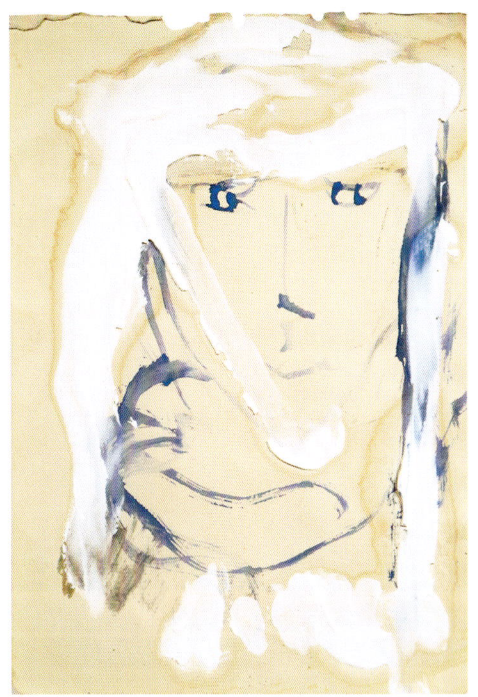
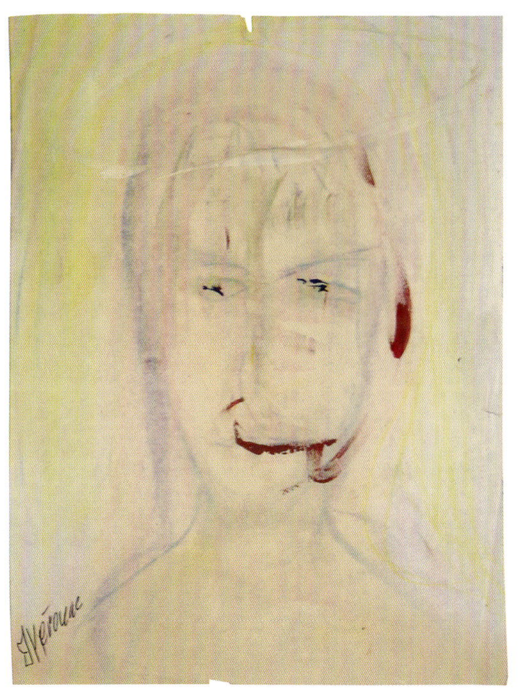
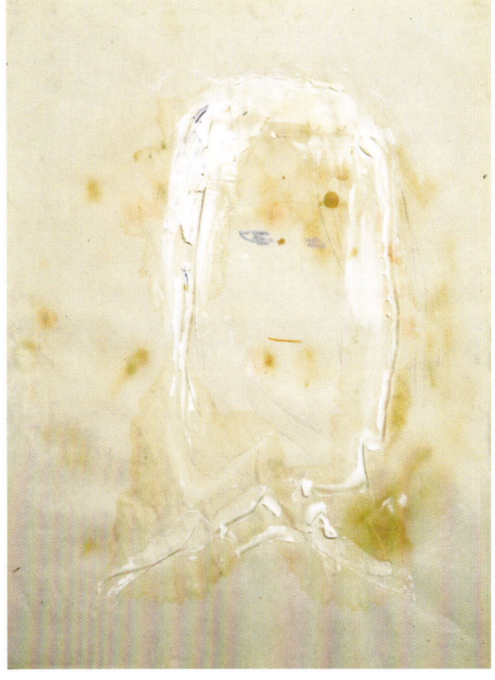

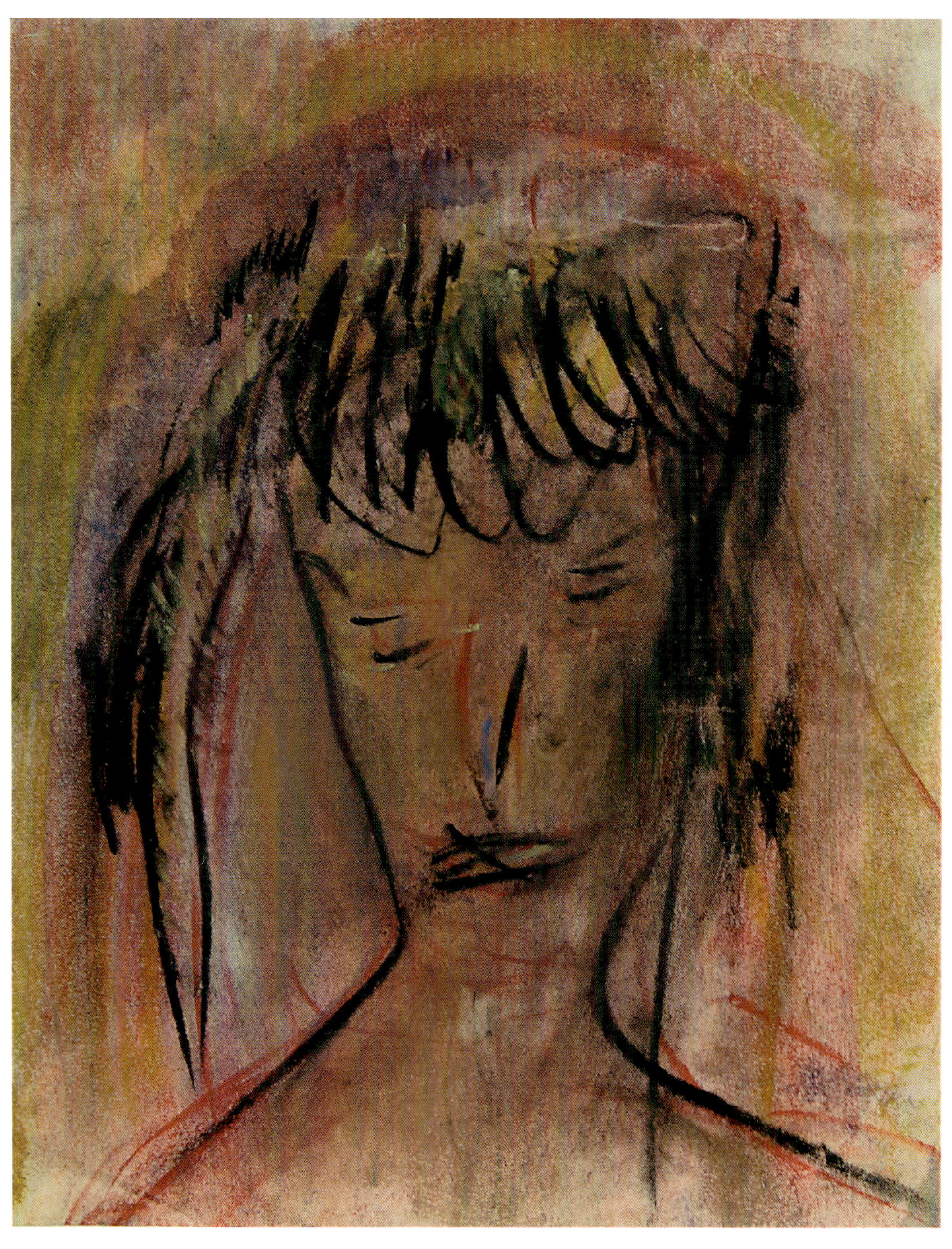

60 *Untitled*, n.d.,
oil pastel on paper,
27.5 x 21.6 cm

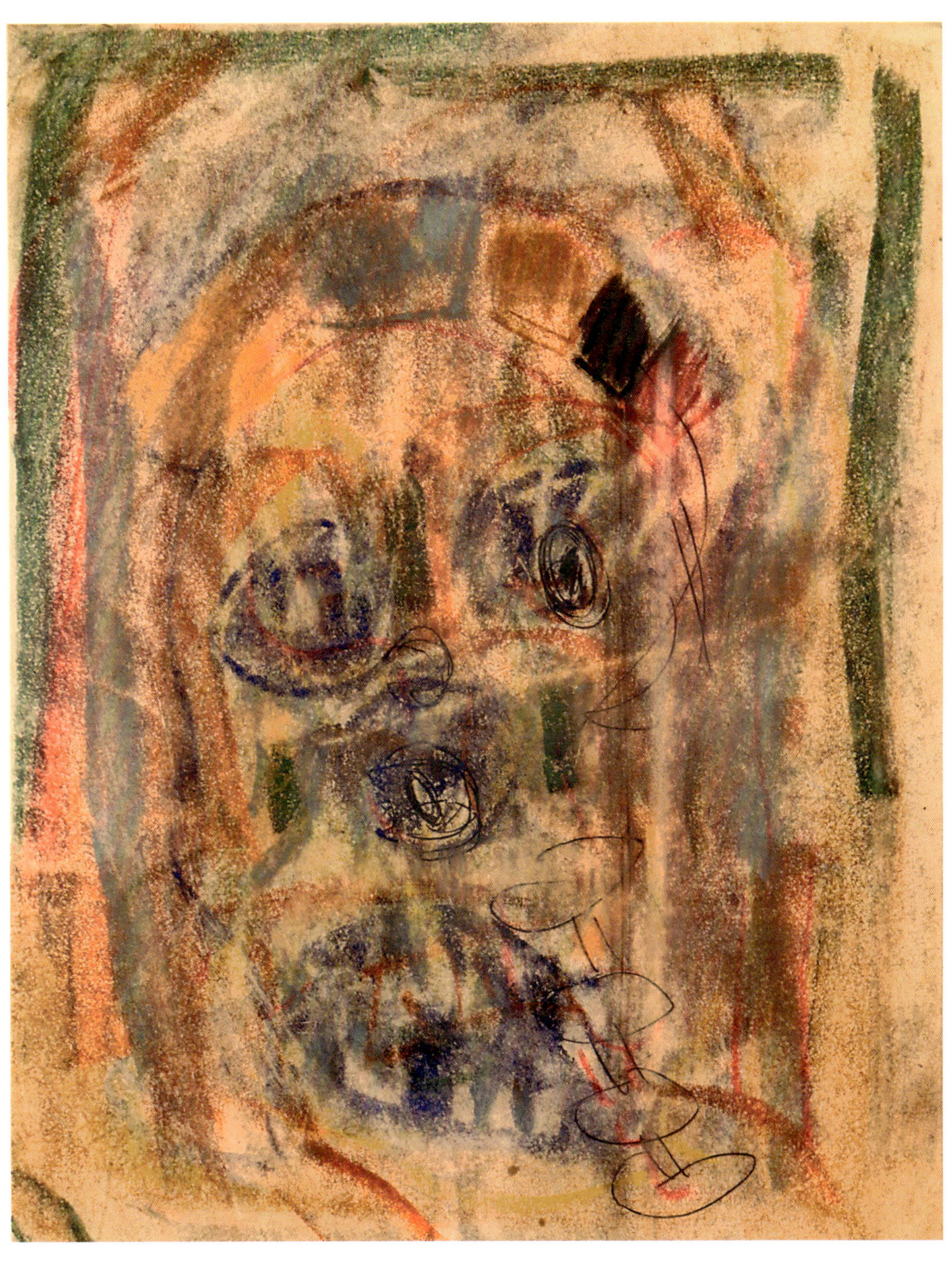

61 *Untitled*, n.d.,
oil pastel and pencil
on paper, 27 x 20.5 cm

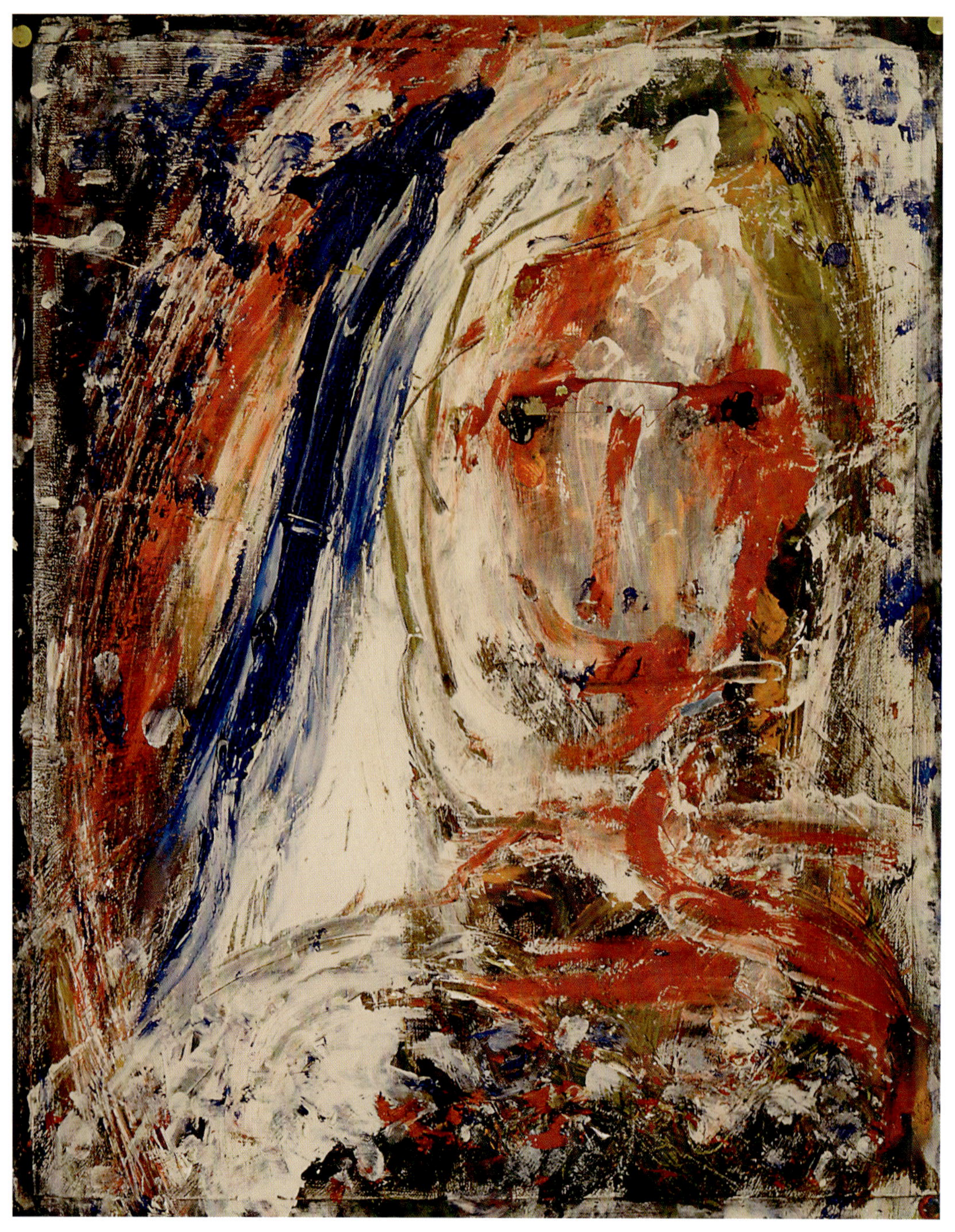

62 *Untitled*, 1960 ca.,
acrylic on canvas,
51 x 40.3 cm

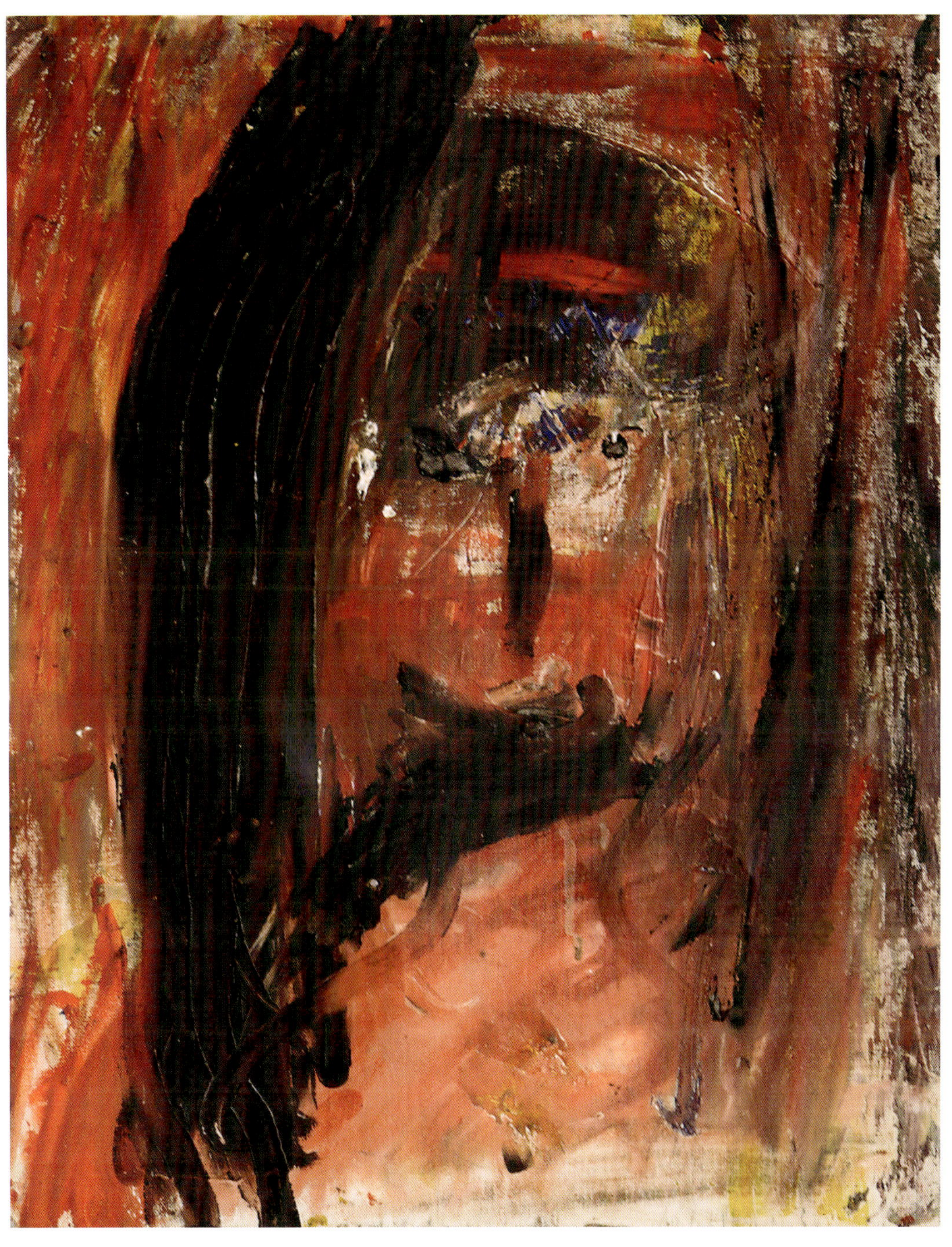

63 *Untitled*, n.d.,
oil on canvas,
50 x 40 cm

64 *Figures on a Red Ground*, n.d., oil on paper, 22 x 29 cm

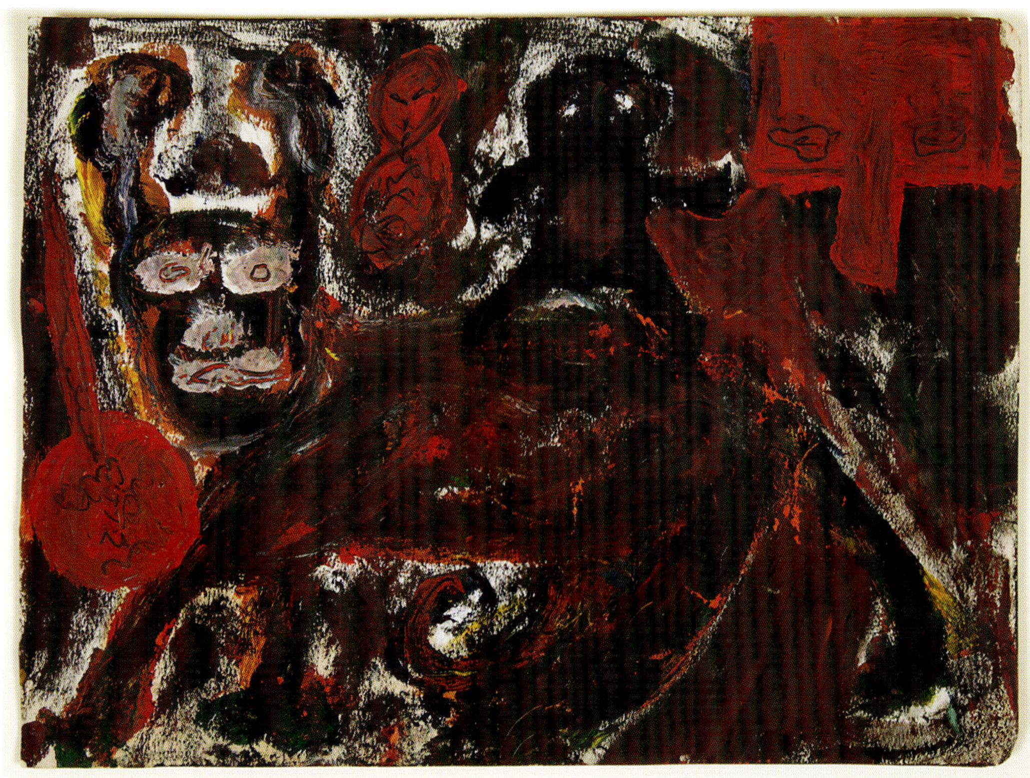

The painting is one of the works that most clearly demonstrates Kerouac's attraction to the more brutal potential of Expressionist language, in terms of both color and iconography. Here, the powerful image can be recognized as an animal, perhaps a cat, since cats were mentioned repeatedly in Kerouac's diaries, notebooks and poems. More mysterious and cryptic is the presence of a small red Buddha flying over the scene, a faint suggestion of the "departed angels" so typical of his religious paintings.

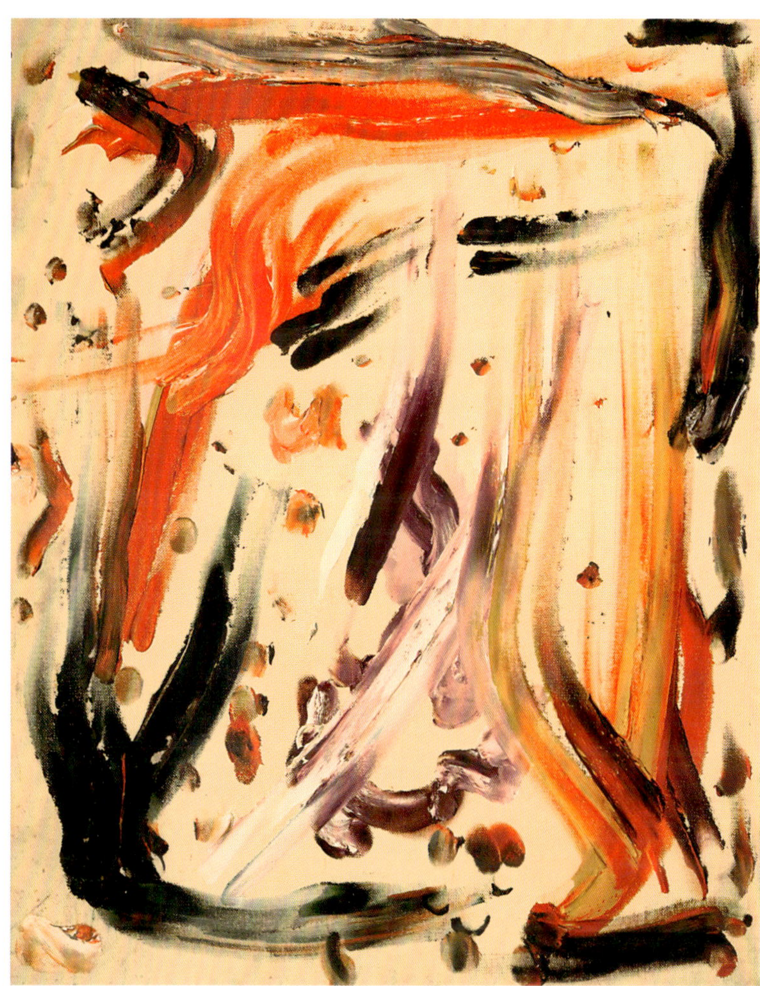

Referring again to the letter dated October 10, 1956, this painting reveals just how important Abstract Expressionism had become for Kerouac. The composition vaguely recalls the features of a woman's face, but the painting is actually rather formless, improvised, free, and strictly bound to the artist's gestuality. This freedom is particularly evident as Kerouac apparently painted the work almost entirely with his fingers directly upon the canvas, without resorting to a paintbrush.

66 *Untitled*, n.d.,
oil on canvas,
49.5 x 40 cm

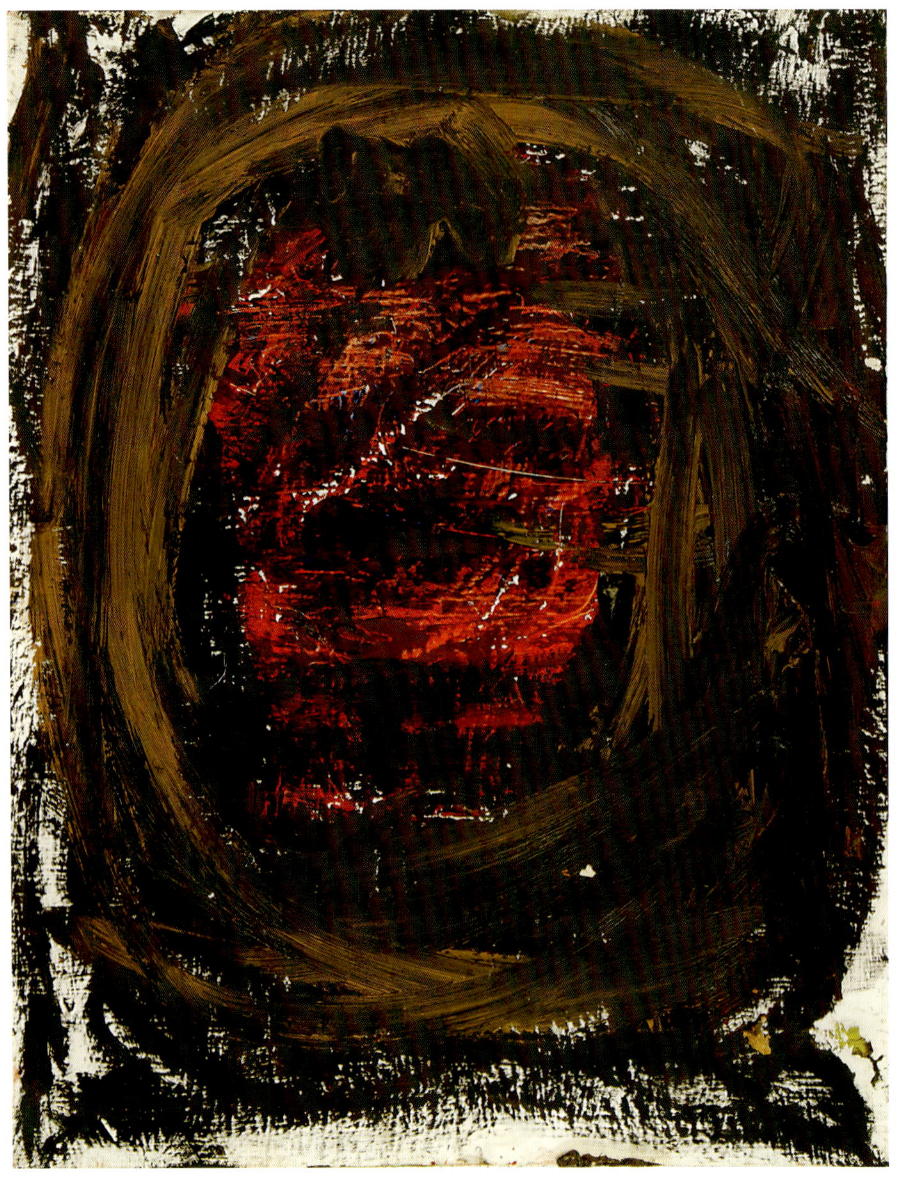

67 *Untitled*, n.d.,
paint on paper,
38 x 45.5 cm

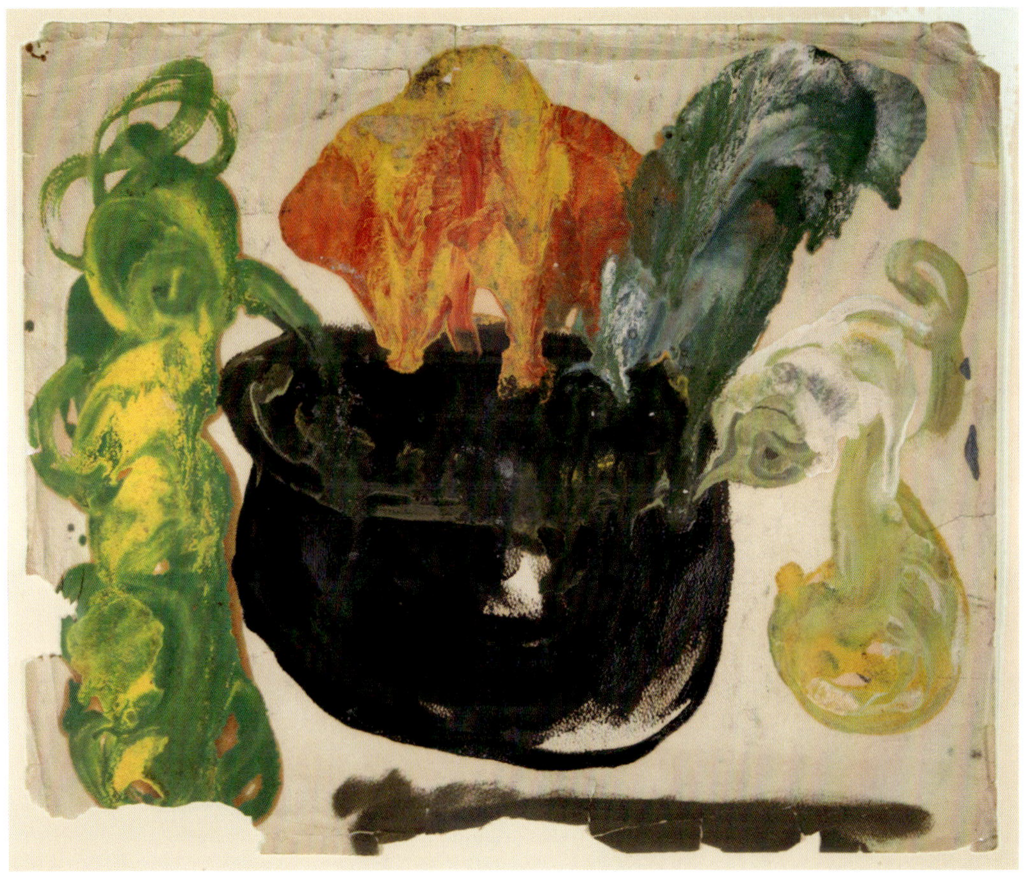

68 *Untitled*, n.d.,
oil pastel and pencil on paper,
30.5 x 23 cm

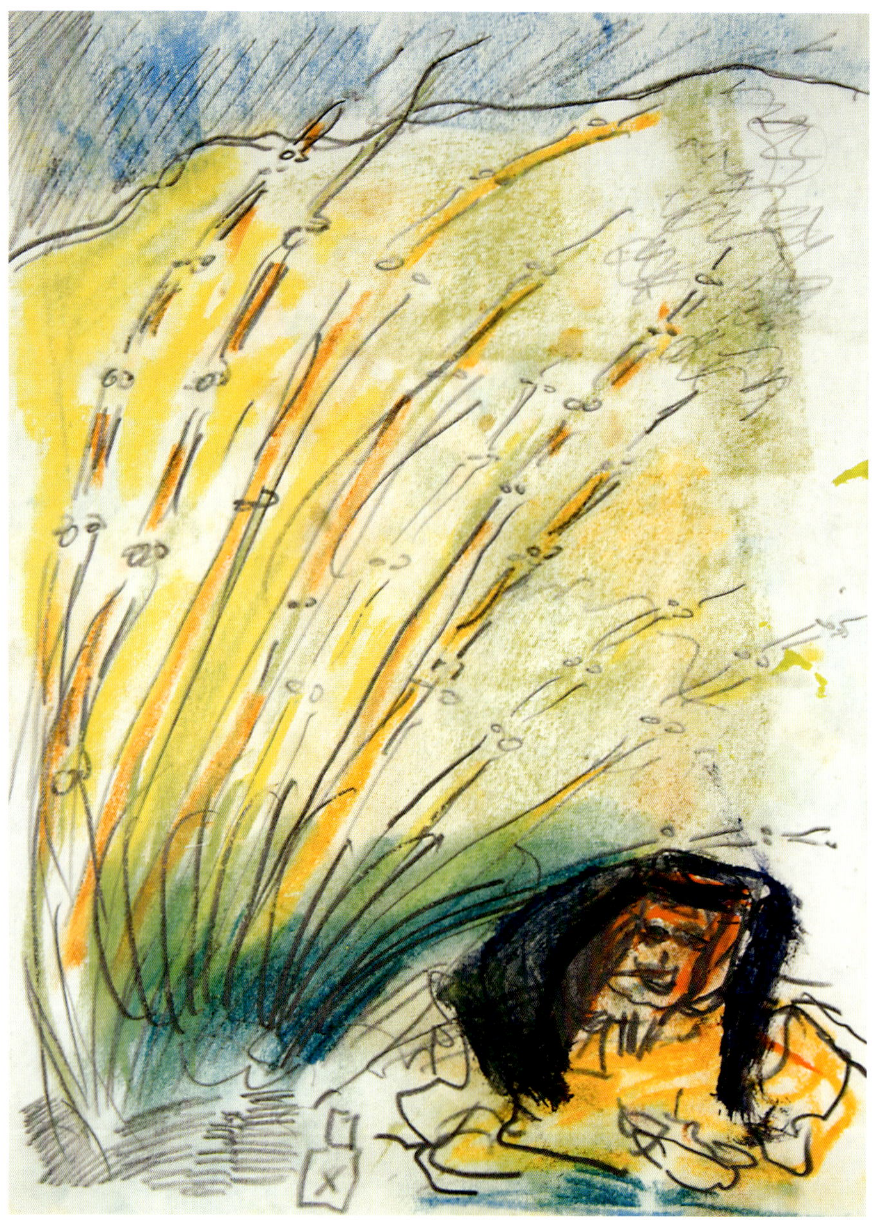

69 *Untitled*, n.d.,
tempera, Indian ink and glue
on paper, 30.5 x 23 cm

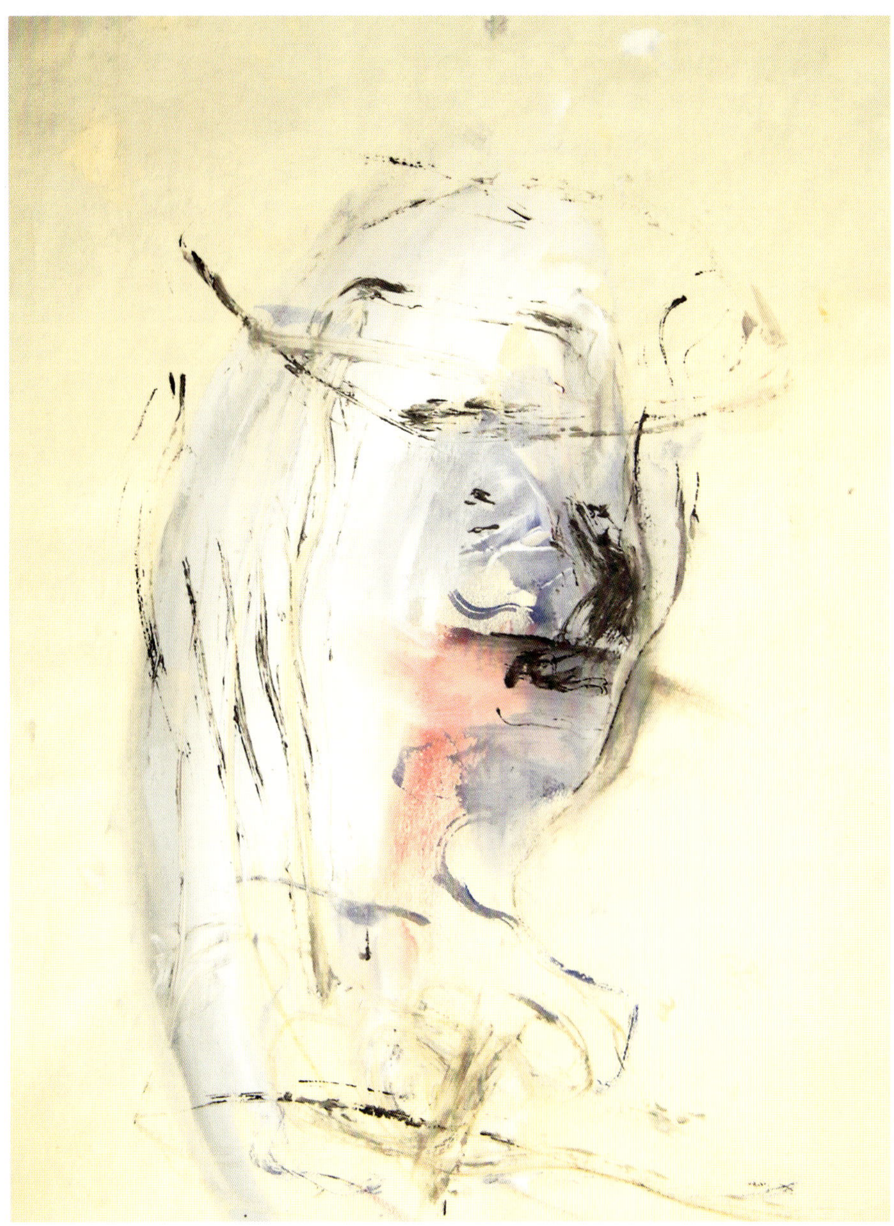

153

154

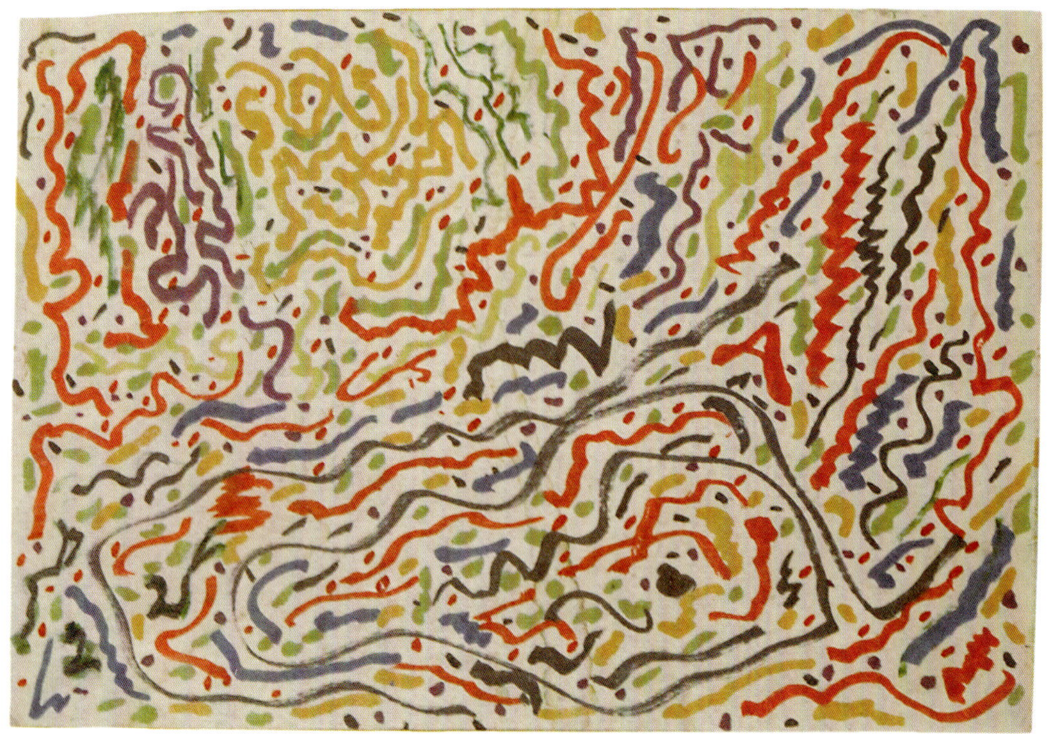

71 *Untitled*, 1959,
watercolor and oil on paper,
30.5 x 23 cm

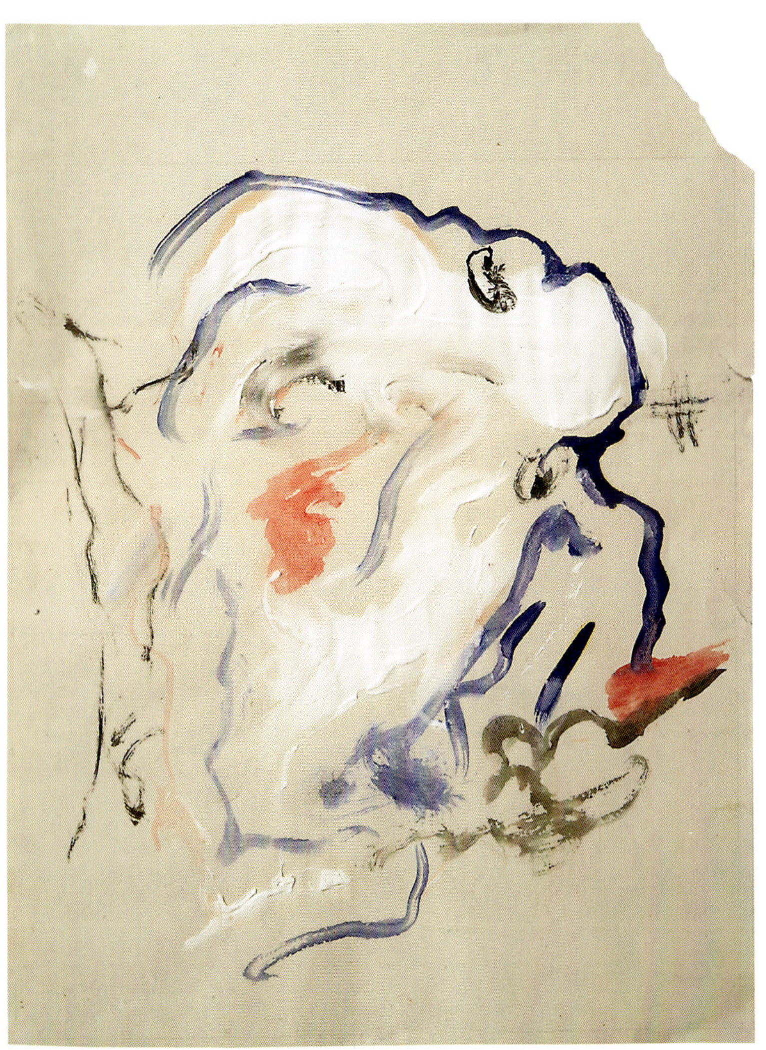

72 Untitled, n.d.,
pen on paper, 13 x 8 cm

156

73 Untitled, n.d.,
marker and ink on paper,
20 x 12.5 cm

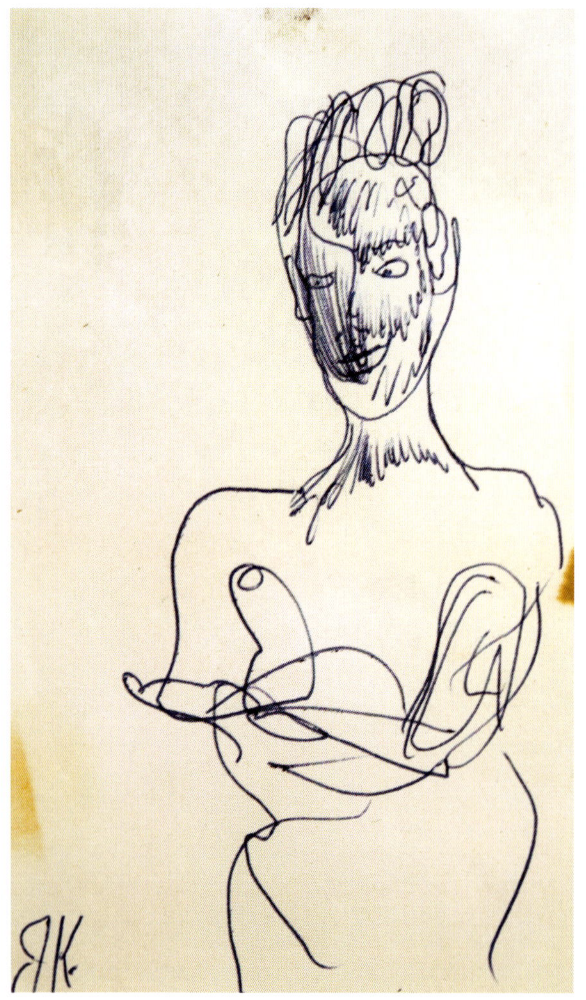

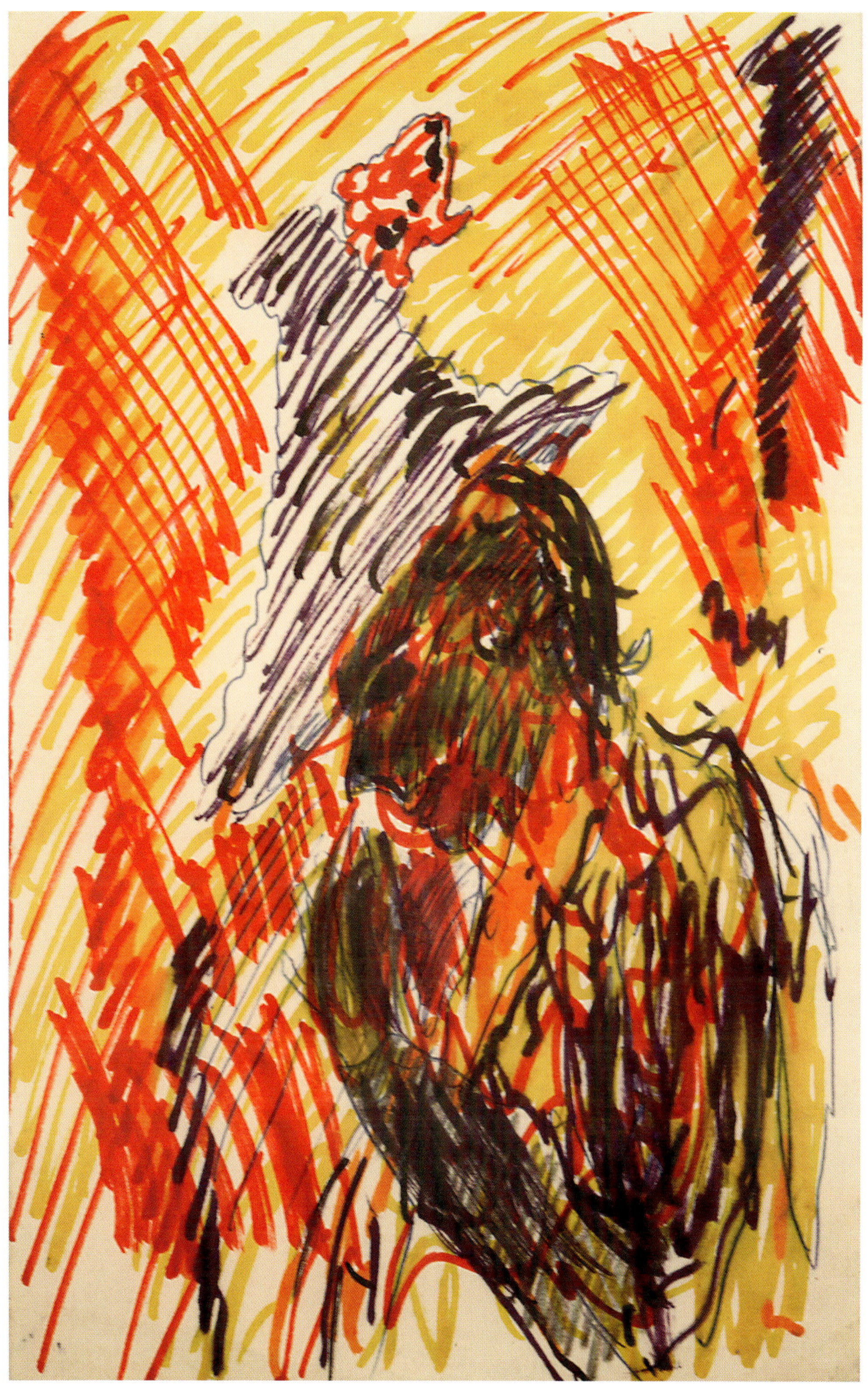

74 *Untitled*, n.d.,
mixed media on paper,
30 x 22.5 cm

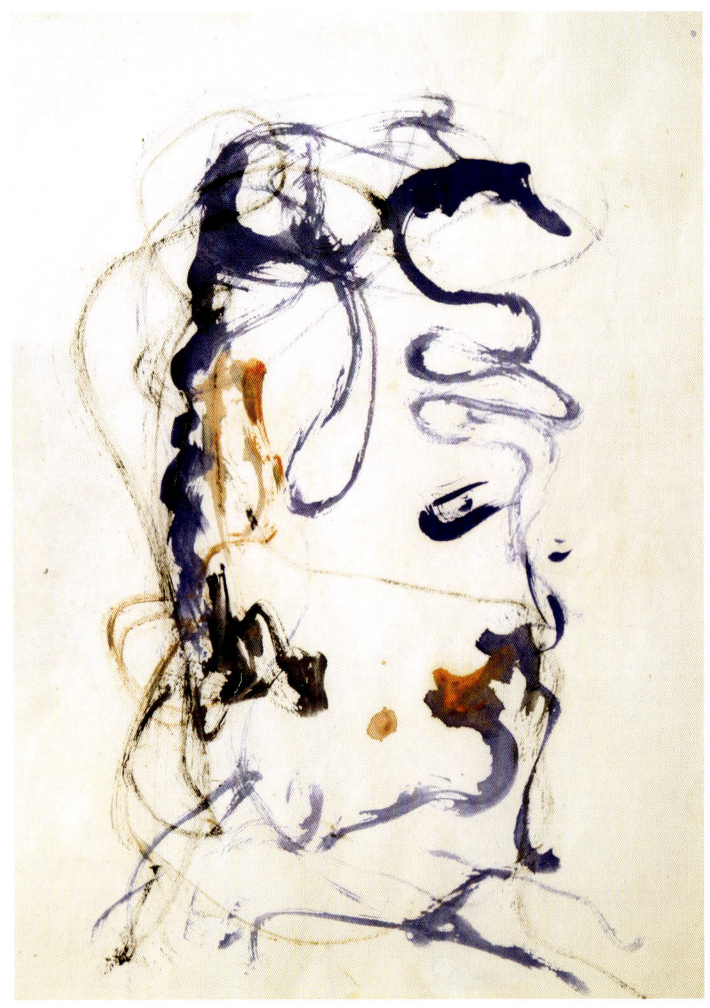

75 *Untitled*, n.d.,
oil, watercolor and pencil
on paper, 46 x 31 cm

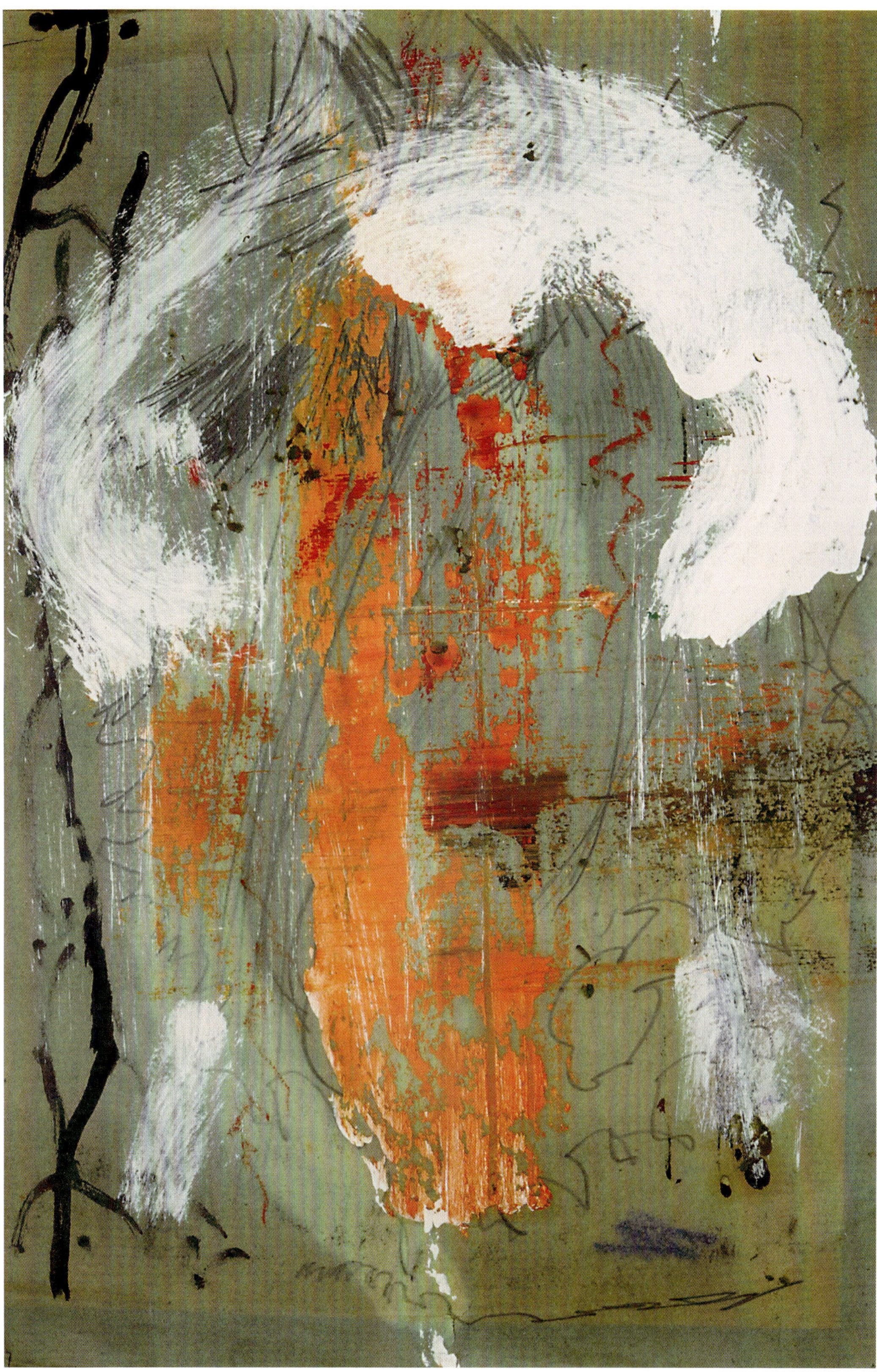

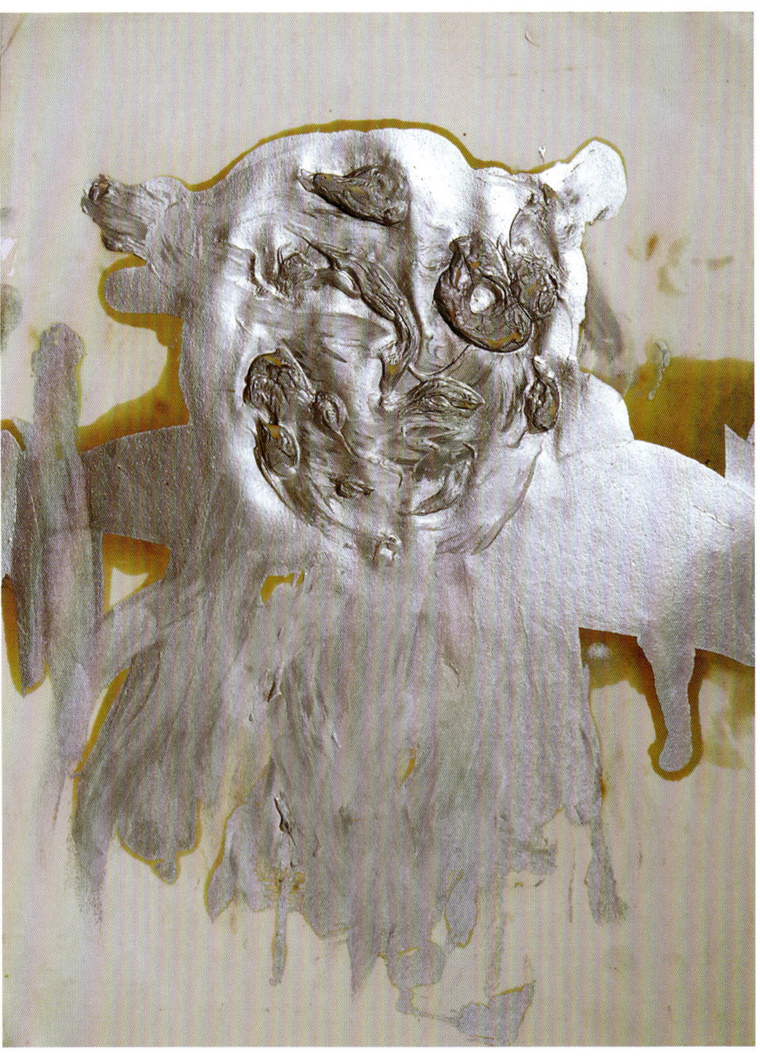

The section ends with a series of experimental
works in which the artist totally abandoned all
figurative and naturalistic references. The works are
distinguished by the experimentation with signs
and gestures (Fig. 76), color, almost as if they were
preparatory boards (Fig. 77), and materials, thanks
to the introduction of dense strata of metallic paint
(Fig. 78) which form the basis of a renewed
Expressionism in Kerouac's pictorial language.

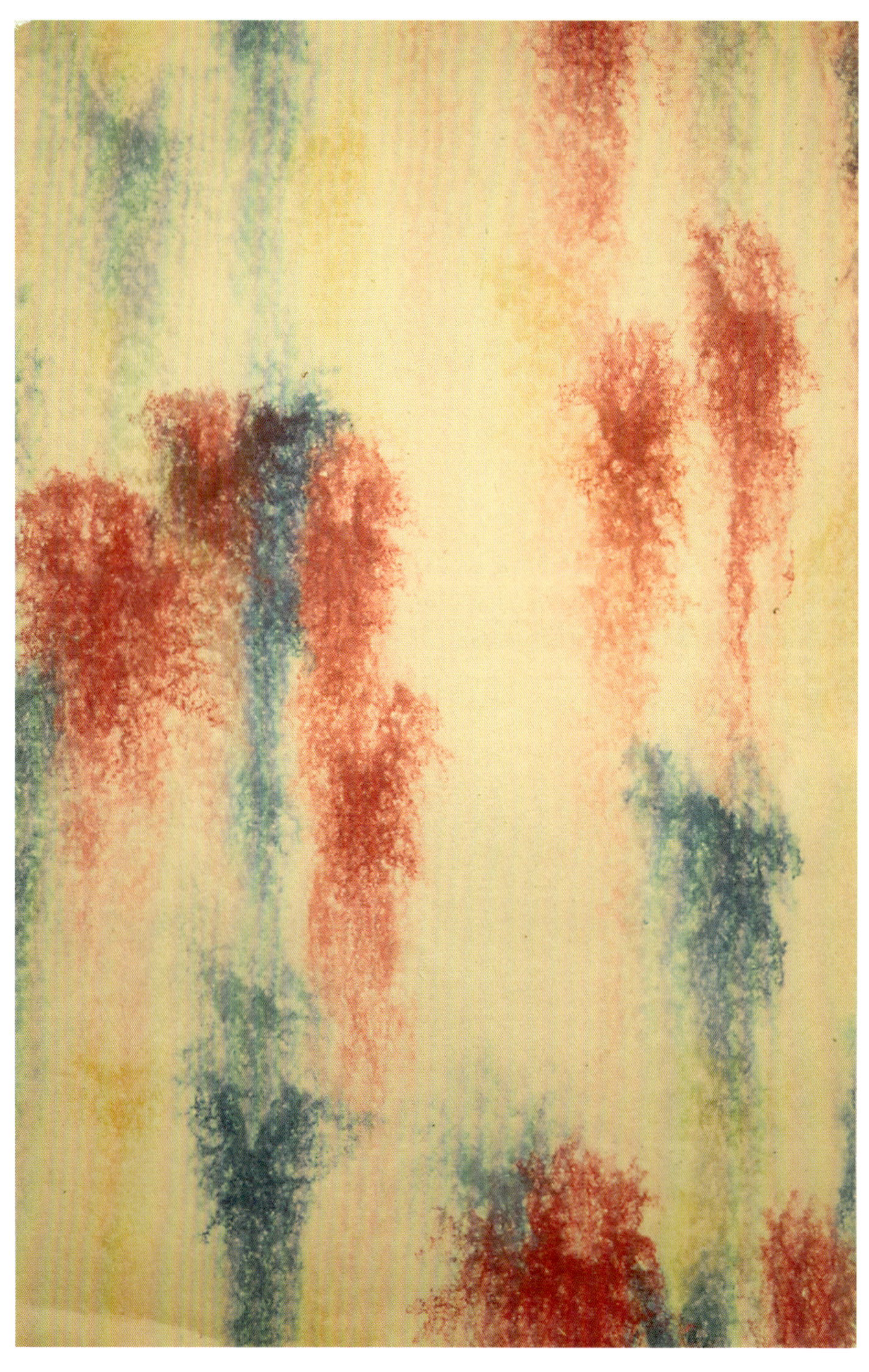

77 *Untitled*, n.d.,
pastel on paper,
45 x 29.5 cm

78 *Untitled*, n.d.,
mixed media on canvas,
30 x 22.5 cm

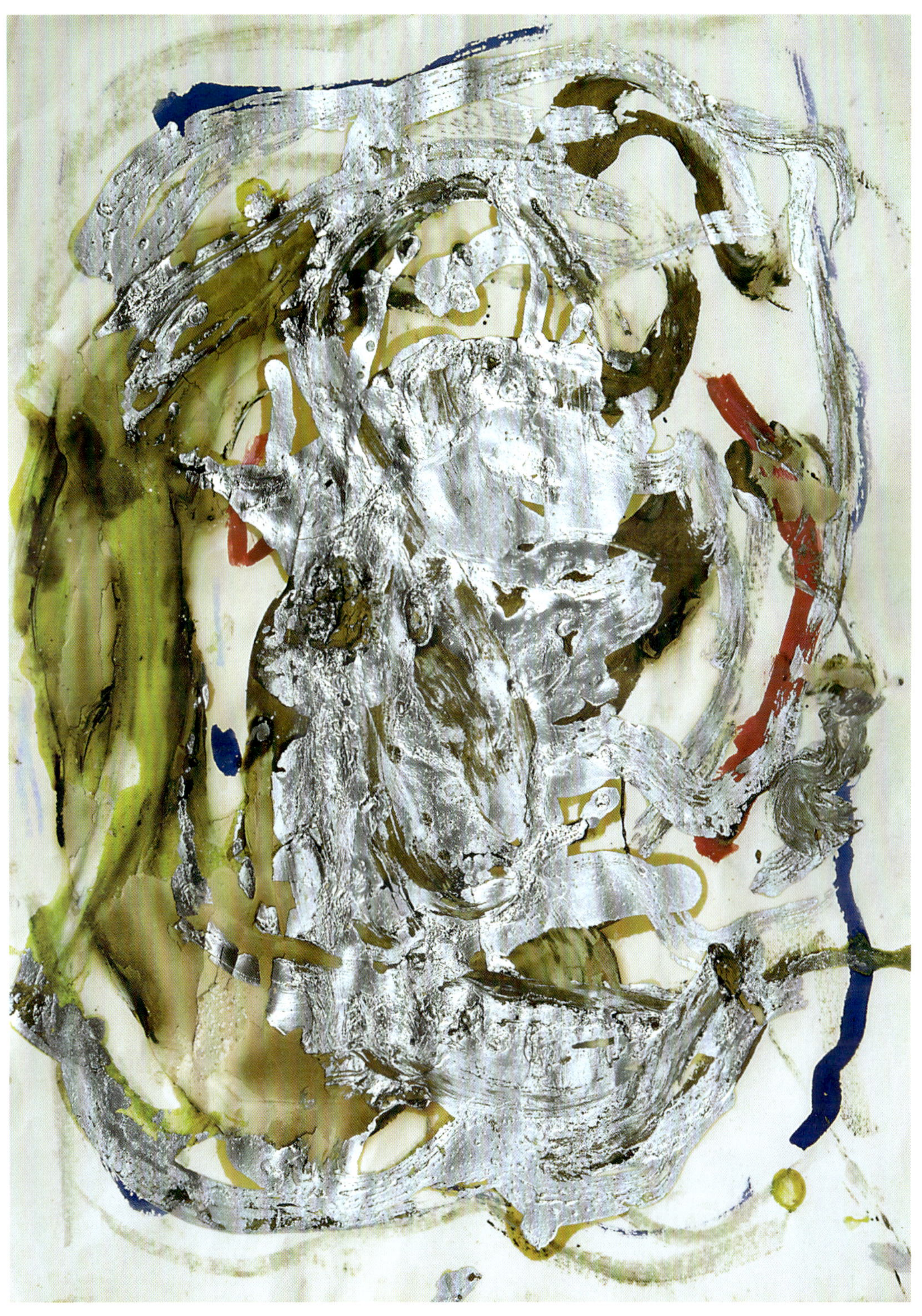

Chronology

	Historical Events
1922	October 28, Benito Mussolini's March on Rome. Benedict XV dies and Achille Ratti is elected as pope, Pius XI. Abolishment of the Ottoman Empire by Atatürk. The Union of the Soviet Socialist Republics is born. Joseph Stalin becomes secretary of the Central Committee. Gandhi is arrested in Bombay.
1926	Francisco Franco becomes the youngest general in Spain and Europe. Mussolini dissolves parties and labor unions in Italy and abolishes elections. Hirohito becomes Emperor of Japan. Umberto Nobile and Roald Amundsen fly over the North Pole on the Norge dirigible.
1939–40	Pact of Steel between Germany and Italy. Pope Pius XI dies. Eugenio Pacelli elected pope, Pius XII. Germany occupies Czechoslovakia. Molotov-Ribbentrop Pact of non-aggression between Germany and Soviet Union. Invasion of Poland. England and France declare war on Germany. Outbreak of Second World War. Russia invades eastern Poland. Franco conquers Barcelona and Madrid. Spanish Civil War ends.
1940–41	Italy and Germany at war against France and England. Germany, Italy and Japan sign Tripartite Pact. Germany invades Denmark, Norway, Belgium, Netherlands and Luxembourg. Hitler invades France. Auschwitz begins operation as concentration camp. Paris occupied. Pétain leads collaborationist government of France, Republic of Vichy. Churchill becomes British Prime Minister. Russia invades Baltic countries. Germany invades USSR. American naval base at Pearl Harbor attacked by Japanese. USA enters war. Trotsky assassinated in Mexico City.

| --- | --- |
James Joyce publishes *Ulysses*. T.S. Eliot publishes *The Waste Land*. Francis Scott Fitzgerald publishes *The Beautiful and Damned*. *Sodom and Gomorrah* by Marcel Proust released. Ludwig Wittgenstein publishes *Tractatus Logico-Philosophicus*. Major exhibition in Berlin of contemporary Russian art, focusing on Suprematism and Constructivism. Albert Barnes founds the Barnes Foundation in Pennsylvania, near Philadelphia.	Born on March 12 in Lowell to Gabrielle-Ange Lévesque and Léo-Alcide Léon Kerouac, baptized Jean Louis Kirouac. The couple has three children: Gerard, Caroline (Nin) and Jack, the youngest. At home, they speak Joual, a dialect of French-Canadian immigrants. Jack has a visceral relationship with his mother and a problematic one with his father, a printer by trade but alcoholic and often out of work.
Luigi Pirandello publishes *One, No One and One Hundred Thousand*. Ernest Hemingway publishes *The Sun Also Rises*. *The Castle* by Franz Kafka released posthumously. William Faulkner publishes *Soldier's Pay*. D. H. Lawrence publishes *The Plumed Serpent*.	Gerard dies of rheumatic fever. The trauma has a tremendous impact on Jack's entire life. Gerard joins the family pantheon, along with saints and sacred images kept by the mother as devotional object of her bigoted, anti-Semitic, homophobic religiousness, from which Jack never completely frees himself. Later, in 1963, Jack writes the novel *Visions of Gerard*, an elaboration of his bereavement, where he recounts his childhood memories in the framework of a hagiographic vision of his brother's life.
Sigmund Freud dies. Jean Paul Sartre publishes *The Wall*. James Joyce publishes *Finnegans Wake*. John Steinbeck publishes *The Grapes of Wrath*. Henry Miller publishes *Tropic of Capricorn*. Raymond Chandler publishes *The Big Sleep*. Matta, Salvador Dalì, Kurt Seligmann and Yves Tanguy leave Europe for New York. World's Fair in New York. Picasso exhibition at MoMA in New York features *Guernica*.	He graduates from Lowell High School, where he focused on English studies. He meets Sebastian Sampas, with whom he shares first literary interests. He attends Horace Mann Preparatory School in New York thanks to an athletic scholarship. He discovers jazz, and particularly loves Benny Goodman, Lester Young and Charlie Parker. He meets Henri Cru and Frankie Edith Parker, who will become his first wife.
André Breton publishes *Anthology of Black Humor*. Dylan Thomas publishes *A Portrait of an Artist as a Young Man*. Ernest Hemingway publishes *For Whom the Bell Tolls*. Richard Wright publishes *Native Son*. Film of *The Grapes of Wrath* by John Ford released. Graham Greene publishes *The Power and the Glory*.	He enrolls at Columbia University, with another athletic scholarship. Due to an accident, he does not train, immersing himself instead in the life of New York jazz clubs and in reading Céline, Whitman, Saroyan, Hemingway, Thomas Wolfe. After a conflict with his trainer, he leaves university and moves to Hartford, Connecticut, where he works for a time in a gas station. He reads voraciously – Dostoevsky, Conrad, Twain, Dos Passos, William James, Mann and Joyce.

1942	Nazis create Warsaw ghetto where the city Jews are deported. Battle of Stalingrad. Russians resist German advance. Allies land in Morocco and Algeria. Battle of El-Alamein. Battle of the Midway. Americans wrest control over Pacific from Japanese. Battle of Guadalcanal. Gandhi arrested in Bombay.
1944	English air force bombs Berlin. In January, Allies land in Anzio. Battle of Montecassino. Deportation of Hungarian Jews to Auschwitz. Allies control Rome. On June 6, Allies land in Normandy. Bretton Woods Conference creates International Monetary Fund and World Bank. On July 20, failed attempt on Hitler's life. Battle of Guam in the Pacific. Warsaw Uprising. Liberation of Paris and Brussels. V2 rocket attacks on London. Roosevelt re-elected President of the USA.
1945–48	Italian referendum abolishes monarchy. Nuremburg Trial condemns Nazi war criminals. First conflicts of Cold War between the Soviet Union and the West. Churchill coins the term "Iron Curtain" to express the concept of division between Western and Communist blocks. Peron elected president in Argentina. Ho Chi Minh elected President of North Vietnam. 1947. US launches Marshall Plan. Soviets create Cominform. UN opts for partitioning of Palestine, vigorously opposed by Arab League. Francisco Franco reinstates monarchy and appointed regent for life. India and Pakistan declare independence. Civil War in China. Creation of CIA, Department of Defense and National Security Council in USA.

Albert Camus publishes *The Stranger*. Maurice Merleau-Ponty publishes *The Structure of Behavior*. Anna Seghers publishes *The Seventh Cross*. John Steinbeck publishes *The Moon is Down*. Jean Anouilh publishes *Antigone*. T.S. Eliot publishes *Little Gidding*.
Artists in Exile exhibition opens at Pierre Matisse Gallery in New York, with Chagall, Mondrian, Léger, Ernst, Tanguy, Masson and others.

In 1942, he ships out on *SS Dorchester*, merchant marine ship heading for Greenland. He is sexually abused on the trip, as he recounted years later. He lands in New York and returns briefly to Columbia University but, once again excluded from the football team, he decides to return to sea. He enlists in the Naval Reserve but is discharged after being found mentally unfit for service. He moves in with his parents in Ozone Park, Queens.

Camus publishes the play *Caligula*. William Somerset Maugham publishes *The Razor's Edge*. Tennessee Williams publishes *The Glass Menagerie*. Saul Bellow publishes *Dangling Man*. Jorge Luis Borges publishes *Fictions*. First major exhibition in France opens only days after Paris is liberated; an entire room is devoted to Picasso. Betty Parsons, future promoter of Abstract Expressionism, works as modern art curator at a New York gallery on 57th Street. Sidney Janis publishes essay *Abstract and Surrealist Art* comparing works of European art with others by American artists of the new generation. *Abstract and Surrealist Painting in America* exhibition in San Francisco.

Through Lucien Carr, a charismatic Columbia student, Jack meets William Burroughs and Allen Ginsberg, nucleus of the future Beat Generation. With Burrough's encouragement, Jack reads Kafka, Cocteau, Apollinaire, Nietzsche and Oswald Spengler. Arrested for aiding and abetting Carr in the murder of David Kammerer, ex-teacher at Carr's school, Kerouac obtains bail money from the family of his friend Edith Parker on condition that he marry her. He does and moves to Michigan to live with her. The marriage ends after two months and Kerouac returns to New York.

Primo Levi publishes *If This is a Man*. Albert Camus publishes *The Plague*. Raymond Queneau publishes *Exercises in Style*. Jean Genet publishes *Querelle of Brest*. Thomas Mann publishes *Doctor Faustus*. Max Horkheimer and Theodor Adorno publish *Dialectic of Enlightenment*. Tennessee Williams publishes *A Streetcar Named Desire*. Malcolm Lowry publishes *Under the Volcano*.
Jean Dubuffet coins term *Art Brut* for art produced by individuals with no artistic culture or with mental illness. First museum in Germany after WWII opens in Hamburg. Term "Abstract Expressionism" used for first time by Robert M. Coates referring to artist Hans Hoffman and later to artists of the New York School. Betty Parsons Gallery opens in New York, exhibiting key artists of Abstract Expressionism over the years, including Pollock, Rothko, Motherwell, Still and Newman. Charles Egan Gallery opens in New York, exhibiting in the following decade the first works of Franz Kline and Willem de Kooning.

In New York, Jack rents a room in apartment of Joan Vollmer Adams, who becomes Burroughs' wife. Ginsberg also comes to live there. Jack meets Vicky Russell, who introduces him to Benzedrine, which facilitates marathon writing sessions. He is hospitalized after thrombophlebitis attack due to excessive use of Benzedrine. He writes *The Town and the City*. In 1946, Jack's father Leo dies of cancer of the spleen. Jack discovers be-bop, drugs, and falls into depression after the illness and death of his father.
In this period, he draws a portrait of a man with a cross around his neck, probably an image of his father (Fig. 11), despite word "Stanley" on the back.
1946. Kerouac meets Neal Cassady in New York, the Dean Moriarty of *On the Road*, and is drawn to the energy and charisma of this voracious intellectual and car thief. Neal is 20, had left school at 14 and wandered with his alcoholic father around the United States, obtaining a high school diploma through an equivalency test. Now he wants to attend Columbia University. Jack obtains permission from his mother to join Cassady and Ginsberg in Denver, in what is the first of his *On the Road* adventures.

1948–50

1948. Elections in Italy won by Christian Democrats. Assassination attempt against Togliatti. State of Israel born. First Arab-Israeli War begins. Rupture between Stalin and Tito. American President Truman ends racial discrimination in US Armed Forces. Gandhi assassinated in New Delhi.
1949. Birth of Federal Republic of Germany with capital in Bonn and German Democratic Republic with capital in Berlin. NATO founded. Soviet COMECON established. Ireland obtains independence from United Kingdom. David Ben Gurion becomes Prime Minister of Israel. Soviet Union conducts atomic tests. People's Republic of China born, led by Chairman Mao Ze-dong. Apartheid instituted in South Africa.
1950. Truman orders development of hydrogen bomb. McCarthyism in United States, purging of alleged Communist sympathizers. India becomes a republic. North Korean army invades South Korea. Korean War breaks out. Egypt demands English withdraw troops from Suez Canal. China invades Tibet and North Korea.

1951

European Coal and Steel Community (ECSC) established. Flooding in Po Valley. Anti-English riots in Egypt. Libya proclaims independence. Seoul occupied by North Korea, then reconquered by Americans. Peron re-elected President of Argentina. Julius and Ethel Rosenberg accused of being Soviet spies. Introduction of color TV in USA.

1952

Elizabeth II crowned Queen of England. Fighting between France and Tunisian nationalists. Republic of Egypt proclaimed. Independence of Sudan. University of Tennessee admits first African-American student. Nehru becomes Prime Minister of India. French offensive in Hanoi. England announces its atomic bomb. Batista military coup d'état in Cuba. First transoceanic jet flight. Eisenhower elected President of United States.

1953

Korean War ends with division of country into North Korea and South Korea. Soviet Union able to produce hydrogen bomb. Josef Stalin dies. Rise of Khrushchev. Tito becomes President of Yugoslavia. Edmund Hillary and Tenzing Norgay reach summit of Mt. Everest. Rosenbergs executed. DNA discovered.

The World of Art and Literature	Life of Kerouac: Literary and Figurative Works
Jean Paul Sartre writes *Dirty Hands*. György Lukács publishes *Essays on Realism*. Ezra Pound publishes *The Pisan Cantos*. Truman Capote publishes *Other Voices, Other Rooms*. At Venice Biennale, conflict between advocates of Realism and those of Abstraction. COBRA movement begins in Paris. Mark Rothko, William Baziotes and Robert Motherwell found private art school, The Subject of the Artist. 1949. Jean Paul Sartre publishes *Iron in the Soul*. George Orwell publishes *1984*. Konrad Lorenz publishes *King Solomon's Ring*. Arthur Miller publishes *Death of a Salesman*. Jorge Luis Borges publishes *The Aleph*. Yukio Mishima publishes *Confessions of a Mask*. Peggy Guggenheim Collection of modern art opens to public in Venice. *L'Art Brut* exhibition in Paris. Experimental COBRA exhibition in Amsterdam. Exhibition on art of Italian Novecento at MoMA in New York. *Life* magazine article on Jackson Pollock. Martin Heidegger writes *Existence and Being*. Eugène Ionesco publishes *The Bald Soprano*. Ray Bradbury publishes *The Martian Chronicles*. Pablo Neruda publishes *Canto general*.	Kerouac reads Melville, Sinclair Lewis, and Fitzgerald. He stays with Cassady in Denver, then goes to San Francisco and explores California. He meets John Clellon Holmes and invents the term "Beat Generation." He starts working on *On the Road*. First trips with Neal Cassady. Cassady marries Carolyn Robinson. 1950. Kerouac publishes *The Town and the City*. Reviews are mediocre. He drives with Cassady to Mexico City, where he tries morphine at Burroughs' house. Back in New York, he has an affair with Joan Haverty, who becomes his second wife.
Marguerite Yourcenar publishes *Memoirs of Hadrian*. Albert Camus publishes *The Rebel*. Eugène Ionesco publishes *The Lesson*. Theodor Adorno publishes *Minima Moralia*. Truman Capote publishes *The Grass Harp*. William Faulkner publishes *Requiem for a Nun*. Yukio Mishima publishes *Forbidden Colors*. French critic Tapié uses the term *"informel"* for first time to refer to genre of abstract painting infused with powerful existential component. January 15 issue of *Life* features photo of New York School artists, labeled "the Irascibles." Included are De Kooning, Pollock, Baziotes, Stamos, Tomlin, Motherwell, Rothko, Still, Newman, Gottlieb, Reinhardt and others. *Abstract Painting and Sculpture in America* exhibition at MoMA.	He reads manuscripts of *Junkie* by William Burroughs and *Go* by Holmes. In New York, in April, he rewrites the manuscript of *On the Road* on a telex roll in three weeks. The marriage with Joan is on the rocks; when she becomes pregnant and refuses to abort, he leaves her. In October, he elaborates his writing method of "sketching," or spontaneous prose, and begins to rewrite *On the Road*. In San Francisco, in December, he works on *Visions of Cody*, an experimental novel.
Samuel Beckett publishes *Waiting for Godot*. Ernest Hemingway publishes *The Old Man and the Sea*. John Steinbeck publishes *East of Eden*. Jerome David Salinger publishes *The Catcher in the Rye*. Jorge Luis Borges publishes *Other Inquisitions*. *Fifteen Americans* exhibition at MoMA, presenting leading exponents of Abstract Expressionism. Term "action painting" coined by art critic Harold Rosenberg.	John Clellon Holmes publishes the article "This is the Beat Generation" in *New York Times*, where the term "beat" is used to mean "a weariness with all the conventions of the world." Kerouac works on *Visions of Cody* under the effect of peyote and writes *Doctor Sax*. The work *Sax on the River* (Fig. 35) is a disturbing vision of Doctor Sax, the book's protagonist. Alluding to a chapter in *Visions of Cody*, the painting *Woman (Joan Rawshanks) in Blue with Black Hat* (Fig. 4) depicts Joan Crawford on the set of *Sudden Fear* in 1952. Kerouac begins a *ménage a trois* with Carolyn and Neal Cassady. In February, Joan Haverty gives birth to Janet; Kerouac refuses to recognize her as his daughter for nine years, until 1962.
Roland Barthes publishes *Writing Degree Zero*. Alain Robbe-Grillet publishes *The Erasers*. Samuel Beckett publishes *The Unnamable*. Ray Bradbury publishes *Fahrenheit 451*. Raymond Chandler publishes *The Long Goodbye*. Martha Jackson Gallery opens in New York, specializing in international abstract and Informal art. *Dada 1913-1923* exhibition at Sidney Janis Gallery in New York, with collaboration of Marcel Duchamp.	In six months, he writes *Maggie Cassidy*, the story of his first love with Mary Carney during high school days in Lowell. He writes *The Subterraneans* on a telex roll in spontaneous prose, writing based on free association, broken syntax and minimal punctuation, in accordance with principles outlined in *Essentials of Spontaneous Prose*.

1954 | French forces in Dien Bien Phu conquered by North Vietnamese. At Geneva Conference, Vietnam is divided in two, Democratic Republic of Vietnam in the North and State of Vietnam in the South. Jonas Salk develops polio vaccine. Nasser becomes President of Egypt. US Supreme Court declares racial segregation in schools unconstitutional.

1955 | Bandung Conference of non-aligned developing countries. Warsaw Pact between Communist block countries. West Germany becomes sovereign state. Rose Parks refuses to sit at the back of bus in area reserved for non-whites. Martin Luther King Jr. organizes African-American boycott of public transport in Montgomery, Alabama. Independence of Morocco and Tunisia.

1956 | Soviet invasion of uprising Hungary. At 20th CPSU Congress, Secretary Khrushchev condemns policies of Stalin government and opens to West. First hydrogen bomb tested in Bikini Atoll. Battle for liberation begins in Algeria. Suez Canal nationalized.

1957 | Rome Treaty institutes European Economic Community (EEC). European Common Market born. Ghana becomes first country of Central Africa to become independent. Independence of Malaysia. Soviets launch orbital satellite Sputnik.

The World of Art and Literature	Life of Kerouac: Literary and Figurative Works
Simone De Beauvoir publishes *The Mandarins*. William Golding publishes *Lord of the Flies*. J.R.R. Tolkien publishes first part of *The Lord of the Rings* trilogy. Tennessee Williams publishes the play *Cat on a Hot Tin Roof*.	He begins to study Buddhism, after finding the tenth volume of *The Sacred Books and Early Literature of the East* in the library in San Jose, where he was living with Carolyn and Neal Cassady. He begins to write *Some of the Dharma*. When tensions arise with his hosts, Kerouac leaves for San Francisco, where he writes *San Francisco Blues*. Then he returns to his mother's house.
Claude Lévi-Strauss publishes *Tristes Tropiques*. Elie Wiesel publishes *The Night*. Herbert Marcuse publishes *Eros and Civilization: A Philosophical Inquiry into Freud*. Eugène Ionesco publishes the play *Jack, or The Submission*. J.R.R. Tolkien publishes second and third parts of *The Lord of the Rings* trilogy. Patricia Highsmith publishes *The Talented Mr. Ripley*. Vladimir Nabokov publishes *Lolita*. City of Paris Museum of Modern Art holds exhibition on 50 years of art in USA, survey of modern and contemporary American art. Kinetic art born in Paris. First *Documenta* exhibition in Kassel.	He writes *Mexico City Blues* upon returning to Mexico City. He begins the novella *Tristessa*, based on a Mexican prostitute addicted to heroin, whom he met through Burroughs. In October, he participates in *Six Poets at Six Gallery* poetry reading in San Francisco, where Ginsberg reads *Howl* for the first time.
Albert Camus publishes *The Fall*. Allen Ginsberg publishes *Howl and Other Poems*. Jun'ichiro Tanizaki publishes *The Key*. Philip K. Dick publishes *The Minority Report*. Anthony Burgess publishes *Time for a Tiger*. Saul Bellow publishes *Seize the Day*. James Baldwin publishes *Giovanni's Room*. American Expressionism exhibition at Tate Gallery in London. Pollock called "Jack the Dripper" in February issue of *Time*; in August, he dies in car accident.	On large doses of benzydrine in the ten days after New Year's Day, 1956, Kerouac writes *Visions of Gerard*. While guest of Gary Snyder in Corte Madera, California, he begins two new projects: *The Scripture of the Golden Eternity* and *Old Angel Midnight*. Working as a fire lookout in Washington's Cascade Mountains, he lives for weeks in utter drug-free solitude on Desolation Peak and keeps a diary. The text is included in the first part of *Desolation Angels*, completed in 1961. In September, after a few days in Seattle, he goes to San Francisco, then to the Cassadys', and then again to Mexico City, where he finishes *Tristessa*. Some of Kerouac's California drawings (Figs. 45, 46, 47, 48, 49) are from 1956. Ginsberg's *Howl* is published by City Lights in San Francisco.
Roland Barthes publishes *Mythologies*. Boris Pasternak's *Doctor Zhivago* published in Italy. Samuel Beckett publishes *Endgame*. Truman Capote publishes *Breakfast at Tiffany's*. Bernard Malamud publishes *The Assistant*. Alain Robbe-Grillet publishes *Jealousy*. Jean Genet publishes *The Balcony*. Tennessee Williams publishes *Baby Doll*. Pier Paolo Pasolini publishes *Gramsci's Ashes*. Carlo Emilio Gadda publishes *That Awful Mess on the Via Merulana*.	After time in Florida, where his sister lives, Kerouac is on the road again, this time to Tangier in Morocco to visit Burroughs. The visit becomes oppressive so in April he takes a ship to Marseilles, and then visits Paris and London. *On the Road* is published on September 4 by Viking Press in New York, which ends up changing Kerouac's life drastically; he becomes famous as an icon of the Beat Generation, hounded by the press. In late autumn, he is again in Florida, working on revisions of *The Subterraneans* and writing *The Dharma Bums*, published in 1958, after *The Subterraneans*. *The Crucifixion* (Fig. 16) is from 1958.

1959

Charles de Gaulle elected President of France. United States support South Vietnam against Viet Cong guerilla force supported by North Vietnam. Cuban President Batista flees Cuba and Fidel Castro enters Havana. Cuba allies with Soviet Union. Dalai Lama flees from Tibet to India.

1961

Katanga secedes from ex-Belgian Congo. Patrice Lumumba assassinated. United States break diplomatic relations with Cuba. John Fitzgerald Kennedy elected President of USA. Bay of Pigs in Cuba invaded by Cuban exiles supported by USA: invasion blocked. Berlin Wall built. At PCUS Congress, Khrushchev denounces Stalin personality cult. Buddhist monks self-immolate to denounce South Vietnamese dictatorship. Yuri Gagarin orbits Earth. First flight of American astronauts. Russia explodes 50-megaton hydrogen bomb.

1965

Vatican II Council ends. Second mandate of President De Gaulle in France. Winston Churchill dies. Martin Luther King Jr. and 2600 others arrested in Selma, Alabama, for protesting against voter registration system. Medicare, national health care for elderly, begins in USA. Race riots in Watts, Los Angeles, cause 34 deaths and thousands of arrests. Malcolm X assassinated.

Raymond Queneau publishes *Zazie in the Metro*. Ernst H. Gombrich publishes *Art and Illusion*. Ernst Bloch finishes publishing *The Principle of Hope*. Günter Grass publishes *The Tin Drum*. William S. Burroughs publishes *Naked Lunch*. Saul Bellow publishes *Henderson, the Rain King*. William Faulkner publishes *Sanctuary*. Norman Mailer publishes *Advertisements for Myself*. Philip Roth publishes *Goodbye, Columbus and Five Short Stories*. John Updike publishes *The Same Door*. Kurt Vonnegut publishes *The Sirens of Titan*. Jean Paul Sartre publishes *The Condemned of Altona*. Another major exhibition at Tate Gallery on American Abstract Expressionism organized by MoMA. Guggenheim Museum opens in New York in circular building by Frank Lloyd Wright. Large Willem De Kooning exhibition at Sidney Janis Gallery in New York.

Difficult period for Kerouac. *Doctor Sax*, *Maggie Cassidy* and *Mexico City Blues* are published but receive negative reviews. Given the writer's visibility after the success of *On the Road*, this critical failure has a vast resonance, which devastates Kerouac. He works on *Lonesome Traveler* and *Book of Dreams*, but by now he is a full-fledged alcoholic. He does the voiceover for the film *Pull My Daisy*, by Robert Frank and Alfred Leslie.
Kerouac's portrait of Truman Capote (Fig. 5) is from 1959. This is the year Capote witheringly insults Kerouac and other Beat Generation authors saying, "[it] isn't writing at all – it's typing." In 1959 Kerouac paints the famed portrait of Cardinal Montini (Fig. 3), taken from a photograph in *Life*, and the Expressionist *The Silly Eye* (Fig. 6), probably the profile of William Burroughs. He also painted abstracts (Fig. 71). In this period, he frequents Dody Muller, widow of Jan Muller, a renowned Expressionist painter. They are lovers for two years, in which Kerouac paints and draws extensively. Dody connects him with Willem de Kooning and the other New York School painters, all "regulars," like Jack, at Cedar Tavern, along with his Northport neighbor, Stanley Twardowicz.

Georges Bataille publishes *The Tears of Eros*. Jean Cocteau publishes *The Testament of Orpheus*. John Steinbeck publishes *The Winter of Our Discontent*. Yasunari Kawabata publishes *House of the Sleeping Beauties*. *The Art of the Assemblage* exhibition at MoMA in New York. J.D. Salinger publishes *Franny and Zooey*. Frantz Fanon publishes *The Wretched of the Earth*.

In 1960, *Lonesome Traveler* is released. Kerouac paints *The Slouch Hat* (Fig. 1), seemingly a figurative, abstract version of the Beat world, with male and female figures arranged "spontaneously" and simultaneously on distinct planes of the canvas like visions engulfed by an abstract aura. In July 1961, Kerouac writes second half of *Desolation Angels* in Mexico City. Back in Florida, he finishes *Big Sur*, an account of his experience the previous year in Ferlinghetti's cabin in Bixby Canyon in Big Sur, California; he goes looking for solitude but finds delirium tremens and terrifying visions instead.
In this period (1962), he paints *Untitled* (Fig. 53).

Bohumil Hrabal publishes *Closely Watched Trains*. Peter Weiss publishes the play *The Investigation*. Norman Mailer publishes *An American Dream*. Sylvia Plath publishes *Ariel*. Alex Haley and Malcolm X publish *The Autobiography of Malcolm X*. American critic Barbara Rose publishes "ABC Art" on minimalist art in *Art in America*. *The Responsive Eye* exhibition on optic, kinetic and programmed art at MoMA. First official exhibition on Minimalism at Tibor de Nagy Gallery in New York. Parke-Bernet auction house in New York auctions off 13 Abstract Expressionist works from Robert C. Scull Collection, marking its definitive canonization but also end of American Abstract Expressionist movement.

After Kerouac moves still another time, going to live with his mother in St. Petersburg, Florida, his sister Nin dies suddenly. *Desolation Angels* released. In one week, in a state of continual drunkenness, he writes *Satori in Paris*.

1966 | Cultural Revolution begins in China. Flooding in Florence. Indira Gandhi elected Prime Minister of India. George Pompidou becomes Prime Minister in France. General Suharto leads coup d'état in Indonesia. Soviet spacecraft Luna 10 first to orbit Moon. Stokely Carmichael launches Black Power movement. Black Panther Party founded. Soviet spacecraft Luna 13 lands on Moon.

1967 | Six-Day War between Israel, Egypt and Jordan. Sinai conquered by Israel. Robert Kennedy assassinated. Coup d'état of the colonels in Greece. USA launch Lunar Orbiter 3. Pope Paul VI publishes *Populorum Progressio* encyclical. Race riots in many cities in USA.
China has H bomb. Che Guevara captured in Bolivia. Nguyên Văn Thiệu elected President of South Vietnam. Surveyor 6 lands on Moon. First heart transplant by Christiaan Barnard in South Africa.

1968 | Student and worker demonstrations in France, then in Germany and Italy. Reforms by Alexander Dubček in Czechoslovakia and repression of Prague Spring. Leonid Brezhnev institutes doctrine of "limited sovereignty" justifying Soviet military intervention in Warsaw Pact countries. Têt offensive in Vietnam with Viet Cong guerilla attacks in South Vietnam. My Lai massacre. Martin Luther King Jr assassinated in Memphis, Tennessee. Richard Nixon elected President in USA.
Pope Paul VI issues Encyclical Humanae Vitae. Tlatelolco massacre in Mexico City during student demonstration 10 days before Olympics. Apollo 7 launched. Apollo 8 orbits Moon and astronauts see dark side of moon and Earth viewed from moon for the first time.

1969 | De Gaulle resigns in France. In Prague, Jan Palach self-immolates to protest Soviet occupation of his country. Alexander Dubček removed and expelled from Czech Communist Party. Willy Brandt becomes Chancellor of West Germany. American astronauts of Apollo 11 land on moon. Piazza Fontana bombing in Milan. Martial law in Spain. Soviet spacecrafts Sojuz 4 and Sojuz 5 hook up to become first experimental space station. Yasser Arafat elected leader of Palestine Liberation Organization. Golda Meir becomes Prime Minister of Israel. Georges Pompidou elected President in France. Woodstock Festival. Colonel Gaddafi gains power through coup d'état in Libya. First computer network ARPANET developed.

Truman Capote publishes *In Cold Blood*. Thomas Pynchon publishes *The Crying of Lot 49*. Mario Vargas Llosa publishes *The Green House*. Bulgakov's *The Master and Margarita* released posthumously. Leonardo Sciascia publishes *To Each His Own*. Tom Stoppard writes *Rosencrantz and Guildenstern are Dead*. Bernard Malamud writes *The Fixer*. Michel Foucault writes *The Order of Things*. Frances Yates writes *The Art of Memory*. *Systemic Painting* exhibition on systemic art at Solomon Guggenheim in New York, a contrast to gestural Abstract Expressionism.

In May 1966, he finds a house in Hyannis, near Cape Cod, Massachusetts. His mother has a stroke. He travels in Italy and on his return, marries Stella Sampas, sister of his childhood friend Sammy, who died in the war. Along with his mother, the couple moves back to Lowell, Massachusetts.

Jacques Derrida publishes *Of Grammatology*. Roland Barthes publishes *The Fashion System*. Simone De Beauvoir publishes *The Woman Destroyed*. Guy Debord publishes *The Society of the Spectacle*. Desmond Morris publishes *The Naked Ape*. Marshall McLuhan and Quentin Fiore publish *The Medium is the Message*. Thomas Bernhard publishes *Gargoyles*. Milan Kundera publishes *The Joke*. Gabriel García Márquez publishes *A Hundred Years of Solitude*. "Is Not Lichtenstein the Worst Painter of Our Time?" is published in *New York Times*, obviously contrasting with *Life* article praising Pollock in 1949.

In Lowell, he starts the novel *Vanity of Duluoz* on the familiar telex roll in March and finishes it in June.

Marguerite Yourcenar publishes *The Abyss*. Norman Mailer publishes *Armies of the Night*. Noam Chomsky publishes *Language and Mind*. Yukio Mishima publishes *Spring Snow*. Philip K. Dick publishes *Do Androids Dream of Electric Sheep?*. John Updike publishes *Couples*. Christa Wolf publishes *The Quest for Christa T. Documenta 4* dedicated to Pop Art in Kassel. *Art of the Real: USA 1948-1968* at MoMA, analyzing relationship between American art and Realism. Another MoMA show, *The Machine at the End of the Mechanical Age*, focuses on relationship between art and technology. Exhibitions of minimalist, conceptual, and Land art and Anti-Form in various galleries in New York. First signed graffiti appears on walls in New York.

Vanity of Duluoz released to tepid critical response. February 4, Neal Cassady dies in Mexico, found frozen along railroad tracks near San Miguel de Allende after mixing alcohol and barbiturates. Jack leaves for Europe, but fails to pull himself out of his alcoholic abyss. The Kerouacs move back to St. Petersburg, Florida in a house near his previous one.

Gilles Deleuze publishes *The Logic of Sense*. Philip Roth publishes *Portnoy's Complaint*. Rudolf Arnheim publishes *Visual Thinking*. Kurt Vonnegut publishes *Slaughterhouse-Five, or The Children's Crusade*. Mario Vargas Llosa publishes *Conversation in the Cathedral*. Ursula K. Le Guin publishes *The Left Hand of Darkness*. Mario Puzo publishes *The Godfather*. Dario Fo publishes *Mistero Buffo* for theater. Kate Millett publishes *Sexual Politics*. Fernand Braudel publishes *On History*. Mark Rothko gives painting cycle originally commissioned for Seagram Building to Tate Gallery in London. Major *Arte Povera* exhibition at Museum Folkwang in Essen. Mark Rothko Foundation established in New York. *Interview*, art and culture magazine founded and directed by Andy Warhol, in New York. Historic exhibition of conceptual, process and Land Art in Seattle Museum of Art.

He works on *Pic*, a novella about a young African-American boy from North Carolina. The book is written in the "black English" of African-Americans of the South.
On September 3, he gets into a brawl and ends up briefly in prison with broken ribs.
On October 20, he vomits blood. Taken to emergency to the local hospital, he dies of cirrhosis of the liver on October 21. The funeral, plagued by controversy, is held in Lowell, where Kerouac is buried in the Catholic cemetery.

Bibliographical note

The collection on display in the *Kerouac. Beat Painting* exhibition at Museo MA*GA of Gallarate (I) from December 2, 2017 to April 22, 2018 is owned by private collectors of Il Rivellino LDV of Locarno. Rights to use the images were granted by John Shen-Sampas, heir of John Sampas, Kerouac's brother-in-law and estate guardian. John was given the collection of drawings personally by Kerouac. The works were transferred directly from Lowell, Massachusetts to the Swiss collections. There have been very few opportunities to exhibit or study the works.

The bibliography for the works in the exhibition is extremely limited; in fact, there are only two essential sources:
• E. Adler, *Departed Angels. Jack Kerouac. The Lost Paintings* (New York: Thunder's Mouth, 2004) and the catalog *Works of Art by Jack Kerouac*, unpublished, of all the collection's works, edited by John Wronoski directly for John Sampas in 2005.

Over the years, various parts of the collection have been displayed in the following exhibitions:
• *Beat Culture and the New America, 1950 – 1965*, New York (USA), Whitney Museum of American Art, 9 November 1995 – 4 February 1996.
• *Jack Kerouac Painter and Poet*, Lowell (USA), Whistler House Museum of Art, 1–4 October 1998.
• *Jack Kerouac. Ti Jean ou l'Art du Joual*, Locarno (CH), Il Rivellino LDV, 7–17 August 2013.
• *Beat Generation. New York, San Francisco, Paris*, Paris (F), Centre Pompidou, 22 June – 3 October 2016 / Karlsruhe (D), ZKM, 26 November 2016 – 30 April 2017.